ENGLISH
MADE SIMPLE

REVISED EDITION

BY
ARTHUR WALDHORN, Ph.D.

AND
ARTHUR ZEIGER, Ph.D.

MADE SIMPLE BOOKS

DOUBLEDAY & COMPANY, INC.

GARDEN CITY, NEW YORK

PREFACE

If you never hesitate between *because of* and *due to*, or *fewer* and *less*, or *index* and *indices*; if you never puzzle over commas, semicolons, and dashes; if you never pause before spelling *proceed* and *precede*, *conference* and *conferring*, *singing* and *singeing*; if you never doubt which words may and which may not be abbreviated in the heading of a business letter; if you never survey with a melancholy eye an awkward, ambiguous, or ungrammatical sentence of your own construction—then you will find it unnecessary to read past this paragraph.

For *English Made Simple* has been planned for people habitually unsure of their grammar, punctuation, spelling; discontent with the range and flexibility of their vocabulary; uneasy about the clarity and force of their writing. They may, of course, advantageously use this book under the guidance of an experienced teacher. But it has been prepared especially for adult readers working without supervision. Each section forms a self-sufficient unit, including all the information (and sometimes repeating information more extensively supplied in other sections) they require to understand it fully. Moreover, the keyed exercises and answers help them check their progress continually.

The book has another purpose as well: to serve as a work of "ready reference." To facilitate such reference, it contains an unusually full table of contents supplementing the index.

The authors have tried to credit sources from which they have borrowed distinctive material. If they have occasionally omitted an acknowledgment or altered a quotation, they apologize now and will try to rectify their error soon. Mrs. Dorothy Lataner, who has typed the manuscript expertly and criticized it helpfully, deserves separate and particular thanks.

—Arthur Waldhorn
—Arthur Zeiger

Note: Since this book was first published, many events have taken place. The revised edition contains updating where necessary, but the core of the original material is the same.

TABLE OF CONTENTS

SECTION 1—THE SENTENCE AND ITS PARTS

SECTION 2—SENTENCE ERRORS

SECTION 3—PARAGRAPHS AND PARAGRAPHING

Table of Contents

THE SENTENCE AND ITS PARTS

TEST NO. 1

Note: Take this test before proceeding to the first section. Check your answers with those provided at the end of the book. Make note of your major weaknesses, and give particular attention to the sections which try to remedy these weaknesses.

SENTENCE ERRORS

Part I: Choose the correct form for each of the following:

EXAMPLE: Jack and Jill (*is, are*) over the hill. *are*

1. Ken is one of those singers who (*is, are*) always off key.
2. There (*go, goes*) Julia and her favorite parakeet.
3. Each of the contestants (*has, have*) a chance to win a trip to the North Pole.
4. The healthiest specimen among the monkeys (*was, were*) chosen to imitate the television actor.
5. I gave ten dollars to the clerk (*who, whom*) I think works on Saturdays only.
6. Between you and (*I, me*) and the bartender, I find Sazaracs potent cocktails.
7. Leave all arrangements to (*her, she*) and (*me, I*).
8. I expected the gentleman caller to be (*he, him*).
9. If one tries to whistle while laughing, (*he, they*) must be highly optimistic.
10. Each of these bananas has a split in (*its, their*) side.
11. Jean's perfume smells (*sweet, sweetly*).
12. Roy (*sure, surely*) is the best catcher in the big leagues.
13. The posse (*seeked, sought*) in vain to find the murderer.
14. Years ago, I (*saw, have seen*) Scaramouche in silent films.
15. If he had entered the building, I (*saw, had seen, would have seen*) him.

Part II: Rewrite the following sentences to assure clarity and correctness.

1. If we all strive towards peace, one may hope that the world will be a better place to live in.
2. Wash your hair with *Squeaky Lotion* and then you should use *Eeky Hair Tonic*.
3. I expect Bill to arrive early and bringing his cousin Ann.
4. Put the sodas in the refrigerator that is warm.
5. His ankle broken, his owner had the racing colt destroyed.

SPELLING

Correct any misspelled word. If the word is correct, let it remain as is.

embarrased	plagiarize	reciept
forcable	adjustable	picknicing
proceed	hieght	manageable
boundries	supersede	benefitted
marraige	dynamoes	valleys

PUNCTUATION

Insert punctuation wherever needed. If no punctuation is needed, let the sentence remain as is.

1. Jane answer the telephone.
2. The athlete who performs well pleases the crowd.
3. If I draw a thousand dollars from the bank I shall be only nine hundred dollars overdrawn.
4. Millie who has several boy friends loves none of them.
5. Gretchen he begged won't you for goodness' sake share a doughnut with me.

VOCABULARY

Part I: Give the opposite of the following words:

EXAMPLE: good   *bad*
1. symmetrical
2. malevolent
3. polygamy
4. benign
5. loquacious

Part II: Give a synonym for each of the following:

EXAMPLE: happy   *gay*
1. gourmet
2. fortuitous
3. plethora
4. remuneration
5. histrionic

THE SENTENCE

A group of words that express a complete meaning makes a sentence. In order to have a meaning, two elements are necessary: **a subject,** a person or thing to speak about, and **a predicate,** something to say about the person or thing.

SUBJECT AND PREDICATE No sentence can exist without both subject and predicate. Suppose, for example, that somebody speaks the name *Pagliacci*. He has not spoken a sentence; for though he has named a person whom he can speak about, he has supplied no **predicate.**

Now, suppose somebody else utters the word *laughs*. He has not a sentence either, because he has named no **person or thing** to say his word about—he has named no **subject.**

If the two words are joined, however, a sentence emerges: *Pagliacci laughs*. It is a "complete thought," a "full meaning." The sentence may be extended by enlarging the subject:*

<u>Pagliacci</u>, the funniest clown in Europe, laughs.

Or by enlarging the predicate:

<u>Pagliacci</u> laughs mockingly, bitterly, ironically.

Or by enlarging both subject and predicate:

<u>Pagliacci, the funniest clown in all Europe</u>, laughs mockingly, bitterly, ironically.

Consider the following group of words:

The beautiful girl of the fairy tale, a drudge by day and a princess by night.

---

* The subject here is indicated by the single line drawn beneath it, the predicate by the double line.

Here, a person is named and described in some detail, but the group of words appears somehow incomplete: something else is needed. By adding *has vanished*, the need is supplied:

<u>The beautiful girl of the fairy tale, a drudge by day and a princess by night</u>, has vanished.

The long group of words underlined simply enlarges the subject, which essentially consists of the word *girl*; a predicate was required and *has vanished* fulfills the requirement.

Now consider this group of words:

Have been stolen by a highly organized and exceedingly clever gang of international thieves operating from a dozen ports throughout the Near East.

Here, again, something is lacking: much has been said—but about what? The subject is lacking.

<u>The jewels</u> have been stolen by a highly organized and exceedingly clever gang of international thieves operating from a dozen ports throughout the Near East.

RECOGNIZING SUBJECT AND PREDICATE In order to decide which word or words make up the subject, simply ask: **Whom or what are we speaking about?**

Barking dogs never bite.

Plainly, dogs are here spoken about; *dogs*, therefore, is the subject. *Barking* simply describes the subject further.

A rare instance of charity by a miser is news.

Since an instance is being spoken about, *instance* is the subject.

In order to decide which word or words make up the predicate, simply ask: What is said about the subject?

A fool and his money are soon parted.

What is said about the subject (*a fool and his money*)? The answer, [*they*] *are soon parted*, makes up the predicate.

The inclusion of proper names in a dictionary might be defended on the ground that it would be convenient to have them there.

Here, the subject is *inclusion* (the full subject is *The inclusion of proper names in a dictionary*); and the predicate, the statement about the subject, is: *might be defended on the ground that it would be convenient to have them there.*

KINDS OF SENTENCES Sentences have three purposes: to state, to ask, and to command.

1. Sentences that state. A sentence that makes a statement (or denies it) is called a **declarative sentence.**

The boy stood on the burning deck.

2. Sentences that ask. A sentence that asks a question is called an **interrogative sentence.**

Did the boy stand on the burning deck?

3. Sentences that command. A sentence that expresses a command is called an **imperative sentence.**

Boy, stand on the burning deck!

Exercise No. 1

Six of the word-groups below are sentences. Pick them out, underlining each subject once and each predicate twice.

1. Death spares none.
2. Death, which antiquates antiquities and strikes down the innocent.
3. Death, the final adventure, armed with no terrors.
4. Let no man be called fortunate until he is dead.
5. O eloquent, just, and mighty Death!
6. As if every one had meant to put his whole wit in a jest and resolved to live a fool the rest of his dull life.
7. Life is made up of marble and mud.
8. It is life near the bone where it is sweetest.
9. Variety's the very spice of life.
10. Life is just one darned thing after another.

THE PARTS OF SPEECH

The term **part of speech** refers to the job that a word does in a sentence—to its **function** or **use.** Since there are eight separate jobs, words are divided into eight classes or **eight parts of speech: noun, pronoun, verb, adjective, adverb, preposition, conjunction, interjection.**

JOB, FUNCTION, USE	PART OF SPEECH	EXAMPLES
1. To name a person, place, thing, quality, state, or action.	*Noun*	Adam, Washington, pen, wit, joy, laughter.
2. To substitute for a noun.	*Pronoun*	he, she, it.
3. To express action—or nonaction (state of being).	*Verb*	run, talk; think. is, was, will be.
4. To modify (describe or limit) the noun and pronoun.	*Adjective*	*strong* man, *ugly* city, *limited* quantity, *few* hours.
5. To modify any verb, adjective, or adverb.	*Adverb*	think *quickly*, *unusually* ugly, *very* quickly.
6. To show the relationship between a noun or pronoun and some other word.	*Preposition*	cart *before* horse, dog *in* manger, bombs *over* Brooklyn.
7. To join two words or two groups of words.	*Conjunction*	Jack *and* Jill; candy is dandy *but* liquor is quicker.
8. To display emotion.	*Interjection*	Oh! Gosh! Heigh-ho! Hurrah!

A word is a noun, verb, adjective, or other part of speech, depending on its use—and on its use only. That is to say, a word is a noun if it is used like a noun, if it names; it is a preposition if it is used like a preposition, if it shows the relationship between nouns; and so on. In the following passage note that the word **round** is used in **five** different ways:

Our *round* world—which I shall *round* once more before I die—spins *round* and *round* on its axis, at the same time making a circle *round* the sun that results in the *round* of the seasons.

a. *round* world—adjective, because it modifies the noun *world*.

b. I shall *round*—verb, expresses action.

c. spins *round* and *round*—adverb, modifies verb *spins*.

d. circle *round* the sun—preposition, shows relationship between two nouns, *circle* and *sun*.

e. *round* of the seasons—noun, names something.

Exercise: Indicate the part of speech of the italicized words:

Jack and Jill went up the hill
To fetch a pail of water.
Jack fell down and broke his crown
And Jill came tumbling after.

WORD	PART OF SPEECH	REASON
Jack	noun	names a person
and	conjunction	joins two nouns (*Jack, Jill*)
Jill	noun	names a person
went	verb	expresses action
up	preposition	shows relationship of *went* to *hill*
hill	noun	names a thing
pail	noun	names a thing
of	preposition	shows relationship of *water* to *pail*
water	noun	names a thing
fell	verb	expresses action
down	preposition	shows relationship of *Jack* to *hill*
broke	verb	expresses action
his	pronoun	substitutes for noun *Jack's*
crown	noun	names a thing
came	verb	expresses action
after	preposition	shows relationship of *Jill* to *Jack*—she came *after* (him).

Exercise No. 2

Indicate the part of speech of the italicized words:

1. *Mary had a little lamb
   Its fleece was white as snow,
   And everywhere that Mary went
   The lamb was sure to go.
   He followed her to school one day,
   That was against the rule;
   It made the children laugh and play
   To see a lamb in school.*
2. This is my *only* copy, a fact I realized *only* now.
3. I *single* out each *single* woman.
4. He seems a *stone* image—with a heart of *stone*.
5. They *run* wildly to escape the common *run* of people.
6. We all *love* people in *love*.
7. The *quick brown fox jumps over* a *lazy dog*.
8. *He stood hestitantly on the board, gazed longingly at the water, but never dived into it.*
9. *Ouch!*
10. *But me no buts.*

THE NOUN

The noun names some person, place, thing, quality, state, or action.

COMMON AND PROPER NOUNS A common noun is a general name, common to all persons and a proper noun is a particular name, denoting a person or thing different from every other.

COMMON NOUN	PROPER NOUN
man	Henry James
city	Washington, D.C.
hill	Bunker Hill
smith	Captain John Smith
book	*Tom Sawyer*
poem	"Paul Revere's Ride"

Note: Proper nouns are always capitalized. Common nouns are capitalized only when they begin sentences.

Exercise No. 3

Capitalize the proper nouns in the following passages:

1. The hudson, a river 306 miles long, flows south

to new york bay. It was discovered by a dutch explorer named henry hudson.

2. The students—who came from china and japan—preferred science to history, esperanto to english, mechanics to music. All, however, were required to take a course entitled introduction to american government.

3. Both mammon and mercury were gods once. To-day, *mammon* means "riches" and *mercury* signifies "a heavy silver-white metallic element."

CONCRETE AND ABSTRACT NOUNS A concrete noun is the name of anything physical, anything that can be touched, seen, heard, smelled or otherwise perceived by the senses.

An abstract noun is the name of a quality, state, or action. It is an idea, and so may not be touched, seen, heard, smelled or otherwise perceived by the senses.

CONCRETE NOUN: coward, democrat, beggar.
ABSTRACT NOUN: fear, democracy, poverty.

Exercise No. 4

Pick out the concrete and the abstract nouns in the following passages.

1. In proportion as the manners, customs, and amusements of a nation are cruel and barbarous, the regulations of their penal code will be severe.

2. In proportion as men delight in battles, bull-fights, and combats of gladiators, will they punish by hanging, burning, and the rack.

COLLECTIVE NOUNS A collective noun names a group of individuals as if they were one individual. Singular in form, it is plural in meaning.

jury	flock	committee
family	mob	regiment

The collective noun is considered either as a singular or as a plural, depending on the purpose it serves.

The committee was unanimous.

(That is, the committee acted as a unit, as a single individual.)

The committee were arguing among themselves.

(That is, the committee were obviously acting as individuals, not as a unit.)

Exercise No. 5

Underline the collective nouns in the following list:

board, journey, classics, class, ministry, churchmen, nation, people, group, Chinese, books, assembly.

INFLECTION Inflection denotes the change in spelling that a word undergoes to show a change in meaning. Noun inflection, which is termed **declension**, shows changes in number (*man, men*), gender (*man, woman*), and case (*man, man's*).

NUMBER Number is the form of a noun that shows whether it is singular or plural—whether it refers to one or more than one.

SINGULAR: *girl, country, joy.*
PLURAL: *girls, countries, joys.*

The Plural Number a. Regularly, the plural of nouns is formed by adding *-s* to the singular: *lands, lovers, books, battles.*

b. Singular nouns ending in *-s, -x, -z, -sh,* or *-ch* form the plural by adding *-es: kisses, misses; taxes, waxes; mazes, blazes; dishes, wishes; churches, birches.*

Note: The ending *-s,* is added when the plural has no more syllables than the singular; the ending *-es* is added when the plural has one more syllable than the singular. Thus the singular *book* and the plural *books* alike have one syllable; therefore *-s* only is to be added in forming the plural. But singular *kiss* has one syllable and plural *kisses* has two syllables; therefore *-es* is to be added in forming the plural. As a cue to spelling, pronounce the singular and plural of the noun.

c. Singular nouns ending in *-y* preceded by a consonant form the plural by changing the *-y* to *-i* and adding *-es: fly—flies; vanity—vanities; soliloquy—soliloquies.**

Note: Singular nouns ending in *-y* preceded by a vowel form the plural by adding *-s: day—days; chimney—chimneys; monkey—monkeys.*

d. Singular nouns ending in *-o* preceded by a consonant generally form the plural by adding *-es: hero—heroes; Negro—Negroes; potato—potatoes.* (But there are many exceptions to the

* The *u* of soliloquy has the sound of the consonant *w* and so does not violate the principle.

generalization: *solo—solos; halo—halos; piano —pianos.*)

e. Singular nouns ending in -*o* preceded by a vowel form the plural by adding -*s: seraglio— seraglios; curio—curios; cuckoo—cuckoos.*

f. Singular nouns ending in -*f* or -*fe* generally form the plural by changing the *f* to *v* and adding -*es: thief—thieves; calf—calves; self— selves; wife—wives; life—lives; knife—knives.* (But there are many exceptions to the generalization: *grief—griefs; turf—turfs; cliff—cliffs; fife—fifes; safe—safes; strife—strifes.*)

g. Eight nouns form their plural by **mutation**—by changing an inside vowel: *man— men; woman—women; tooth—teeth; foot— feet; mouse—mice; doormouse—doormice; louse—lice; goose—geese.*

h. Four nouns form their plurals by adding -*en* or *ne: ox—oxen; cow—kine;* child—children; brother—brethren.**

i. Compound nouns form their plurals by adding -*s* to the most important word of the compound: *mother-in-law—mothers-in-law; court-martial—courts-martial; will-o'-the-wisp—will-o'-the-wisps; hand-me-down—hand-me-downs; good-by—good-bys.*

Note: Compounds written solidly regularly add -*s* to form the plural: *pickpocket—pickpockets; spoonful—spoonfuls; stepmother— stepmothers.*

j. Foreign nouns, unless they have been thoroughly naturalized, form their plurals according to their native declension. There are several thousand foreign nouns in occasional English use.

SINGULAR	PLURAL
Latin	
addendum	addenda
alumna	alumnae
alumnus	alumni
datum	data
erratum	errata

* The more frequent plurals are, of course *cows* and *brothers;* however, they have different connotations.

Greek

analysis	analyses
basis	bases
crisis	crises
phenomenon	phenomena
thesis	theses

French

bandeau	bandeaux
Monsieur	Messieurs

k. Foreign nouns in frequent use generally have two plural forms—their native plural and their English -*s* (-*es*) plural.

	ENGLISH	FOREIGN
SINGULAR	PLURAL	PLURAL
Latin		
apparatus	apparatuses	apparatus
cactus	cactuses	cacti
curriculum	curriculums	curricula
formula	formulas	formulae
hippopotamus	hippopotamuses	hippopotami
medium	mediums	media
memorandum	memorandums	memoranda
Greek		
automaton	automatons	automata
criterion	criterions	criteria
gymnasium	gymnasiums	gymnasia
phenomenon	phenomenons	phenomena
French		
beau	beaus	beaux
madam	madams	mesdames
tableau	tableaus	tableaux
trousseau	trousseaus	trousseaux
Italian		
bandit	bandits	banditti
dilettante	dilettantes	dilettanti
Fascist	Fascists	Fascisti
libretto	librettos	libretti

l. Some nouns have two plural forms, each form with its own meaning. Thus:

SINGULAR	PLURAL
index	Books have *indexes*
	Numbers have *indices*
die	Machinists use *dies*
	Gamblers use *dice*
genius	*Geniuses* have high intelligence quotients
	Genii act as guardian or demonic spirits

m. Some nouns are used only in the plural.

alms	blues	dregs

athletics	billiards	economics
bellows	commons	forceps

n. The plurals of letters, signs, numbers, and of words regarded as words form the plural by adding *'s*.

Cross your *t*'s and dot your *i*'s.
Omit +'s and −'s.
Excise all the *this*'s and *that*'s.
They were at *6*'s and *7*'s.

Exercise No. 6

In the list below, convert all singular nouns into the plural number and convert all plural nouns into the singular number. (Consult your dictionary when in doubt—as occasionally you are sure to be.)

duty	swine	appendices
flies	spoonful	series
monkey	lice	*p* and *q*
brethren	courts-martial	strata
goose	passer-by	oasis
mongooses	hanger-on	madam
sheep	dice	beaux
Negro	step-in	seraphim
domino	genius	mathematics
half	apparatus	dilettanti

GENDER In English nouns, **gender** indicates sex or the absence of sex. Four genders are distinguished:

1. **Masculine Gender:** male human beings or animals.

boy, father, Joseph; bull, cock, stallion

2. **Feminine Gender:** female human beings or animals.

girl, mother, Josephine; cow, hen, mare

3. **Neuter Gender:** objects without sex.

flower, fire, furnace

(Note: children and animals are sometimes spoken of as Neuter:

The baby cries because it is bored.

The dog barks because it can't speak.)

4. **Common Gender:** human beings or animals that may belong to either sex.

cousin, parent, child, fish, bird

Denoting Gender In nouns, gender may be indicated in any of three ways: by a **different word**, by a **changed termination**, and by an **added word**.

By a different word.

MASCULINE	FEMININE
buck	doe
bull	cow
cock	hen
colt	filly
lord	lady

By a changed termination.

MASCULINE	FEMININE
actor	actress
baron	baroness
god	goddess
hero	heroine
widower	widow

By an added word.

MASCULINE	FEMININE
billy goat	nanny goat
bridegroom	bride
landlord	landlady

Exercise No. 7

Supply the words that fit the following definitions:
1. An old maid.
2. A female dog.
3. A female foal.
4. The wife of a baron.
5. The Italian for "gentleman."
6. A male cat.
7. The man who owns and leases land.
8. A woman who writes poetry.
9. The female counterparts of *Master, Mr.,* and *M.*
10. The male analogue of *widow.*

PERSONIFICATION Sometimes objects or forces, normally of neuter gender, are **personified**—regarded as persons; consequently, they are endowed with masculine or feminine gender.

Crops fail at times, but Death always reaps his harvest.

Then Ire came in, his hand upon his knife.

She has her sister-ships.

Fame smiled, displaying her false teeth.

Note: Personifications are often capitalized.

CASE In English nouns, **case** refers to the change in form that shows the grammatical relationship of nouns to other words in the sentence.

Whether a noun initiates an action or receives it, the form remains constant (that is, the spelling of the noun does not change):

John threw the *bull*.

The *bull* threw *John*.

The noun changes its form (or spelling) only when it is used to show possession:

John's cape eluded the *bull's* horns.

Therefore, some grammarians insist that English nouns have two cases only: the **common case** and the **possessive case**. However, though the principle is valid, it creates as many difficulties as it solves, since it complicates nomenclature. Throughout this book, consequently, the traditional **three cases of nouns** are recognized.

The Nominative Case A noun is said to be in the **nominative** (or **subjective**) case when it acts as the **subject** of a verb, as a predicate nominative, as a word in direct address (vocative), or as an appositive of another word in the nominative case.

Subject of a Verb To determine the word or words acting as its subject ask **who?** or **what?** before the verb. The answer yields the subject.

Jonah was in the belly of the whale for three days and three nights.

Who was in the belly of the whale? The answer, *Jonah,* is the subject of the verb *was*.

Shadrach, Meshach, and *Abed-nego* fell down bound into the midst of the burning fiery furnace.

Who fell down? The triple subject is *Shadrach, Meshach, Abed-nego*.

The *nations* are as a drop of a bucket.

What are as a drop of a bucket? The *nations*-subject.

How beautiful upon the mountains are his *feet*.

Here the subject does not precede the verb, as normally it does. Nevertheless, the method of finding the subject remains the same. What are beautiful: *feet*-subject.

A bruised *reed* shall he not break, and the smoking *flax* shall he not quench.

There are two verbs in the preceding sentence: *shall break* and *shall quench; he,* the subject of each, is located by asking **who?** before the relevant verb.

Predicate Nominative After the **copula** or **linking verb** (a verb that expresses a state of being rather than an action and acts as a kind of equal sign linking subject and predicate) the nominative case is used. The most common of the linking verbs is *be* (*is, was, will be, have been, had been,* etc.); but *become, seem, appear, prove, look,* and about fifty other verbs may be used as linking verbs.

Note in the following examples how the predicate nominative (italicized) serves to define or explain the subject.

God is *one*.

The Bible is a little-known *book*.

The Bible has become a little-known *book*.

We shall have been *friends*.

We remain *enemies*.

The poet turned *traitor*.

Direct Address The word used to address a person directly is termed **the nominative of direct address.**

Villain, unhand me!

Oh *Judgment,* thou art fled to brutish beasts!

Will you roam, *Romans?*

Your enemies, *my friends,* are my enemies.

Appositive A noun is said to be an appositive of another noun, or in **apposition** with another noun, when it **identifies the same person or object under another name.** A noun is in the nominative case if it is in apposition with another noun in the nominative case.

Tom, the piper's son, stole pigs.

A bugler, Little Boy Blue, went into hiding.

Mary, a gardener, planted cockle-shells.

Possessive Case A noun is in the possessive (also called **genitive**) case when it adds *'s* (*apostrophe s*), or simply the apostrophe, to **indicate ownership** (possession), **source or origin** (genesis), **manufacture or authorship, association or connection,** and similar relationships.

Uses of the Possessive Ownership: Marco's millions, Edward's eye teeth

Source or origin: Adam's sin, God's country, the pope's encyclical, mother's son

Manufacture or authorship: Johnson's baby lotion, Johnson's *Lives of the Poets*

Association, connection, attribute, or duration: a woman's work, a month's delay, at swords' point

Formation of the Possessive To form the possessive singular, add **apostrophe s** to the simple (nominative) form of the noun.

child's play	Keats's odes
woman's work	Thomas's doubts
Harold's hope	Dickens's novels

Note: Only the apostrophe is added if another s would cause sibilants (*s*-sounds) to pile up: rather than *Aristophanes's comedies, Dr. Seuss's cartoons,* prefer *Aristophanes' comedies, Dr. Seuss' cartoons.*

To form the possessive plural, add **only the apostrophe** when the simple (nominative) plural form of the noun ends in *s,* but add **apostrophe s** when the simple plural does not end in *s.*

PLURAL ENDING IN S	PLURAL NOT ENDING IN S
horses' tails	children's play
Thomases' doubts	people's voices
devils' delights	freshmen's folly
ladies' day	oxen's burdens
Negroes' advance	brethren's resolve

Note: The methods of forming the possessive case described and illustrated in the foregoing paragraphs have gained wide acceptance; they are as valid as any and far more lucid than most. Unfortunately, other systems are in vogue.

To form the plural of a group of words containing a single idea (**group genitive**) add **apostrophe s** to the last word.

brother-in-law's virtues

brothers-in-law's virtues

The Y.M.C.A.'s program

Kaufman and Hart's *The Man Who Came to Dinner.*

In formal usage, inanimate objects do not take the possessive case, except for some constructions that have long been in the language.

pages of a book (rather than *a book's pages*)

principles of grammar (rather than *grammar's principles*)

process of evolution (rather than *evolution's process*)

leaves of a tree (rather than *a tree's leaves*)

BUT:

goodness' sake	*day's march*
conscience' call	*hair's breadth*
razor's edge	*earth's surface*

Objective Case A noun is said to be in the objective case when it acts as **the direct object of a verb, the indirect object of a verb, the object of a preposition,** or as an **appositive** of another word in the objective case.* (Object implies the person or thing receiving an action: *John hit Mary. Mary,* the object, receives the action that *John,* the subject, initiates.)

Direct Object of a Verb To determine the word or words acting as object of the verb ask **whom?** or **what?** after the verb. The answer yields the object.

Well hast thou fought the better *fight.*

Well hast thou fought what? The answer, [the better] *fight,* is the object of the verb *hast fought.*

She approved my *reason.*

She approved what? The object of approved is *reason.*

God, sitting on his throne, sees *Satan.*

God sees whom? *Satan* is the object of the verb *sees.*

Spirits, when they please, can either *sex* assume.

Spirits can assume what? The answer, *sex,* is the object of the verb *can assume,* even though it comes before *assume.*

Death his *dart* shook.

Death shook what? His *dart.* Here, again, the object precedes the verb.

Indirect Object of a Verb Besides naming the **direct object,** the person or thing receiving an action, a verb may also have an **indirect object,** the person for whom or to whom, or the thing for which or to which an action is performed. To determine the indirect object (which usually comes before the direct object) ask **to**

* The noun is in the objective case when it acts as the *subject of the infinitive.* (See *infinitive.*)

whom? to what? or for whom? for what? after the verb.

The professor taught his *students* grammar.

The professor taught to whom? The answer, [his] *students*, yields the indirect object.

The actress showed *producers* her talents.

Showed to whom? *Producers* is the indirect object.

She wrote the *soldier* a "Dear John" letter.

Wrote to whom? The answer, *soldier*, is the indirect object.

He bought his *wife* a floor-mop.

He bought for whom? *Wife* is the indirect object.

He gave the museum a shrunken head.

Gave to what? *Museum* is the indirect object.

Object of Preposition The preposition shows the relationship between its object and some other word or words in the sentence.

shade of a *tree*

water in the *bucket*

rain on the *roof*

lady into *fox*

Navy versus *Army*

Appositive A noun is in the objective case if it is in apposition with another noun in the objective case.

He arrested Tom, *the piper's son*.

They found the bugler, *Little Boy Blue*.

The wedding guest listened to the mariner, an old *loon*.

Exercise No. 8

In the following sentences, state *what case* each of the italicized words is in and explain briefly the reasons for your statement.

Example:

Truth, crushed to earth, shall rise again.

Truth is in the nominative case because it is the subject of the verb *shall rise*.

1. *Cleo* refused *Tony* his request.
2. It was *David*, the *king*, *priest*, and *prophet* of the Jewish *people*.
3. *Man* is the *architect* of his own *character*.
4. O *Judgment*, thou art fled to brutish *beasts*.
5. Well, Brando, you have played *Brutus*; *Brutus* has lost.
6. The *King of England's palace* is a quarter of an *hour's ride* from the *center* of *London*.
7. The *plural* of the possessive *forms* baffled the *ingenuity* of *grammarians* for a considerable *time*.
8. Try *Guiness's Stout* for *goodness' sake*.
9. Did you see *Shelley* clearly?
10. The happy *man's* without a *shirt*.

THE PRONOUN

The pronoun substitutes for the noun (as its derivation from Latin *pro* meaning "for" and *nomen* meaning "name" indicates). Like the noun, it designates a person, place, or thing; but, unlike the noun, it designates without supplying the name. The following sentence exemplifies the difference.

He butters parsnips.

The pronoun *he* designates someone but does not supply his name; the noun *parsnips* designates and names as well.

Usually the pronoun refers to a word that names the person, place, or thing being discussed. Such a word is called an antecedent:

Jukes has no problems because *he* has no mind.

Here the pronoun *he* has for its antecedent the noun *Jukes*: the noun establishes the identity of the person whom the pronoun merely designates.

KINDS OF PRONOUNS If it were not for the substitutions that the pronouns make possible, repetitious and awkward sentences, rife with distorted meanings, would be inevitable. Consider the following sentences, the first of which employs and the second of which avoids pronouns:

When Abdul looked at his wives and listened to their cackling, he wondered about polygamy.

When Abdul looked at the wives of Abdul and listened to the cackling of the wives of Abdul, Abdul wondered about polygamy.

Depending on the kinds of substitutions they effect, pronouns are generally divided into eight classes: personal, demonstrative, indefinite, relative, interrogative, numerical, reflective, reciprocal.

THE PERSONAL PRONOUN—indicates the speaker (first person), the person spoken to (second person), or the person, place, or thing spoken about (third person).

The declension of the personal pronoun (the forms it takes to show different relations) follows:

FIRST PERSON (MASCULINE AND FEMININE)

	SINGULAR	PLURAL
NOMINATIVE	I	we
POSSESSIVE	my *or* mine	our *or* ours
OBJECTIVE	me	us

SECOND PERSON (MASCULINE AND FEMININE)

NOMINATIVE	you	you
POSSESSIVE	your *or* yours	your *or* yours
OBJECTIVE	you	you

THIRD PERSON

	MASCU-LINE	FEMININE SINGULAR	NEUTER	PLURAL
NOMINATIVE	he	she	it	they
POSSESSIVE	his	her *or* hers	its	their *or* theirs
OBJECTIVE	him	her	it	them

THE DEMONSTRATIVE PRONOUN—*this, that, these,* and *those*—points out a person or thing specifically:

This (that) is the forest primeval.
These (those) were the happy days.

Note: When the demonstrative is followed by a noun which it limits or restricts, it is classified as an adjective:

This forest is primeval.
Those days were happy.

THE INDEFINITE PRONOUN—refers to persons or things generally rather than specifically. Often the antecedents are understood but not stated.

I know *something.*
Somebody loves me.
One must do his duty.

The following list includes the indefinite pronouns most commonly employed.

all	everybody	nobody
another	everyone	nothing
any	everything	nought
anybody	few	one
anyone	least	one another
anything	many	oneself
aught	more	other
both	most	several
each	much	some
each one	neither	somebody
each other	none	someone
either	no one	something

THE RELATIVE PRONOUN—plays two parts at once: **pronoun** and **connective**. As a pronoun it acts as subject or object in a subordinate part of the sentence. As a connective it joins the subordinate to a more important part of the sentence:

It was a silence *that* could be heard.

The relative pronoun *that* acts as the subject of one group of words (*that could be heard*) and at the same time joins it to a more important group (*It was a silence*) by referring or relating back to the noun *silence*. The noun *silence* is the antecedent of the relative pronoun.

He saw the man *who* was invisible.

The relative pronoun *who* connects two parts of the sentence by relating back to its antecedent *man,* and acts as the subject of one part (*who* was invisible).

She is the woman *whom* I heard.

Here, *whom* connects two parts of the sentence by relating back to its antecedent *woman,* and acts as the object of one part (*whom I heard*).

In the following declension, note that only *who* has different case forms, and that *which, that* and *what* have no distinctive possessive forms:

SINGULAR AND PLURAL

NOMINATIVE	POSSESSIVE	OBJECTIVE
who	whose	whom
which	of which	which
that	of that	that
what	of what	what

Several **compound relative pronouns** are in general use. They are formed by adding *ever* and *soever* to the simple forms *who, which,* and *what:*

SINGULAR AND PLURAL

NOMINATIVE	POSSESSIVE	OBJECTIVE
whoever	whosoever	whomever
whichever	of whichever	whichever
whatever	of whatever	whatever
whosoever	whosesoever	whomsoever
whichsoever	of whichsoever	whichsoever
whatsoever	of whatsoever	whatsoever

Who refers to either a masculine or a feminine antecedent: *The man who smiles* or *The woman who smiles.*

Which refers to things (or animals) only: *The bed which broke, The dog which snarled.*

That refers to masculine, feminine, or neuter antecedents: *The man or woman that smiles, The bed that broke.*

The compound relative pronouns frequently include their own antecedents:

Whoever writes must sweat.

Whoever in the preceding sentence equals "the one who"—the antecedent being self-contained.

What, too, though simple in form, is compound in meaning, since it equals "that which":

What is to be will be.

THE INTERROGATIVE PRONOUN—helps ask a question.

Who will go with me to Ramoth-Gilead?

Which of you, without taking thought, can add to his stature one cubit?

SINGULAR AND PLURAL

NOMINATIVE	POSSESSIVE	OBJECTIVE
who	whose	whom
which	of which	which
what	of what	what

Note that only *who* changes the form to show case.

THE NUMERICAL PRONOUN—definitely cites a number, either a **cardinal number** (*one, two, three,* etc.) or an **ordinal number** (*first, second, third,* etc.). They are pronouns when they take the place of an understood noun:

The opposing team cut him off and *one* of them tackled him—the *eleventh* to try.

THE REFLEXIVE AND THE INTENSIVE PRONOUN—are formed by adding *-self* or *-selves* to the personal pronouns:

SINGULAR	PLURAL
myself	ourselves
yourself	yourselves
himself, herself, itself	themselves

Their usage, however, varies.

The **reflexive** pronoun is used as **object**, referring to the same person as the subject:

He loves *himself.*

Here, *himself,* the reflexive pronoun which is the object, and *he,* the personal pronoun which is the subject, refer to the same person. The subject acts on itself—the action reflecting back upon the subject.

The reflexive may also follow a linking or copulative verb:

I feel *myself* again.

The **intensive** pronoun is used simply to emphasize:

The people *themselves* sinned.

They sinned *themselves.*

The intensive pronoun is appositive with the noun or pronoun to which it refers.

THE RECIPROCAL PRONOUNS—represent two or more persons or things interactive—interchanging the action denoted by the verb:

They cheat *each other.*

They cheat *one another.*

Note: Some excessively careful people use *each other* when two people are involved and *one another* when more than two. But the distinction is generally disregarded, even by meticulous writers.

Exercise No. 9

(1) Choose the correct form of the pronouns bracketed, then name the class and case of the word chosen.

(2) Name the class to which each of the pronouns italicized belongs (personal, reflexive, demonstrative, etc.) and its case.

1. *He* was loyal to (whoever, whomever) trusted *him.*
2. He was loyal to (whoever, whomever) he was trusted by.

3. I bit (me, myself) on the elbow.
4. Psychologists know (we, us, ourselves) sometimes despise (us, ourselves).
5. There we were—*all* of us—Einstein, Fermi, and (I, me, myself).
6. The lover and his lass slugged (each other, one another).
7. I heard it from the man (who, whom) knew the janitor to (who, whom) the president of the company had dropped a significant word.
8. He stood on a hill (whose haughty brow, the haughty brow of which) frowned at *everything*.
9. This gismo is a useful gadget (whose use, the use of which) *nobody* knows.
10. Let's you and (I, me) kill rats.

AGREEMENT OF PRONOUNS Pronouns agree with their antecedents—the words for which they stand—in number, person, and gender.

Agreement in Number If the antecedent is singular, the pronoun must be singular; if the antecedent is plural, the pronoun must be plural.

Harry the Horse gave *his* smallest "hello."

The men bred *their* white elephants.

In the first sentence the singular pronoun *his* refers to the singular noun *Harry the Horse;* in the second sentence the plural pronoun *their* refers to the plural antecedent *men*. In sentences like those quoted, few difficulties crop up—at least for those people whose native language is English. Difficulties multiply, however, in two allied situations:

1. When the antecedent is an indefinite pronoun:

Wrong: Each man gets to heaven in *their* own way.

Right: Each man gets to heaven in *his* own way.

Each is singular—and so are *either, neither, everyone, no one, everybody, nobody*. Avoid using a plural pronoun to stand for any of them.

Note: *None* may be either singular or plural.

2. When the antecedent refers to a collective noun:

Wrong: The jury were divided. *It* was unable to bring in a verdict.

Right: The jury were divided. *They* were unable to bring in a verdict.

Here *jury* seems to be plural, a deduction supported by the plural verb *were*.

When *either . . . or* and *neither . . . nor* connect two antecedents:

Wrong: Neither the Republican Party nor the Democratic Party wants Jojo as *their* candidate for dogcatcher.

Right: Neither the Republican Party nor the Democratic Party wants Jojo as *its* candidate for dogcatcher.

The pronoun *its* refers to one party or the other—not to both; the pronoun must consequently be singular.

Agreement in Person The pronoun must be in the same person—first, second, or third—as its antecedent.

Error in person-agreement occurs principally in shifting points of view.

Wrong: The school insists on right behavior: *we* are not Prussians, but *one* must teach children discipline or else *you* will turn out moral monsters.

Right: We insist on right behavior at our school: *we* are not Prussians, but *we* believe that *we* must teach children discipline or else turn out moral monsters.

The first sentence shifts from third person (*school*), to first (*we*), to third (*one*), to second (*you*). The second maintains a first-person point of view throughout.

Note: *We* ought to be used with a specific antecedent, either stated or clearly understood: *we*—the editors; *we*—the authors; *we*—the people of the United States of America. Avoid a vague or ambiguous or shifting signification for *we*.

Agreement in Gender Pronouns—personal pronouns—must be in the same gender—masculine, feminine, or neuter—as their antecedents.

The man has *his* duty, the woman has *hers*, the child has *its*.

Note that *his* corresponds in gender with its antecedent *man, hers* with its antecedent *woman, its* with its antecedent *child*.

Note: The neuter *it* (*its*) may refer to animals and to young children, even though they are of male or female sex and so ought theoretically to be of masculine or feminine gender.

Exercise No. 10

Correct all errors in agreement of pronoun and antecedent.
1. Everybody has a right to their own opinion, right or wrong.
2. Either the marines or their gallant commander, Captain Jinks, may be relied upon for their customary rescue, to occur just before the final curtain.
3. "In America," he said, "one knows that he is free, but sometimes he becomes a little afraid, for we are not yet acclimated to freedom."
4. What a sweet child it is! He seems the image of your friend Jack.
5. If the pig or the fool are of a different opinion, it is because they know only their side of the question.

CASE OF A PRONOUN—depends on its use in the sentence. The pronoun agrees with its antecedent in number, person, and gender, but not in case.

Joan loved John, but *he* spurned *her*.

The pronoun *he* is in the nominative case, whereas its antecedent *John* is in the objective case; *her* is in the objective case, whereas its antecedent *Joan* is in the nominative case.

Like the noun, the pronoun may be in the nominative, possessive, or objective case. Unlike the noun, the objective case of the pronoun undergoes a change in form—is spelled differently from the nominative case.

In the sentences *John struck Jim* and *Jim struck John*, the noun is spelled the same whether it acts as subject or as object. Only the word order shows who initiates and who receives the action.

But in the sentences *He struck John* and *John struck him*, the pronoun is spelled one way (*he*) when functioning as subject and another way (*him*) when functioning as object.

Actually, though, the variations in form to indicate change in case may be easily exagger-

ated. Only six pronouns, for example, have distinct forms for the objective case:

NOMINATIVE: I, we, he, she, they, who
OBJECTIVE: me, us, him, her, them, whom

Note: If compound pronouns (*whoever, whosoever*) and archaic forms (*thou, ye*) are counted, the number is slightly larger.

The case of pronouns depends on the same sentence-relations as the case of nouns. The following analysis of case is therefore abbreviated.

The Nominative Case

SUBJECT OF A VERB
He strains at a gnat.
We are no braver than they [are brave].

PREDICATE NOMINATIVE
It is *I.*

DIRECT ADDRESS
You, come here!

APPOSITIVE
The captain and his company—*he and they alone*—attacked the position.

The Possessive Case

To indicate possession, source, authorship, and similar relationships.
'Twas *mine,* 'tis *his.*

Mill read Wordsworth *whose* verse he praised for *its* healing power.

The Objective Case

DIRECT OBJECT OF A VERB
Jane likes *him* although he loathes *her.*
Jane, *whom* he loathed, liked *him.*

Note: To decide whether the nominative or the objective case of the relative pronoun ought to be employed, substitute a personal pronoun for the relative:

who/whom he loathed
she/her he loathed

Few people would decide that *she* was the proper form; consequently the nominative form is incorrect and *whom* ought to be employed.

He was the detective *who/whom* found the obvious clue.

he/him found the obvious clue. Here, the nominative *he* is plainly the correct form; therefore *who* ought to be employed.

The criminal *who/whom* he sought eluded him.

he/him he sought

Here, the objective *him* is in order; therefore *whom* ought to be employed.

She likes Jane more than [she likes] him.

Note: The words in brackets complete the thought. When unexpressed, they must be silently supplied in order to determine whether the nominative or the objective form is correct. If the sentence read

She likes Jane better than he.

the meaning would be

She likes Jane better than he [likes Jane].

INDIRECT OBJECT OF A VERB

He taught *her* Esperanto.

She gave *him* a package of cyanide.

OBJECT OF PREPOSITION

We know with *whom* we must deal.

Whom are you speaking to?

Note: The preposition may properly come at the end of a sentence, if it seems natural to place it there.

APPOSITIVE

I poisoned Wainewright, his wife, and his dog —*him, her,* and *it,* all three.

Exercise No. 11

Supply the correct case form of the pronoun and give the reasons for each entry.

1. Between you and (I, me) and the lamppost, I think neither (he, him) nor (she, her) knows the time of the day.
2. Knuckleheads like (they, them) need keepers.
3. It was (we, us) children who fired the arsenal.
4. I believe (they, them) to be the dastards.
5. He pointed to the most intelligent person present; namely, (I, me).
6. You are, very obviously, as ugly as (he, him).
7. (Who, whom) the gods love, they grind to dust; those (who, whom) are of the devil's

Pronouns

PERSONAL	DEMON-STRATIVE	INDEFINITE	RELATIVE	INTERROGA-TIVE	NUMERICAL	REFLEXIVE AND INTENSIVE	RECIPROCAL
I; we my, mine; our, ours me; us you your, yours he, she, it; they his, hers; its; their, theirs him, her, it; them.	this; these; that; those.	all, any, anything, both, each, either, one, everyone, everybody, everything, few, many, more, neither, none, somebody, someone, something	who, whose, whom; which, of which; that, of that; what, of what;	who, whose, whom; which, of which; what, of what;	one, two, three; first, second, third.	myself, ourselves; yourself, yourselves; himself, herself, itself; themselves.	each other one another
I speak to *him,* but *he* turns *his* deaf ear towards *me.*	What is *this* or *that* to me who talked it out in Tartary.	In Adam's fall We sinned all.	This is the cock *that* crew in the morn.	*What* light is that, and *whose* hand holds it aloft?	*One* for the money, and first things *first.*	He that wrongs his friend wrongs *himself* more.	The people do not cherish *one another.*

party, however, receive much of the same treatment.

8. Richard Cory is a man (who, whom) we suppose envies no one.

9. All but (he, him) had fled from the burning deck.

10. Than (who, whom) would you say is he more audible?

THE VERB

The verb states something about the subject. Usually the verb expresses action, but also it may express condition or state of being.

He *walks, falls, gets up, continues*.
He *is, was*, and always *shall be*.

TRANSITIVE AND INTRANSITIVE VERBS A transitive verb needs an object to complete its meaning—to receive the action or motion which it expresses:

He *struck* the board.

Here, the *board* completes the meaning of the verb; the action passes over from subject (*He*) to object (*board*). *He struck* alone would seem incomplete, the statement unfinished.

An intransitive verb needs no object to complete its meaning; the action or motion is confined to the subject:

He sleeps.

The action seems complete, the statement finished.

Note: The distinction between transitive and intransitive verbs helps solve one of the recurrent problems of usage. These verbs are transitive: *set, raise, lay* (to place); these are intransitive: *sit, raise, lie* (to recline). Thus:

I *lay* (*laid, have laid*) the book down.
I *lie* (*lay, have lain*) asleep.

LINKING (COPULATIVE) VERBS The linking or copulative verb is a special kind of intransitive, deserving special treatment. Such a verb joins subject to predicate:

Time *is* money.
God *is* love.

Note that *is* establishes a sort of equality between the word which precedes it and the word which follows. Nouns and pronouns following *is*, or any part of *to be*, are in the nominative case; but since they appear in the predicate rather than the subject they are termed predicate nominatives. The bearing on usage becomes apparent when a pronoun functions as a predicate nominative:

The man is *he*.

Note that *he* is not an object.

An adjective may follow the linking verb:

The bells are *joyful*.

Such an adjective, describing or defining the subject, is termed a **predicate adjective**.

Other verbs may serve as joining verbs: *appear, become, feel, grow, look, prove, remain, seem, turn*:

Hopes *prove* false.
All *seems* lost.
Dictators *turn* tyrants.

AUXILIARY VERBS An auxiliary verb helps another verb express action or condition or state of being, foregoing its use as a principal or main verb for that purpose:

He *has* tried Herpecide.

Here, *has* helps *tried* make its statement, thus functioning as an auxiliary. In the following sentence, however, *has* is employed as a principal verb:

He *has* no hair.

The auxiliary verbs are: *can, could, do, did, have, had, is* (and the parts of *to be*), *may, might, must, shall, should, will, would*.

Note: The auxiliary may be separated from the other parts of the verb by a modifier:

I *can* hardly *lie* down and die.
He *has* rarely or never *exhibited* human intelligence.

Exercise No. 12

Indicate by marking them, *T, I, L*, or *A*, whether the italicized verbs are transitive, intransitive, linking (copulative), or auxiliary.

1. I sometimes *sit* and *pity* Noah; but even he *had* this advantage over all succeeding navigators,

that wherever he *landed,* he *was* sure to get no ill news from home. He *should be* canonized as the patron saint of newspaper correspondents, being the only man who ever *had* the very latest authentic intelligence from everywhere.

2. However good you *may* be, you *have* faults; however dull you may *be,* you *can* find out what some of them *are;* and however slight they may be, you *had* better make some—not too painful, but patient—effort to get quit of them.

3. The division of labor—and *let* us say also of play —between poets and scientists, and the cleavage of the two commodities they *make, does* not any more *mean* the end of poetry than of science.

STRONG AND WEAK VERBS

Strong (or irregular) verbs show past time by varying a vowel within the present form of the verb:

PRESENT:	sing,	drink,	know
PAST:	sang,	drank,	knew
PAST PARTICIPLE:*	sung,	drunk,	known

Weak (or regular) verbs show past time by adding *-ed, -t,* or *-d,* to the present form of the verb:

PRESENT:	talk,	feel,	love
PAST:	talk*ed,*	fel*t,*	lov*ed*
PAST PARTICIPLE:	talk*ed,*	fel*t,*	lov*ed*

Note: "Strong verbs" acquired their name because they seemed to form the past without requiring the assistance of any endings, whereas "weak verbs" needed such assistance.

"Regular" and "irregular" are more meaningful (though not precise) terms. In Old English, verbs were inflected in several ways. With the passage of time, however, most verbs assumed some regularity—that is, people began forming them according to a dominant pattern. But the irregular verbs resisted conversion because they were so commonly used that people remembered their inflection.

Of the thousands of verbs in English, fewer than three hundred are strong or irregular. Unable to withstand the process of analogy, most verbs (all verbs newly added to the language) tend to adhere to the regular models.

* A participle (discussed later) is an adjective formed from a verb. The past participle generally ends in *-ed* (*bided*), *-d* (*laid*), *-t* (*wrought*), *-n* (*mown*), *-en* (*ridden*).

PRINCIPAL PARTS OF VERBS

The principal parts of the verb are the **infinitive,** the basic or root part of the verb—usually the same in form as the present form used with *I* (*hop, skip, jump*); the past tense, first person singular (*hopped, skipped, jumped*); and the past participle (*hopped, skipped, jumped*). From the principal parts, the other verb-forms are constructed:*

The **infinitive** yields the **present and future.**
(love)   (I *love*) (I shall *love*)
The past tense yields the past tense only.
(loved)   (I *loved*)
The past participle yields the present perfect,
(loved)   (I *have loved*)
the past perfect, the future perfect.
(I *had loved*)   (I *shall have loved*)

PRINCIPAL PARTS OF IRREGULAR VERBS

The principal parts of the irregular verbs that give the most trouble are included in the following list.

PRESENT (INFINITIVE)	PAST	PAST PARTICIPLE
awake	awaked, awoke	awaked
be (am)	was	been
bear	bore	borne
begin	began	begun
bid	bade	bidden
break	broke	broken
burst	burst	burst
dive	dived, dove	dived
do	did	done
drink	drank	drunk
flee	fled	fled
fly	flew	flown
forsake	forsook	forsaken
get	got	got, gotten
go	went	gone
hang	hung, hanged	hung, hanged
have	had	had
know	knew	known
lay	laid	laid
lie	lay	lain
light	lit, lighted	lit, lighted
ring	rang	rung

* The verb *be* and the defective verbs (those lacking one or more inflectional forms) *may, can, must, ought, will,* and *shall* are exceptions.

rise	rose	risen
see	saw	seen
sing	sang	sung
slay	slew	slain
slink	slunk	slunk
speak	spoke	spoken
sting	stung	stung
stink	stank, stunk	stunk
swear	swore	sworn
swim	swam	swum
wake	woke, waked	waked
wring	wrung	wrung
write	wrote	written

FIRST PERSON:	I love	we love
SECOND PERSON:	you love	you love
THIRD PERSON:	he, she, it loves	they love

I *am* your obedient servant.

I, who *am* your obedient servant, refuse.

You *are* my ex-servant.

He *is* looking for a job.

He and I *are* looking for jobs.

John, who *seeks* a job, *finds* one.

Note: The noun is always in the third person; therefore it always takes a verb in the third person.

Exercise No. 13

Correct the errors in verb form. (If a form other than the given one is preferred supply it.)

1. Because he busted my balloon, I busted him on the nose.
2. He dove fifty feet into a wet handkerchief.
3. He has gotten gold, but the process has froze the gentle current of his soul.
4. I have laid awake on rainy mornings, wondering why I had lain away money for them.
5. When the warden rung the bell, the prisoner was hung.
6. I beared the burden that I was borne to bear.
7. Because he had drank so much, his wife wrang his neck.
8. The sun shined over Ruth as she binded the sheaves.
9. The Romans loaned Antony their ears.
10. When the bee stang him, he sprung to his feet.

VERB INFLECTION: CONJUGATION Verbs change their form or spelling to show **person** (which tells whether the subject is speaking, is spoken to, or is spoken of); **number** (which tells whether the subject is singular or plural); **tense** (which tells whether the subject is involved in a present, past, or future action); **mood** (which tells whether the speaker regards an action as a fact, a command, or a condition); and **voice** (which tells whether the subject performs an action or is acted upon). Verb inflection is termed **conjugation**.

PERSON IN THE VERB The verb agrees with its subject in person. The verb has three persons:

NUMBER IN THE VERB The verb agrees with its subject in number. The verb has two numbers:

SINGULAR: I *love*, you *love*, he, she, it *loves*.

PLURAL: We *love*, you *love*, they *love*.

A compound subject takes a plural verb.

Nero and Caligula *need* shock therapy.

Note: When the compound subject denotes a single idea it may take a singular verb.

The tumult and the shouting *dies*.

The sum and substance of her objection *amounts* to this: she does not like him.

A subject plural in form but singular in meaning takes a singular verb.

Electronics *was* a science and *has become* an industry.

The gallows *seems* her destiny.

A collective noun takes a singular or a plural verb, depending on the way it is understood:

The class *is* unanimous.

The class *are* divided.

After a construction like *one of those who* or *which* or *that*, the temptation is to use a singular verb. The temptation should be resisted:

Wrong: He is one of those men who *gets* bitten by non-existent mosquitoes.

Right: He is one of those men who *get* bitten by non-existent mosquitoes.

The relative pronoun (serving as subject of the verb *get*) is plural, since its antecedent *men* is plural. Therefore the verb ought to be plural.

An easy test consists of relocating the troublesome group of words:

Of those men who get bitten by non-existent mosquitoes, he is one.

When the sentence is revised in such a manner, the temptation to use a singular verb disappears.

It is one of the mosquitoes that (or which) *zing* as they *sting*.

Of the mosquitoes that *zing* as they *sting*, it is one.

Exercise No. 14

Correct the errors of person and number in the verbs included below.

1. Neither John or I are utterly senseless.
2. The herd of cattle which are grazing on the field has been sold down the river.
3. He is one of the men who needs lobotomy like a hole in the head.
4. There is a table, a chair and a tape-recorder: now talk!
5. Tactics win battles.
6. He is one of those pedagogues who has given *pedantry* its signification.
7. It is I, not he, who is at fault.
8. There's gold pieces in plenty here.
9. Seven days without water make one week.
10. The general, together with five thousand picked troops, storm the tavern.

TENSE IN THE VERB The tense of a verb shows the time of an action—present, past, or future. There are six tenses, however—three simple and three perfect.

Simple Tenses The present tense shows that an action takes place now:

He *fills* the cup and *drinks*.
God *is* just and *has* His reasons.

The forms of the verb in the present tense follow.

Note: The verb *fill* is regular; the verbs *drink, am, have,* are irregular.

SINGULAR	PLURAL
1. I fill, drink, am, have	We fill, drink, are, have
2. You fill, drink, are, have	You fill, drink, are, have
3. He, she, it fills, drinks, is, has	They fill, drink, are, have

The past tense shows that an action took place at some previous time.

SINGULAR	PLURAL
1. I filled, drank, was, had	We filled, drank, were, had
2. You filled, drank, were, had	You filled, drank, were, had
3. He, she, it filled, drank, was, had	They filled, drank, were, had

The future tense shows that an action will take place in time to come.

SINGULAR	PLURAL
1. I shall fill, drink, be, have	We shall drink, fill, be, have
2. You will fill, drink, be, have	You will drink, fill, be, have
3. He, she, it will fill, drink, be, have	They will drink, fill, be, have

Perfect Tenses—denote that an action is completed or perfected at the present, at some past time, or at some future time. They are formed by prefixing *have (has)* or *had* or *shall have (will have)* to the past participle.

Present Perfect Tense—shows that an action is complete at present. The action indicated began in the past and extends to the present or bears on the present:

I *have tried* kindness always.

Here the indication is that "I have up to the present tried kindness always." The implication, perhaps, is that the speaker considers altering his course (but other inferences are possible).

Compare the simple past tense:

I *tried* kindness.

Here, the indication is that "At a specific time in the past, I tried kindness." Note that the perfect tense may not be used to describe a definite time in the past.

Wrong: I *have graduated* from college last year. (Perfect)

Right: I *graduated* (or *was graduated*) from college last year. (Past)

Compare also the following statements:

I *ate*. (Past)
I *have eaten*. (Perfect)

In the first sentence, the action indicated took place at a definite (but unstated) time in the past. In the second sentence, the action indicated took place so recently that it has some influence on the present—perhaps it means: "I have eaten so recently that I do not want to eat now." The perfect tense, then, implies some relationship to the present; the past tense reports only that an action is past.

SINGULAR	PLURAL
1. I have filled, drunk, been, had	We have filled, drunk, been, had
2. You have filled, drunk, been, had	You have filled, drunk, been, had
3. He, she, it has filled, drunk, been, had	They have filled, drunk, been, had

Past Perfect Tense—shows that an action was completed before another action in the past, or completed before a definite time in the past:

Before the audience *arrived* [past], he *had memorized* his impromptu speech.

When he *had finished* his second glass of brandy, he *saw* [past] things more clearly.

For twenty years they *had considered* the plunge they *have taken* [perfect].

In the last sentence cited, *they* apparently considered for twenty years the feasibility of taking the plunge, and *then* took it.

SINGULAR	PLURAL
1. I had filled, drunk, been, had	We had filled, drunk, been, had
2. You had filled, drunk, been, had	You had filled, drunk, been, had
3. He, she, it had filled, drunk, been, had	They had filled, drunk, been, had

Future Perfect Tense—shows that an action will be completed before another action in the future, or before a given time in the future.

Note: The future perfect tense is seldom employed.

They *will have hanged* the man while the committee debate.

They will try to stop you, but you *will have passed* beyond their reach.

SINGULAR	PLURAL
1. I shall have filled, drunk, been, had	We shall have filled, drunk, been, had
2. You will have filled, drunk, been, had	You will have filled, drunk, been, had
3. He, she, it will have filled, drunk, been, had	They will have filled, drunk, been, had

Exercise No. 15

Give the tense of each italicized verb in the following sentences:

1. I fell in love before I *had reached* years of discretion.
2. I wonder how many souls the devil *will have collected* before he returns to his winter home.
3. With the continued growth of specialization, the experts *have* necessarily *had* more and more to say in the affairs of industry.
4. The true friend of property, the true conservative, is he who *insists* that property *shall be* the servant and not the master of the commonwealth.
5. During this Gilded Age the standard of the best building *had risen* almost as high as it *had been* in America in any earlier period; but the mass of good buildings *had* relatively *decreased;* and the domestic dwellings in both country and city *lost* those final touches of craftsmanship that *had lingered* here and there, up to the Civil War.
6. Many people *believe* that it *was* a sad day indeed when Benjamin Franklin *tied* that key to a kite string and flew the kite in a thunderstorm; other people *believe* that if it *hadn't been* Franklin, *it would have been* someone else.
7. What *made* Poe particularly acceptable to the French, however, was what *had distinguished* him from most of the other Romantics of the English-speaking countries: his interest in aesthetic theory.
8. No one *can be found* who *will deny* that in the case of any single individual the greatest prosperity *can exist* only when that individual *has reached* his highest state of efficiency; that is, when he *is turning* out his largest daily output.
9. It *is* well for the world that in most of us, by the age of thirty, the character *has set* like plaster, and *will* never *soften* again.
10. In a few years the Octogenarian Club *will have been decimated.*

MOOD IN THE VERB The mood (or *mode*) of a verb shows the manner in which a statement is made. There are three moods: indicative, imperative, and subjunctive. For a statement of fact, a verb in the indicative mood is used:

I *ask* questions.

For a command or request, a verb in the imperative mood is used:

You, *ask* questions.

For an idea presented as doubtful, contrary to fact, conditional, or imaginary, the subjunctive mood is used.

Indicative Mood is the mood of fact, or rather of statement presented as fact. Though the statements which follow contradict each other, both employ the same (indicative) verb:

Rum is an alcoholic liquor.

Rum is a non-alcoholic liquor.

Questions employ verbs in the indicative mood (since questions expect statements of fact in reply).

Is rum an alcoholic liquor?

The indicative mood is much the most important in English; perhaps ninety-eight percent of the verbs employed in speaking and writing are in the indicative mood. Almost every function of the subjunctive may be assumed by the indicative. Thus, *If he ask questions, he will receive answers* has been instanced as subjunctive. But unquestionably the indicative alternative, *If he asks questions, he will receive answers* is the more normal. Moreover, the uses of the subjunctive shrink continually, the indicative increasingly embracing them.

The indicative forms for the six tenses are listed under **Tense in the Verb.**

Imperative Mood is the mood of command and request.

Consider the ant.

Join the marines.

Hold your tongue.

Note: *You* is understood but generally not expressed in the imperative.

The imperative has only one tense and one number. It has both numbers, but the form for the singular is identical with the form for the plural.

Subjunctive Mood is the mood of doubt, condition, wish, imagination, and the like.

The forms of the subjunctive follow. Note that the subjunctive implies future time (it has been called "the mood of futurity"); consequently, the subjunctive, requiring no future forms, includes only four tenses. (*If*, though no part of the subjunctive, precedes each form because the subjunctive most often appears in *if*-constructions.)

PRESENT TENSE: (If) I, you, he, we, they *fill, drink, be, have.*

PAST TENSE: (If) I, you, he, we, they *filled, drank, were, had.*

PRESENT PERFECT TENSE: (If) I, you, he, we, they *have filled, have drunk, have been, have had.*

PAST PERFECT TENSE: (If) I, you, he, we, they *had filled, had drunk, had been, had had.*

Note that most verbs have only one form of the subjunctive different from the corresponding indicative form—the third person singular of the present tense:

SUBJUNCTIVE: (If) he, she, it *drink, fill, have.*

INDICATIVE: He, she, it *drinks, fills, has.*

The verb *be* (the sole verb currently used in the subjunctive to any extent) has two distinctive forms:

Be for all persons of the present tense.

Were for the first and third persons of the past tense.

SINGULAR		PLURAL	
PRESENT TENSE			
SUBJUNCTIVE	INDICATIVE	SUBJUNCTIVE	INDICATIVE
1. (If) I *be*	I am	(If) we *be*	We are
2. (If) you *be*	You are	(If) you *be*	You are
3. (If) he, she, it *be*	He, she, it *is*	(If) they *be*	They are
PAST TENSE			
1. (If) I *were*	I was	(If) we *were*	We were
2. (If) you *were*	You were	(If) you *were*	You were
3. (If) he, she it *were*	He, she, it was	(If) they *were*	They were

The subjunctive has only two live uses—and neither exhibits so much liveliness as formerly. They are:

(1) In a "condition contrary to fact" construction:

If he *were* to fall into the pond, he would come up with a fish in his mouth.

I wish you *were* here—instead of me.

Note: If the condition is presented not as contrary to fact—untrue—but merely as doubtful or uncertain, the present subjunctive is used:

If he *be* innocent, we are all guilty.

If he *survive*, the doctor's fees will kill him.

(2) In a *that*-construction after verbs or adjectives which denote asking, agreeing, demanding, determining, directing, enacting, insisting, ordering, proposing, recommending, suggesting, and the like. Most such usages are formal:

He moved that the meeting *be* adjourned.

The prisoner asks that he *be* allowed to take courses for credit.

It is necessary that justice *be* done.

Is it just that the poor man *suffer?*

The subjunctive persists, too, in many idioms, formulas, and fossilized expressions.

Far *be* it from me.

O that it *were* possible!

Peace *be* with you.

Be it ever so humble, there's no place like home.

Though he *slay* me, yet will I trust in him.

Be that as it may.

Exercise No. 16

In the sentences following, supply the modal form, indicative or subjunctive, to be preferred. (The verb to be used is parenthetically indicated.)

1. If the earth ____ flat, men could perhaps sail *asquare* it. (to be)
2. Since the earth ____ round, men can sail around it. (to be)
3. If wishes ____ horses, beggars would ride. (to be)
4. Since wishes ____ not horses, beggars are pedestrians. (to be)
5. They proposed formally that he ____ admitted. (to be)
6. They will do their best to see that he ____ admitted. (to be)
7. I suggest that the student ____ carefully the shifty nature of mood. (to consider)
8. It is necessary that every citizen with a small capacity for disappointment ____ campaign promises. (to suspect)
9. I wish I ____ your widow. (to be)
10. Far ____ it from me to split infinitives, or hairs, to dangle participles or babies, to modify substantives or opinions. (to be)

VOICE IN THE VERB The voice of a verb shows whether the subject is active or passive: the verb is active if the subject performs an action, passive if the subject receives an action.

ACTIVE: A misinformed electorate *put* him into office.

PASSIVE: He *was put* into office by a misinformed electorate.

In the first sentence the subject *electorate* acts; in the second the subject *He* receives the action.

Note: The object (*him*) of the active verb becomes the subject (*he*) of the passive verb. Since transitive verbs have objects, only transitive verbs have a passive voice.

The passive voice of the verb is made by adding its past participle to some form of the verb *be*. The following table gives the conjugation of *fill* in the passive voice for the third person singular, indicative mood.

PRESENT: It is filled

PAST: It was filled

FUTURE: It will be filled

PRESENT PERFECT: It has been filled

PAST PERFECT: It had been filled

FUTURE PERFECT: It will have been filled

The active voice is the norm in English: it is more direct and more forceful than the passive:

ACTIVE: I *pitied* him.

PASSIVE: He *was pitied* by me.

Moreover, the passive construction often leads to awkward expression, especially in long sentences: Compare the passive translation of Emerson's famous sentence with the original.

Awkward Passive If good corn *is had* by a man, or wood, or boards, or pigs *to be sold*, or better chairs or knives, crucibles or church organs *can be made* by him than by anybody else, a broad, hard-beaten road to his house, though it be in the wilderness, *will be found* by you.

Active If a man has good corn, or wood, or boards, or pigs to sell, or can make better chairs or knives, crucibles or church organs than anybody else, you will find a broad, hard-beaten road to his house, though it be in the wilderness.

There are, however, legitimate uses for the passive:

(1) To emphasize the recipient of an action: The fuse *was ignited* by someone.

Here, the fuse, not the igniter, is the center of interest.

(2) To eliminate mention of the agent: The fuse was ignited.

Much *has been written* and much *has been said*, but nothing *has been done.*

Note: Since the doers of the action are irrelevant here, the passive voice seems preferable.

Exercise No. 17

In the following sentences, several of the verbs in the passive voice are ineffective because they are awkward, unnatural or unemphatic. Convert such passive verbs into active verbs; recast the sentence if necessary.

1. A most enjoyable time was had by everybody.
2. It is believed by most teachers that sentences are written in the passive by people when the communication they intend has not been thought out before the pen has been set to the paper.
3. Joe's head is being examined by some quack.
4. He saw that she wanted to be kissed, and she was kissed by him.
5. After Jonathan J. Logorrhea had spoken for an hour, nobody listened to what was being said.
6. I admit that I was impressed by the bank notes which were flashed before my eyes by her father.
7. We wandered aimlessly until we were rescued by a passing garbage truck.
8. Caesar was first conquered then cuckolded by Cleopatra.
9. Books are read by soldiers—comic books, chiefly.

10. Belloc hoped that when he died people would say: "His sins were scarlet, but his books were read."

OTHER VERB FORMS: THE PROGRESSIVE AND EMPHATIC FORMS A meaning somewhat different from any indicated by the tense-forms previously described can be achieved by employing the **progressive** or the **emphatic** forms of the verb.

Progressive Forms—of the verb show that an action is still continuing. They may present duration more graphically than the simple tenses.

Progressive tense-forms consist of some part of the verb *be* followed by the present participle. A synopsis in the third person singular follows. Note that only the present and past forms of the progressive are used in the passive voice.

ACTIVE

PRESENT: *He is filling*
PAST: *He was filling*
FUTURE: *He will be filling*
PERFECT: *He has been filling*
PAST PERFECT: *He had been filling*
FUTURE PERFECT: *He will have been filling*

PASSIVE

PRESENT: *He is being filled*
PAST: *He was being filled*

SUBJUNCTIVE

PRESENT: *(If) he be filling*
PAST: *(If) he were filling*
PERFECT: *(If) he have been filling*
PAST PERFECT: *(If) he had been filling*

Note: In the passive voice, the past is the only subjunctive form used: *(If) he were being given.*

Emphatic Forms—of the verb are used for emphasis or stress.

Emphatic tense forms consist of *do* or *did* followed by the infinitive without *to*. The emphatic forms are used only in the present and past tense of the active voice; they are not used at all in the passive voice.

PRESENT: *I do fill*
PAST: *I did fill*

Exercise No. 18

Keeping tense and mood constant, supply the progressive form and the emphatic form (if one exists) of each verb in the following list.

1. I *play*	5. they *had asseverated*
2. you *fiddled*	6. he *will have explicated*
3. it *will fizz*	7. (if) he *laugh*
4. she *has constituted*	8. he *is slugged*

THE ADJECTIVE

The adjective modifies or qualifies a substantive (noun or pronoun), altering in some way its meaning or range.

KINDS OF ADJECTIVES Adjectives are classified according to the work they do:

DESCRIPTIVE ADJECTIVE—describes or characterizes a substantive—readers its meaning more precise. There are two kinds of descriptive adjectives:

COMMON ADJECTIVE—applies to a class of things, rather than to a particular thing.

mauve decade, *industrious* beaver, *lone* ranger, *happy* moron, *little* man, *yellow* journalism.

PROPER ADJECTIVE—applies to one particular member of a class, rather than to the class as a whole. Proper adjectives derive from proper nouns—often proper nouns are used to modify.

Sunday punch, *Roman* holiday, *American* way, *Panama* hat, *Protestant* tradition, *English* literature.

NOTE: Often the proper adjective has a limiting as well as a descriptive function, as in *Panama hat;* however, *Panama hats* has become a general name for a variety of plaited hat, and the limiting function of the adjective seems to be of minor importance. Ultimately, it may be written with a lower-case *p.* For when the origin of a proper adjective is disregarded, it generally is spelled without an initial capital:

quixotic gesture, *india* ink, *italic* type, *venetian* blinds, *satanic* wiles, *paris* green, *pasteurized* milk.

LIMITING (OR DEFINITIVE) ADJECTIVE—limits or defines the meaning of the noun—restricts its application. There are several kinds of limiting adjective.

PRONOMINAL ADJECTIVE—is a word, commonly used as a pronoun, that modifies a substantive.

DEMONSTRATIVE
this book, *these* books
that man, *those* men

INTERROGATIVE
What directions did the doctor give?
In *which* direction does the dog point?
By *whose* direction are we held?
The italicized adjectives each modify *direction.*

RELATIVE
Select *which* rapier you like.
I selected the rapier *whose* metal had been tested.
Whose may refer either to persons (as commonly) or to things.

INDEFINITE
some days, *any* stick, *no* islands, *every* man, *each* age, *other* times, *neither* alternative, *both* ends

POSSESSIVE
my eyes, *mine* eyes (archaic), *your* tooth, *his* hair, *her* lips, *its* tongue; *our* bodies, *your* heads, *their* appendixes

Note: The possessive adjectives agree in number with their antecedents, not with the nouns they modify:
my word, *my* words

INTENSIVE
the *very* likeness

IDENTIFYING
the *same* story

NUMERICAL
three men (cardinal)
the *third* man (ordinal)

Exercise No. 19

Underline each adjective and indicate the kind it is.

1. The full African moon poured down its light into the wide, lovely plain.
2. O may I join the choir invisible
   Of those immortal dead who live again
   In minds made better by their presence.
3. I can tell you which lie you prefer.
4. Which lie seems better?
5. The pixilated man offered to fight any woman or any child in the house.
6. Coffee, say the Spaniards, ought to be black as the devil, hot as hell, and sweet as sin.
7. The argument, subtle and specious, convinced everyone who could not follow it.
8. He suffered (or, rather, other people did) from the Holmesean delusion that the worst puns are the best.
9. He called the argument brilliant but corrupt.
10. "Like a mackerel by moonlight," he said, "it shines and stinks."

ARTICLES The definite article *the* and the indefinite articles *a* and *an* function as limiting adjectives.

Definite Article *The* particularizes the noun; that is, it specifies a particular thing, distinct from others of the same kind.

The monkey has a beard.
The children are monsters.
He is not *the* man I thought he was.

The derives from the old form of the demonstrative *that*, and still has demonstrative force:

He is *the* Johnson McThirlwall Dickson.

The preceding an adjective may form a plural noun:

Only *the* brave deserve *the* fair.
The valiant never taste of death but once.

The preceding a singular noun may have a generalizing effect, equal to the indefinite *any* or *every*:

The child is father to *the* man.
The lunatic, *the* lover, and *the* poet.
Are of imagination all compact.

Note: Repetition of *the* before the nouns of a series stresses their individual quality.

The before a proper noun converts it into a common noun.

He was *the* Solomon of our asylum.
She was *the* Jezebel of the old ladies' home.
In the sentences cited, *Solomon* equals "wise man," and *Jezebel* "wicked woman."

Indefinite Article *A* is used before words beginning with a consonant sound:

a boy, *a* crowd, *a* girl, *a* union, *a* European

Note: Both *union* and *European* begin with a consonant sound; consequently each is preceded by *a*.

An is used before words beginning with a vowel sound.

an apple, *an* eagle, *an* idiot, *an* omen, *an* urn

Note: *An* is preferred before "silent" *h*:

an heir, *an* hour, *an* herb

A is preferred before "sounded" *h*:

a history, *a* historical novel (but *an* historical novel is also in good usage), *a* hotel, *a* hump, *a* hill

A and *an* generalize the noun; that is, they point to an object as one of a general class:

And this is the sum of lasting love:
Scratch *a* lover, and find *a* foe.

Though he seemed *a* man of distinction, he acted like *an* ape.

A Book of Verses underneath the Bough,
A Jug of Wine, *a* Loaf of Bread—and Thou

A and *an* derive from the old form of *one*, and sometimes have the force of the numeral:

A stitch in time saves nine.

A and *an* sometimes have the force of each:

Her perfume costs *a* dollar *an* ounce.
He works seven days *a* week.

Note: *A* and *an* are preferred to *per*, save in Latin phrases or commercial locutions.

Exercise No. 20

Insert *a* (*an*) or *the*, whichever seems the more logical, in the following blanks. (If neither article is appropriate, make no change.)

1. Every man has ——— good angel and ——— bad angel attending on him in particular.
2. His wisdom has became ——— proverb and ——— byword, but ——— half was not told me.
3. There ——— wicked cease from troubling and there ——— weary be at rest.
4. I saw ——— very strange couple yesterday,

——— monkey leading ——— man; today my oculist saw ——— same pair, ——— monkey still leading ——— man.

5. It was ——— Honorable Trismagestus Q. Terwilliger.
6. ——— adobe as well as ——— hotel often has ——— history.
7. Lo! Death has reared himself ——— throne
In ——— strange city lying alone
Far down within ——— dim West,
Where ——— good and ——— bad and ——— worst and ——— best
Have gone to their eternal rest.
8. ——— Thames, England's principal river, rises in ——— Gloucestershire on ——— east slope of ——— Cotswold Hills and bounds part of ——— Gloucestershire, Middlesex, Essex, Wiltshire, Berkshire, Surrey, and Kent.
9. ——— *h* in "heaven" is aspirate.
10. We will now consider that charming beast, ——— hippocampus.

POSITION OF ADJECTIVES An adjective regularly precedes the noun it modifies directly:

Brave men and *fair* women
Kind hearts and *gentle* folk
Cold hands and *warm* heart

But in some relatively established phrases the adjective follows:

Streets *wide* and *narrow*
Life *everlasting*
Time *enough*

Note: An adjective coming before the noun, listing one of its attributes, is called an **attributive adjective**.

An adjective sometimes acts like a noun in apposition, following and explaining the noun.

The devil, *unholy* and *unabashed*, stood before Cotton Mather.

The Byronic hero—*passionate, tormented, world-weary*—was fashioned after Byron's own image.

He scorned our simple ways, *simple* but *joyous*.

Note: An adjective used like a noun in apposition is called an **appositive adjective**.

An adjective may complete the meaning of the verb while modifying the subject:

The sea is *calm* tonight, the tide is *full*.
The problem proved *insolvable*.

The child became *difficult* first, then *impossible*.

Note: An adjective that is part of the predicate but functions as a modifier of the subject, is called a **predicate adjective**.

COMPARISON OF ADJECTIVES Most adjectives denote variable qualities—qualities that exist in various degrees. The adjective is inflected (its spelling is altered) to show the degree of the quality. Such modification is termed **comparison**.

There are three degrees of comparison, the positive, the comparative, and the superlative.

1. The positive degree names the simple quality:

Socrates was a *wise* man.
Shakespeare was a *great* poet.

2. The comparative degree expresses a higher degree of the quality:

Socrates was a *wiser* man than Protagoras.
Shakespeare was a *greater* poet than Jonson.

The comparative degree is used in comparing two persons or two things.

3. The superlative degree expresses the highest degree of the quality:

Socrates was the *wisest* Greek of all.
Shakespeare was the *greatest* English poet.

The superlative degree is used in comparing three or more persons or things.

FORMING THE DEGREES OF COMPARISON The positive degree is the form the dictionary supplies; it is the simple (uninflected) form of the adjective.

Regular adjectives form the comparative degree in two ways:

Almost all adjectives of one syllable form the comparative by adding *-r* or *-er* to the simple adjective:

braver, higher, lower, smaller, larger, thinner, thicker.

Most adjectives of two syllables (disyllables) and almost all adjectives of three or more syllables (polysyllables) form the comparative by using *more* before the simple adjective:

disyllables { more careful, more distinct, more active, more recent.

polysyllables { more beautiful, more dangerous, more practical, more primitive.

Regular adjectives form the **superlative** degree in two ways:

Almost all adjectives of one syllable form the superlative by adding -st or -est to the simple adjective:

bravest, highest, lowest, smallest, largest, thinnest, thickest.

Most adjectives of two syllables and almost all adjectives of three or more syllables form the superlative by using most before the simple adjective:

disyllables { most careful, most distinct, most active, most recent.

polysyllables { most beautiful, most dangerous, most practical, most primitive.

Some commonly used adjectives are compared irregularly:

bad	worse	worst
far	farther, further	farthest, furthest
good, well	better	best
late	later, latter	latest, last
little	less, lesser, littler	least, littlest
much, many	more	most
old	older, elder	oldest, eldest

Many adjectives of two syllables may be compared by adding the suffix -er and -est to form the comparative and superlative, or by prefixing more and most.

lovely	lovelier *or* more lovely loveliest *or* most lovely
handsome	handsomer *or* more handsome handsomest *or* most handsome
narrow	narrower *or* more narrow narrowest *or* most narrow
serene	serener *or* more serene serenest *or* most serene
remote	remoter *or* more remote remotest *or* most remote

Note: Whether the -er, -est method of comparison or the *more, most* method of comparison is to be preferred depends upon euphony and emphasis: if either form of the comparative or superlative sounds better than the other, or more effectively achieves the emphasis desired, it is to be preferred.

"Down-hill" comparison (to show decreased degree of a quality) may be effected by using *less* **and** *least***:**

strong	less strong	least strong
worthy	less worthy	least worthy
repulsive	less repulsive	least repulsive

Absolutes, adjectives denoting the highest or lowest degree of a quality, are theoretically incapable of being compared. When a thing is *unique,* only one of its kind exists—itself; consequently, *more unique* and *most unique* are logically impossible. The following adjectives do not logically admit of degrees:

almighty	empty	matchless	square
certain	eternal	perfect	supreme
circular	everlasting	perpetual	triangular
complete	heavenly	round	universal
dead	infinite	single	unique

However, language is often illogical, and in practice absolutes like *perfect* are frequently used as a kind of shorthand for "more nearly perfect."

Exercise No. 21

Insert the appropriate comparative or superlative forms of the simple (positive) adjectives italicized below.

1. Of two evils, choose the *little.*
2. My aunt is the *old* of eighteen sisters.
3. Thank you; you are *kind.*
4. Get there *first* with the *much*—that is the *fundamental* principle of tactics.
5. Cats are *clean* than monkeys, but monkeys are *intelligent* than cats.
6. He is the *wellknown* and the *bloodthirsty* of that nefarious crew.
7. Put your *good* foot forward.
8. He had rarely listened to a (an) *absurd* proposal, or to one *happy* in its phrasing.
9. He had never eaten a sausage that was *big, red, hot.*
10. He penetrated to the *in* sanctum.

THE ADVERB

The adverb modifies or qualifies a verb, an adjective, or another adverb, altering in some way its meaning or range.

He speaks *bitterly*.

The adverb *bitterly* modifies the verb *speaks*.

He speaks in an *exceedingly* bitter fashion. The adverb *exceedingly* modifies the adjective *bitter*.

He speaks *very* bitterly.

The adverb *very* modifies the adverb *bitterly*.

KINDS OF ADVERBS Depending on their use, adverbs are classified as **simple** or **conjunctive**.

SIMPLE ADVERB—alters the meaning of a single word in some way. The simple adverb answers one of several questions, deriving its name from the kind of answer it gives:

ADVERB OF TIME The adverb of time answers the question *when?*

He will come *today, tomorrow, by and by*.

ADVERB OF PLACE The adverb of place answers the question *where?*

He has gone *here, there*, and *everywhere*.

ADVERB OF MANNER The adverb of manner answers the question *how?*

He talks *well—slowly, distinctly*, and *lucidly*.

ADVERB OF DEGREE OR MEASURE The adverb of degree or measure answers the question *how much?*

He seemed *quite* rich, *very* knowledgeable, *hardly* enthusiastic, but *not* unenthusiastic.

ADVERB OF CAUSE OR PURPOSE The adverb of cause or purpose answers the question *why?*

Why does the fat lady walk through the fields in gloves?

Note: *Why* in the sentence just cited may be called an **interrogative adverb** as well, since it is used to introduce a question. (Similarly, in *How tall she is!* the adverb *how* may be called an **exclamatory adverb**, since it is used to make an exclamation.)

CONJUNCTIVE ADVERB—acts like a conjunction and it acts like an adverb. As a conjunction it joins two independent clauses; as adverb, it modifies the independent clause in which it appears.

He knows nothing; *moreover*, he doesn't know that he knows nothing.

Note: *Moreover* is said to be an adverb, though it modifies the whole idea of the independent clause in which it appears, rather than a specific verb, adjective, or adverb. It is called an **adverb** for arbitrary reasons: words that do not fit into any other category are accounted adverbs—for convenience of classification.

He laughs at psychoanalysis; he believes in dianetics, *however*.

Note: The conjunctive adverb *however* modifies the whole independent clause *he believes in dianetics*, not any particular word in the clause. Compare *however* as a simple adverb:

However ridiculous psychoanalysis seems theoretically, it has proved itself clinically.

However here modifies the adjective *ridiculous*.

The more common conjunctive adverbs are:

accordingly	hence	nevertheless
additionally	however	no
also	indeed	on the contrary
at any rate	in other words	on the other hand
anyway	in short	still
besides	likewise	then
consequently	moreover	therefore
furthermore	namely	yes
		yet

Note: Unlike the conjunction, which stands first in the clause it introduces, the conjunctive adverb may stand in any position in the clause which it modifies. The italicized words in the following sentences are conjunctions.

He gave generously *because* he was kind.

He gave generously, *for* he was kind.

Neither *because* nor *for* may be displaced: each must stand first in the clause it introduces. Compare the variously placed conjunctive adverbs in the following sentences:

He gave generously; *consequently*, he was kind.

He gave generously; he was, *consequently*, kind.

He gave generously; he was kind, *consequently*.

FORMS OF ADVERBS Most adverbs are formed by adding *-ly* to the corresponding adjective:

ADJECTIVES: *swift, slow, hot, cold.*

ADVERBS: *swiftly, slowly, hotly, coldly.*

Many adverbs (especially those long in common use) do not end in *-ly*.

very, much, little, almost, often, there

Note: The ending *-ly* is not the invariable sign of an adverb. The italicized words in the following sentence are all adjectives:

A *lovely* lady of *queenly* bearing, she married an *ugly* man of *slovenly* habits.

Note, too, that sometimes adverbs have the same form as the corresponding adjectives: their use determines their classification.

ADJECTIVE: He had a *fast* hold.

ADVERB: He held *fast*.

Exercise No. 22

In the following sentences, underline each adverb and indicate the class to which it belongs.

1. He played mumblety-peg almost professionally.
2. I eat; therefore, I exist.
3. He formerly hunted mongooses.
4. The goose has gone west; it is, consequently, a gone goose.
5. There she blows!
6. He feels bad and behaves badly.
7. His nerve endings are anesthetized; hence, he feels badly.
8. Yes, we have no bananas.
9. He seldom talks sensibly; she, never.
10. Well, what now?

COMPARISON OF ADVERBS Adverbs, like adjectives, have their degrees of comparison: the positive, the comparative, and the superlative.

Most adverbs form the comparative degree by using *more* and the superlative degree by using *most*.

bravely	more bravely	most bravely
beautifully	more beautifully	most beautifully
seldom	more seldom	most seldom

Adverbs of one syllable generally form the comparative degree by adding *-er* and the superlative degree by adding *-est*.

fast	faster	fastest
soon	sooner	soonest
late	later	latest
hard	harder	hardest

Note: A few adverbs of two syllables, especially those having the same form as the corresponding adjective, add *-er* and *-est* to form the comparative and superlative:

early	earlier	earliest
little	littler	littlest
icy	icier	iciest

Note: To achieve euphony or special emphasis, these adjectives may form comparative and superlative degrees by prefixing *more* and *most*.

A few adverbs may be compared either by adding *-er* and *-est* or by prefixing *more* and *most*:

common	commoner or more common	commonest or most common
often	oftener or more often	oftenest or most often

A few adverbs are compared irregularly:

far	farther, further	farthest, furthest
ill or badly	worse	worst
little	less	least
much, many	more	most
well	better	best

Note: In standard English, *farther* expresses greater distance; *further* expresses greater degree or quantity.

Heaven is *farther* than hell.

He received *further* reports from Screwtape.

Adverbs (like adjectives) may be downgraded by using *less* and *least*.

soon	less soon	least soon
keenly	less keenly	least keenly
agreeably	less agreeably	least agreeably

Some adverbs theoretically do not admit of comparison:

| fatally | quite | certainly |
| absolutely | entirely | |

In practice, however, they are frequently compared.

Exercise No. 23

Insert the appropriate comparative or superlative forms of the simple adverbs italicized below.

1. Extremes of fortune are true wisdom's test,
   And he's of men *wise* who bears them *well*.

2. The *far* we go, the *ill* we fare.

3. The steaks are *tough* than ours, but the women are *tender*.

4. Of them all, she spoke *distinctly*.

5. His kite went *high* of all, and he was the *highly* elated of fliers.

THE CONJUNCTION

The conjunction joins words or groups of words.

KINDS OF CONJUNCTIONS There are two kinds of conjunctions, **coordinating** and **subordinating**.

COORDINATING CONJUNCTION—joins words or groups of words that are coordinate—that is, of the same order or rank.

> WORDS: Jack *and* Jill
> wind *or* weather
> not angles *but* angels
> GROUPS OF WORDS: of cabbages *and* of kings
> not to live in *but* to look at
> what we want *and* what we get
> if we live *or* if we die
> Knowledge comes *but* wisdom lingers.
> We must die, *for* men are mortal.

There are six simple coordinating conjunctions: *and, but, for, nor, or, yet.*

Because they are regularly coupled with each other, some coordinating conjunctions are termed **correlatives**:

both . . . and	not only . . . but (also)
either . . . or	neither . . . nor
so . . . as	whether . . . or

Neither fish *nor* fowl *nor* good red herring
He *not only* marks his cross *but also* signs his name.

SUBORDINATING CONJUNCTION—joins a subordinate clause to a main clause.*

* A clause is a group of words containing a subject and predicate. A main clause can stand alone; it is a self-sufficient unit. A subordinate clause cannot; it depends upon some other word or words to make its meaning clear.

I whistle *while* he works.
The subordinate clause *while he works* is joined to the main clause *I whistle* by the subordinating conjunction *while*. The subordinating conjunction introduces its clause (**subordinating it**) and at the same time links it to the main clause upon which it depends for its relevance and force.

Before the sun rose, the hens set.
The hens set *before* the sun rose.

In these two sentences, note that *before* is the link-word, though in the first sentence the clause it introduces precedes and in the second sentence follows the main clause. The logic of the connection remains the same.

The most commonly used subordinating conjunctions, together with the relations they indicate, follow:

Time: as, as long as, as soon as, often, before, since, till (until), when, while.

Reason or Cause: as, because, inasmuch as, since, why.

Supposition or Condition: although (though), if, unless, whether . . . or.

Purpose: in order that, so, that, lest.
Comparison: than.

Exercise No. 24

Pick out each conjunction in the following sentences and tell whether it is a coordinating or a subordinating conjunction.

1. Neither heat nor cold daunts the postman.
2. A man is shorter when he is walking than when at rest.

3. As good cooks go, she went.
4. He pores over books when it rains.
5. Though all men deny thee, yet will not I.
6. It is certain because it is impossible.
7. He maintains a discreet silence so that no one will be able to swear he is stupid.
8. Tarry, lest you be on time.
9. But the conclusion must be false, for the premises are false.
10. He is not only dull himself, but the cause of dullness in others also.

THE PREPOSITION

A preposition shows the relationship between a noun or a pronoun and some other word in the sentence.

water *under* the bridge
age *before* beauty
dog *in* the manger

The prepositions (italicized) connect two words, like the conjunction; unlike the conjunction the preposition shows the relationship existing between them.

OBJECT OF A PREPOSITION The noun or pronoun that the preposition introduces or governs is in the objective case.

cannon *before them*
the secret *between us*
a headache *to him*

The pronouns *them, us,* and *him* are all objects of the prepositions upon which they depend.

POSITION OF THE PREPOSITION The preposition generally precedes its object (is in the *pre* position). However, it may legitimately follow, and in idiomatic expressions or commonly employed locutions it often does:

Whom are you speaking *about?*
This is the type of arrant pedantry *which* I will not put up *with.*
Peace is *what* we must prepare *for.*

In each of the sentences above the pronoun (*whom, which, what*) is the object of the terminal preposition.

Note: The object of the preposition may be omitted:

The lady [*whom*] we look *for.*
The ground [*which*] we stand *on.*

MEANINGS OF THE PREPOSITION The preposition generally expresses the relation of one thing to another with respect to place or position:

He stood *on* a hill, looking *at* the lake; then ran *along* the valley, *between* rows of trees.

However, the preposition may express other relations as well: time (*before* dawn, *after* noon, *during* the night), instrumentality (*through* neglect, *with* swords, *by* Henry W. Longfellow), manner (*with* love, *by* hook and *by* crook), purpose (*for* knowledge, *for the sake of* knowledge).

Exercise No. 25

Underline the preposition and the words it relates to in each of the following sentences.

1. We saw, heraldic in the heat,
   A scorpion on a stone.
2. I never thrust my nose into other men's porridge. It is no bread and butter of mine; every man for himself, and God for us all.
3. What is bred in the bone will never come out of the flesh.
4. He came from Switzerland, through France, over to England, and stayed among us some months.
5. Whom does he speak to?

THE INTERJECTION

The interjection expresses some emotion. It is an exclamation of surprise, anger, delight, grief, consternation, or the like. It is an independent element—one without grammatical relation to the other parts of the sentence. Words normally employed as other parts of speech may, if uttered emotionally, function as interjections.

Oh!	Bang!	Welcome!
So!	Well!	Nonsense!
Help!	Hurrah!	O dear!
	Indeed!	

Note: The interjection is generally followed by an exclamation point.

VERBALS: GERUNDS, PARTICIPLES, AND INFINITIVES

VERBALS Words derived from verbs but used as other parts of speech are called verbals. There are three kinds of verbals: gerunds, participles, and infinitives. Though they function as nouns (gerund and infinitive) or as modifiers (participle and infinitive), they also have some characteristics of the *finite verb* from which they originate. (A finite verb is "limited" or "bounded" in person and number by its subject. Thus *read* and *write* are finite verbs. Their corresponding verbals are *infinite*—"unlimited.")

GERUND The gerund derives from the verb but functions as a noun: it is a **verbal noun.**

1. The tense and voice forms of the gerund follow:

	ACTIVE	PASSIVE
PRESENT	reading	being read
	writing	being written
PERFECT	having read	having been read
	having written	having been written

Marrying is their object.

Marrying, the gerund, is the subject of the linking verb *is.*

The gerund may serve any of the functions of a noun—subject, object, complement, appositive. Compare the sentence cited with

Marriage is their object.

Marriage, the noun, serves the same function and has essentially the same meaning as the gerund *marrying.*

The other forms of the gerund are comparatively unusual.

In retrospect, he could see her object in *having married.*

Shakespeare said that *being married* means being marred.

His *having been married* makes any man a better philosopher, Socrates contended.

Verb Characteristics of the Gerund The gerund may take an object:

Marrying *him* is her object.

The pronoun *him* is the object of the gerund *marrying.* (To determine the object of the gerund, ask *whom* or *what* after it: Marrying

whom? The answer, *him,* supplies the object of the gerund.) The noun *marriage,* of course, never takes an object. We may not say: *Marriage him.*

The gerund may be modified by an adverb: Though he has several times repented leisurely, he has not been cured of marrying *hastily.*

The adverb *hastily* modifies the gerund *marrying* (in the same way that the adverb *leisurely* modifies the finite verb *repented*).

Note: An adjective may modify the gerund when its naming function is more prominent than its acting function.

Hasty marrying often leads to leisurely repenting.

Hasty, an adjective, modifies *marrying* because the noun sense of the gerund is uppermost.

The gerund may take a subject; such a subject is regularly in the possessive case.

John's marrying her is a necessary prelude to his divorcing her.

John's, a noun in the possessive case, is the subject of the gerund *marrying.* (Note that the pronoun *his,* the subject of the gerund *divorcing,* is also in the possessive case.)

In several circumstances, the subject of a gerund is regularly in the objective case:

(a) When the subject is stressed:

Though I approve of marriage, I cannot approve of *John* (him) marrying.

(b) When the subject is plural:

I cannot approve of minors marrying.

(c) When the subject is modified:

I cannot approve of an immature person marrying.

Exercise No. 26

In the sentences below, underline the gerunds, along with their modifiers, subjects and objects. Correct all errors in case.

1. Desperate for news, the reporter resorted to biting dogs.
2. Jojo's avid reading in abnormal psychology has served one purpose: that of making him feel normal.

3. He spurning her demonstrates his need for both a psychiatrist and an oculist.

4. He thought him gilding lilies was a sufficient career.

5. Their having read all the selections of the book clubs has not raised their intelligence quotients a fraction of a point.

PARTICIPLE The participle derives from the verb but functions as an adjective: it is a verbal adjective.

Coming round the mountain, Susannah saw more mountains.

The participle *Coming* modifies the noun *Susannah*.

The tense and voice forms of the participle follow:

	ACTIVE	PASSIVE
PRESENT	reading, writing	being read, being written
PAST	[lacking]	read, written
PERFECT	having read, having written	having been read, having been written

Tense in the Participle The present participle always ends in *-ing*. It indicates action taking place at the same time as the action of some finite verb.

Hermione left, *scowling* but silent.

The participle *scowling* modifies the noun *Hermione* (just as the adjective *silent* modifies it). The action it describes takes place at the same time as the action of the finite verb *left*.

Scowling but silent, Hermione leaves.

Again the action indicated by the participle is simultaneous with the action indicated by the finite verb.

The past participle is the third "principal part" of the verb. The past participle indicates action taking place before the action of the finite verb:

Neglected and unhappy, Paine retired to New Rochelle.

The past participle *neglected* modifies the noun *Paine* (just as the adjective *unhappy* modifies it). The action indicated by the past participle takes place *prior* to the action indicated by the finite verb: Paine was neglected and unhappy first; he retired to New Rochelle afterward.

Note: The past participle is the third principal part of the verb. In regular verbs, the past participle has the same form as the simple past tense (*talked, walked, balked*). In irregular verbs, the participle is formed in several ways (*taken, rung, won*) which need to be learned separately. See sections on Verbs, Principal Parts.

The perfect participle is formed by prefixing the auxiliary *having* to the past participle. It indicates an action that has been definitely completed, or perfected, before the action of the finite verb.

Having read his Baedeker, he felt ready to tour historic Italy.

The perfect participle *having read* modifies the pronoun *he*. The action indicated by the perfect participle takes place before the action indicated by the verb *felt*.

Note: The distinction between the past participle and the perfect participle is a good deal less stringent in practice than the "rules" imply. Actually, the rhythm of the sentence rather than the rules of tense usually determines the choice.

Verb Characteristics of the Participle The participle may take an object.

Having eaten the *avocado*, Tony saved the pit to plant in a pot.

The noun *avocado* is the object of the participle *having eaten*.

The participle may be modified by an adverb.

Having eaten it *hurriedly*, he digested it poorly.

The adverb *hurriedly* modifies the participle *having eaten* (just as the adverb *poorly* modifies the finite verb *digested*).

Using the Participle The participle, since it is an adjective, must modify a noun or noun-substitute. If it does not clearly and logically relate to a noun, a misconstruction known as the **dangling participle** results.

Dangling: Squirming and wriggling, I tied the little varmint.

Repaired: I tied the squirming and wriggling little varmint.

(Another possible repair—though a clumsy one: Squirming and wriggling, the little varmint was tied by me.)

Dangling: Coming round the mountain, other mountains hove into view.

Repaired: When we came round the mountain, other mountains hove into view.

Repaired: Coming round the mountain, we saw other mountains.

The participle, a verbal adjective, must be distinguished from the gerund, a verbal noun.

Gerund: Four cookies stopped the child's *crying.*

The gerund *crying* is the object of the verb *stopped.*

Participle: *Crying,* the child received four cookies.

The participle *Crying* modifies the noun *child.* Compare *The crying child received four cookies.*

Exercise No. 27

In the following sentences, underline all participles, along with their modifiers, subjects, and objects. Correct all errors.

1. Desperate for news, the reporter had bitten dogs.
2. Having avidly read books on abnormal psychology, Jojo's normality oppressed him.
3. The lady having been spurned by Jojo, proceeded to rival the several furies of hell.
4. Having gilded lilies with loving devotion, he sought roses needing varnish.
5. Having read all the selections of the book clubs, their intelligence quotients remained static.

INFINITIVE The infinitive is the first of the principal parts of the verb. The infinitive is usually introduced by *to*, the "sign" of the infinitive: *to read, to write, to reckon;* the sign, however, may be omitted (especially after the auxiliaries *may, can, shall, will, must*, and after the verbs *dare, bid, make, see, hear, feel*).

The infinitive is a **verbal noun** chiefly; but it may also function as adjective or adverb.

The tense and voice forms of the infinitive follow.

	ACTIVE	PASSIVE
PRESENT	to read, to write	to be read, to be written
PERFECT	to have read, to have written	to have been read, to have been written

The Infinitive as Noun, Adjective, and Adverb
The infinitive is primarily used as a noun:

To see is *to believe.*

To see is used as subject of the linking verb *is* and *to believe* as its complement (predicate nominative).

The infinitive may be used as an adjective.
W. C. Fields liked water *to bathe in* and whiskey *to drink.*

The infinitive *to bathe in* modifies the noun *water*, and the infinitive *to drink* modifies the noun *whiskey.*

The infinitive may be used as an adverb.
The sower went forth *to sow.*

The infinitive *to sow* modifies the verb *went* (*forth*).

Verb Characteristics of the Infinitive The infinitive may take an object.

To see *him* is to believe *her.*

The pronoun *him* is the object of the infinitive *to see;* the pronoun *her* is the object of the infinitive *to believe.*

The infinitive may be modified by an adverb.
To spell *correctly* requires no instruction in voodoo.

The adverb *correctly* modifies the infinitive *to spell.*

The infinitive may take a subject. The subject is in the objective case.

I know *them* to be burners of books.

The pronoun *them* is the subject of the infinitive *to be.* (Compare: *I know that they are burners of books.* Here the pronoun *they* is subject of the finite verb *are* and consequently in the nominative case. However, the two constructions are closely analogous. In each sentence, the group of words following *know* constitutes its object; and in each group of words the pronoun is governed by the infinitive or the verb that follows.)

Note: The subject of the infinitive *to be* (as the subject of all infinitives) is in the objective case.

Tense in the Infinitive The present infinitive indicates action taking place at the same time as the action of the finite verb.

I considered him *to be* only three generations removed from an asparagus.

The action indicated by *to be* and the action indicated by *considered* take place at the same time.

The perfect infinitive indicates action taking place before the action of the main verb.

They believed the soldier *to have taken* unofficial leave.

The action indicated by *to have taken* occurs before the action indicated by *believed*.

Using the Infinitive When the infinitive is used as a modifier (not as a noun) it must be logically related to the word it modifies. Otherwise the dangling infinitive results.

Dangling: To win friends and *influence* people, guile and fraud are necessary, some politicians believe.

Repaired: To win friends and *influence* people, one must employ guile and fraud, some politicians believe.

Note: The sign of the infinitive, *to*, has been omitted before *influence* because it clearly parallels *to win*. Where the parallelism is apparent, the sign of the infinitive may be omitted.

Exercise No. 28

Correct all errors in the employment of the infinitives below.

1. He wanted to have seen the headless horseman.
2. I think the criminal to be he.
3. To write with precision it is necessary to first have thought logically.
4. I know he to be a sheep in wolf's clothing.
5. To invariably be kind to children, angelic qualities are required.

PHRASES AND CLAUSES

A group of words may substitute for a part of speech. Compare the following groups:

The *green-eyed* monster.
The monster *with green eyes*.
The monster *that has green eyes*.

Clearly, *green-eyed* acts as an adjective, modifying the noun *monster*. But *with green eyes* and *that has green eyes* similarly modify *monster*; and consequently they are adjectives too. The group *with green eyes* is called a phrase; the other group *that has geen eyes* is called a subordinate clause. Each forms a sense unit: each acts as a single part of speech expressing a fragmentary thought.

There is a distinction between the two elements, however. The subordinate clause has a subject (*that*) and predicate (*has green eyes*). The phrase has neither subject nor predicate, for it lacks a pivotal word—a verb.

PHRASE A phrase is a group of words, containing neither subject nor predicate, which acts as a single part of speech.

Phrases may be classified according to use as nouns, adjectives, or adverbs.

Noun Phrase *To do* is *to learn.*
The phrase *to do* acts as the subject and the phrase *to learn* as the complement (predicate nominative) of the linking verb *is*.

Adjective Phrase Books *in black and red* were the clerk's delight.
The phrase *in black and red* modifies the noun *books*.

Adverbial Phrase He shouted *on house tops*. The phrase *on house tops* modifies the verb *shouted*.

Note: Since any group of two or more related words constitutes a phrase, it is possible to distinguish:

A Verb Phrase—(consisting of the main verb and its auxiliaries)—*will thrust, will have thrust, will have been thrust;*

A Phrase Preposition—*with reference to, in preference to, in spite of, on account of, by means of;*

A Phrasal Conjunction—*in order that, as if, as though, in so far as, on condition that.*

However, it seems simpler to consider these as compound verbs, compound prepositions, or compound conjunctions.

Phrases may be classified, according to their introductory or pivotal word, as **prepositional, participial, infinitive,** or **gerund.** (Note that this is a classification according to form; it does not contradict the classification according to use.)

Prepositional Phrase The time *for conversation* is not *before breakfast;* let us eat *in silence.* The prepositional phrase *for conversation* functions as an adjective, modifying the noun *time;* the prepositional phrase *before breakfast* functions as a predicate nominative after the linking verb *is;* the prepositional phrase *in silence* functions as an adverb, modifying the verb *eat.*

Participial Phrase *Having joined the Rotary Club,* Sinclair Lewis felt like George Babbitt. The participial phrase modifies the noun *Sinclair Lewis.* (The participial phrase may of course be used only as an adjective.)

Infinitive Phrase *To read books* means to *enlarge one's horizons.*
(Noun use of the infinitive phrase.)
He wanted books *to juggle acrobatically.*
(Adjective use of the infinitive phrase.)
He read *to enlarge his horizons.*
(Adverbial use of the infinitive phrase.)

Gerund Phrase *Reading books* enlarges one's horizons.
(The gerund phrase may of course be used only as a noun.)

Absolute Phrase A phrase may be grammatically detached from the rest of the sentence in which it occurs. Such a construction modifies no one word in the sentence, but instead the whole idea of the sentence.

A participle, plus the noun or pronoun it modifies, may form an absolute phrase.
The albatross having been slain, they were idle as a painted ship upon a painted ocean.
The italicized phrase, an absolute construction, really has an adverbial function, equalling *When the albatross was slain, they were idle* . . . The

noun in the **substantive plus participle** construction is called the **nominative absolute.**

An infinitive may form an absolute phrase.
To tell the truth, I lied.

Note: Appositive and parenthetical phrases are sometimes considered absolute phrases.

Exercise No. 29

Underline the phrases in the following sentences, classifying them as to use and form.
1. A bird in the hand is worth two in the bush.
2. Having seen three birds in the bush, he let the one in his hand fly away.
3. The birds in the bush having been captured, Jojo found his hands full.
4. He lived to snare birds and burn bushes.
5. To part from friends is to die a little.

CLAUSE A clause is a group of words containing a subject and a verb. If the clause makes a statement capable of standing alone—if it "makes a complete statement"—it is called a **main** (or **principal** or **independent**) clause. If the clause makes a statement that cannot stand alone—if it depends for its meaning on some other word or words in the sentence—it is called a **subordinate** (or **dependent**) clause.

Main Clause—is a group of words, containing a subject and a verb, which makes a complete statement.
Men come and go, but *the brook goes on forever.*
The sentence contains two main clauses (italicized), each capable of standing alone. Note, however, that if either of the italicized parts stood alone, it would be classified as a simple sentence, not as a clause. Clause necessarily implies the larger whole of which it is a part.

Subordinate Clause—is a group of words, containing a subject and a verb, which depends on some other word or words in the sentence for its meaning. (It is always joined to the main clause by a joining word—a relative pronoun or a subordinating conjunction.)
Clauses are classified according to use as nouns, adjectives, and adverbs.

Noun Clause He believes *that the devil likes angel cake*.

The noun clause functions as object of the verb *believes*.

Note: A relative pronoun in the objective case may be omitted:

This is the evidence [*which* or *that*] the detectives sought, and now they can arrest the men [*whom* or *that*] they have suspected.

Adjective Clause The lady *who had two heads* could not credit the proverb *which declared* that two heads were better than one.

The first adjective clause modifies the noun *lady*; the second modifies the noun *proverb*.

Adverbial Clause He cried *because he had spilled milk*.

The adverbial clause modifies the verb *cried*.

Elliptical Clause The subject and predicate of a clause may be omitted when they can be supplied from the context:

He needs shock therapy more direly than you [*do* or *need it*].

While [he was] eating, he kept talking relentlessly.

Note: When the elliptical (or omitted) subject differs from the subject of the main clause, a dangling construction results:

While eating, his words tumbled forth relentlessly.

Exercise No. 30

Underline all the subordinate clauses below, noting the function of each.

1. She knew where she was going and how she would get there.
2. He ate when I was hungry and drank whenever he could.
3. He had but a single purpose, which he concealed from everybody, including himself.
4. Criminals who have status in their world frequently serve an apprenticeship in crime.
5. While making hay, you ought to see whether the sun is shining.

THE SENTENCE

A sentence is a group of words containing both subject and predicate and expressing a complete thought.

Sentences may be classified in two ways: by use and by structure.

Sentences Classified According to Use Sentences may function in four ways.

Declarative sentence makes a statement.

In 1492 Columbus sailed the ocean blue.

Note: A declarative sentence may of course make a false statement:

In 1493 Columbus sailed the deep blue sea.

Interrogative sentence asks a question.

Where are the snows of yesteryear?

Imperative sentence issues a command or expresses an entreaty.

Give us this day our daily bread.

Note: Often, the subject of an imperative sentence is understood, not expressed. In the sentence given above, for example, the subject is *you* (understood).

Exclamatory sentence gives vent to strong feelings—of anger, sorrow, grief, surprise, or the like.

Oh, Hamlet, thou hast cleft my heart in twain!

Sentences Classified According to Structure Four kinds of construction may be distinguished in sentences.

Simple sentence contains one subject and one predicate.

Men love.

This is the simplest form of the simple sentence, containing a noun for its subject and a finite verb for its predicate. The simple sentence may of course be lengthened by adding modifiers and a complement.

Neurotic men and women love only themselves. The compound subject (*men and women*) does not alter the simple construction: either subject or predicate or both may be compound.

Note: No matter how structured (simple,

compound, or complex), a sentence may be used to make a declarative, an interrogative, an imperative, or an exclamatory statement.

Compound sentence contains two or more main (principal, independent) clauses.

Man has his will, but *woman has her way.* The independent clauses italicized are joined by the coordinating conjunction *but.* (A semicolon would have served as well: *Man has his will; woman has her way.*)

Complex sentence contains one main clause and one or more subordinate (dependent) clauses.

"A woman is the most inconsistent compound of obstinacy and self-sacrifice *that I have ever seen,*" says a misogynist.
(One main clause, written without italics, and one subordinate clause, with italics.)

"Women are such a provoking class of society *because, though they are never right, they are never more than half wrong,*" says a misogynist.
(One main clause, written without italics, and two subordinate clauses: *because they are never*

more than half wrong and *though they are never right.*)

Compound-complex sentence contains two or more main clauses and one or more subordinate clauses.

However great may be the love that unites them, a man and a woman are always strangers in mind and intellect; they remain combatants *who belong to different races.*
(Two main clauses, written without italics, and two subordinate clauses, with italics. The semicolon, substituting for a comma plus coordinating conjunction, links the two main clauses.)

Exercise No. 31

Convert the following simple declarative sentences into compound and complex sentences.

1. Jack loves Jill. Jill loves herself.
2. The nickel has diminished value. It no longer buys a telephone call.
3. Ideas have consequences. The consequences are sometimes far-reaching.
4. He reached for the moon. He stubbed his toe.
5. The American way of speaking and writing differs from the English way. It is not therefore inferior.

SENTENCE ERRORS

AGREEMENT

AGREEMENT BETWEEN SUBJECT AND VERB

The verb must agree with its subject in number. Number, in English, applies to nouns, pronouns, and verbs. Number distinguishes between one and more than one: words which denote one (*tree, man*) are *singular;* words which denote more than one (*trees, men*) are *plural*. Thus, if the subject is singular, the verb that goes with it must be singular; if the subject is plural, the verb that goes with it must be plural:

The dog barks.   The singular verb *barks* agrees with the singular subject *dog.*

The dogs bark.   The plural verb *bark* agrees with the plural subject *dogs.*

Note: Most nouns form their plurals by adding -*s*, -*es*, -*ies: dogs, masses, ladies*. Most verbs form their singular by adding -*s*: he *barks,* she *walks,* it *moves.*

When the subject comes before the verb, usually no problem about agreement exists. However, when the word order is reversed, or when certain special constructions are used, trouble may crop up. These problems and their solutions are discussed in the sections below.

The number of the noun in a phrase introduced by the preposition *of* does not affect the number of the verb.

SUBJ.   PHRASE   VERB

Right: A *list* (of many things) *has* been drawn up.

The true subject of this sentence is *list,* not *things*. Since *list* is singular, the verb agreeing with it must be singular—*has* (not *have*).

Exercise No. 32

Which of the italicized verbs is correct?

1. One of the cats (*scratch, scratches*) children.
2. The cause of typhoons (*is, are*) known.
3. Three months of my work (*was, were*) wasted.
4. Two ships of the Asiatic fleet (*is, are*) missing.
5. The longest of modern epics (*is, are*) Joyce's *Ulysses.*

Note: A plural verb follows the construction *one of those who* because the antecedent of *who* is plural (*those*).

George is one of those *men who* always *score* high in tests.

Note: Relative clauses introduced by *who, that,* or *which* take verbs agreeing with the antecedent of the pronoun.

Right: Ulysses is one of the most interesting *books that have* ever been written.

Ulysses is the subject of the linking (copulative) verb *is*. The subject of the clause is *that;* its antecedent is the plural noun *books*. Therefore, the verb must likewise be plural—*have.*

Exercise No. 33

Which of the italicized verbs is correct?

1. Tests are one of the difficult ordeals that (*confront, confronts*) mankind.
2. Charles is one of those experienced accountants who never (*fail, fails*) to spot an error.
3. Geriatrics is one of the newest sciences that (*has, have*) commanded public interest.
4. Agreement is one of those points in grammar that always (*confuse, confuses*) me.
5. Joan is one of those mediocre dancers that (*need, needs*) a less talented partner than Bob.

When the subject and predicate nominative differ in number, the verb agrees with the subject, *not* the complement.

SUBJ.   VERB COMPLEMENT

Right: The *theme* of the novel *is* the *experiences* of a Hollywood writer.

SUBJ. VERB COMPLEMENT

Right: The essential *difficulty was* the *hordes* of enemy tribes surrounding our camp.

Compound subjects (A + B) joined by *and* ordinarily take a plural verb.

A + B

Right: The *flower* and the *vine are* decayed. Although each of these subjects is singular, when joined by *and* they become plural, and therefore the verb must be plural.

Note: Reversing normal word-order (that is, the subject-verb pattern) in no way alters the rule about agreement between compound subjects and their verb.

A + B

Right: Here *come John* and his *brother*.

A + B

Right: There *are* the *bread* and the *spice* for the stuffing.

There and *here* are always *adverbs* and can never be subjects.

Exercise No. 34

Which of the italicized verbs is correct?

1. Laughing and giggling (*irritate, irritates*) the dour man.
2. There but for the grace of God (*go, goes*) I.
3. (*Was, were*) there three patients due today?
4. Here in the desk, of all places, (*was, were*) the thermometer and the screwdriver.
5. Candlelight and white wine (*add, adds*) a touch of Venus.

Note: Compound subjects joined by *or, either . . . or, neither . . . nor, not only . . . but also* ordinarily take verbs agreeing in number with the nearer subject.

SUBJ.   SUBJ. VERB
Right: Neither *Norman* nor his *sister is* listening.

SUBJ.   SING. SUBJ.
Right: Not only *laymen* but also the *tax expert*
SING. VERB
makes errors.

SUBJ.   PLURAL SUBJ.
Right: Not only the *layman* but also *tax experts*
PLURAL VERB
make errors.

Exercise No. 35

Which of the italicized verbs is correct?

1. Either Bob or Ann (*has, have*) played a trick on us.
2. Here in Suburbia neither Democrat nor Republican (*dominate, dominates*) local politics.
3. Neither the principal nor the teachers (*understand, understands*) John's behavior.
4. Not only the technician in the studio but also the televiewers (*was, were*) amused by the antics of the comedian.
5. Some think that neither Nash nor Hoffenstein (*is, are*) destined for lasting fame among the comic poets.

Note: Singular subjects (when followed by prepositional phrases introduced by *with, along with, together with, as well as*) ordinarily take a singular verb.

SUBJ.
Right: Cleopatra, as well as her entire retinue,
VERB
was eager to meet Caesar.

SUBJ.
Right: New York, together with 49 other
VERB
states, *votes* for president.

As well as and *together with* introduce phrases which modify the subject, but are not themselves the subjects. Although formally correct, these constructions are often stilted. By substituting *and* for the preposition, a more normal sentence results. Note, however, the change in number.

A + B

Right: Cleopatra and her *retinue were* eager to meet Caesar.

Exercise No. 36

Which of the italicized verbs is correct?

1. The soldier, along with his commanders, (*enter, enters*) the bivouac area.
2. Ellen, as well as the girls of her sorority, (*dislike, dislikes*) classical music.
3. The suspect's attitude, together with the material evidence against him, (*was, were*) decisive in the verdict.
4. Beelzebub, as well as his Satanic cohorts, (*search, searches*) eternally new means to seduce mankind.
5. Bebop, played with Dixieland jazz in the background, (*lead, leads*) one to envy the deaf.

INDEFINITE PRONOUNS Each of the following indefinite pronouns takes a singular verb:

anyone	everybody	nothing
everyone	somebody	anything
no one	someone	everything
each	either	neither

SUBJ.　PHRASE　VERB

Right: Each (of the men) *was* irritated with his work.

Right: Everybody here *knows* the importance of building vocabulary.

Each of the following indefinite pronouns takes a plural verb:

both　many　several　few

Right: Several were present at the meeting, but *few spoke.*

Each of the following indefinite pronouns is singular or plural depending upon the context of the sentence:

none　some　any　most　all　more

Right: None of the inductees *has* yet arrived.

Since *none,* an indefinite pronoun, is too vague to indicate number, we may safely turn to the context of the sentence. Although *inductees* is plural, the context suggests that *no one* of them has yet arrived.

But: *Some* (most, all, more) of the inductees *have* arrived.

Much of the task has been accomplished, but *some* of it still *remains* to challenge us.

All is lost.

Nouns of quantity, although plural in form, are often understood as collective units and therefore take singular verbs.

Right: Three-quarters of his talent *lies* in music.

Right: The *crowd shouts* its approval of the speaker.

Right: Seven *years is* a long time for a famine.

Right: The *jury takes* several hours to reach its verdict.

Note: If, however, the parts of the unit are considered more important than the unit as a collective whole, the verb must be plural.

Right: There *are* a *number* of men who will not accept the opinion of the majority.

Right: The *majority* of the class *are* interested in their work.

AGREEMENT BETWEEN PRONOUN AND ANTECEDENT

The pronoun must agree with its antecedent noun or pronoun in *number, person,* and *gender.*

Almost all errors in agreement between pronoun and antecedent result from confusion about number rather than about person or gender. Few people, for example, would write either:

The Englishman expects every man to do *her* duty. (Error in gender)

England expects every man to do *your* duty. (Error in person)

But many people might write:

England expects every man to do *their* duty. (Error in number) The correct form of this sentence, of course, is:

England expects every *man* to do *his* duty. The pronoun *his* has as its antecedent the noun *man.* Since *man* is singular in number, masculine in gender, and third person, the pronoun which refers to *man* must agree with it in each of these respects.

Note: A plural pronoun is used to refer to two or more singular antecedents joined by *and.*

Right: The *beautiful and* the *damned* have *their* place in fiction.

Right: In American literature *romance* and *realism* have had *their* days.

Note: A singular pronoun is used to refer to two or more singular antecedents connected by *either . . . or, neither . . . nor, or, nor,* and the like.

Right: Neither Sophocles *nor* Aeschylus *has lost his* appeal.

Note: The pronoun is either singular or plural when it refers to a collective noun depending upon whether that noun is singular or plural in meaning.

Right: The jury gave *its* verdict.

Jury here means the members collectively, as a whole unit, and thus the pronoun is singular.

Right: The jury gave *their* verdict.

Jury here means the jurors individually, as if they were polled. Thus, the meaning is plural and the pronoun is plural.

Exercise No. 37

Write the correct form of the pronoun and the antecedent with which it agrees.

EXAMPLE:

Neither Goldilocks nor Red Riding Hood liked (*her, their*) animal friends.

CORRECT FORM	ANTECEDENT
her	Goldilocks
	Red Riding Hood

1. All must heed the laws of (*his, their*) land.
2. Each of the authors received (*his, their*) royalty check.
3. The lass with the delicate air and the lad with the frightful mien went (*his, her, their*) separate ways.
4. Orwell is one of those authors who do (*his, their*) best to irritate the reader.
5. If anyone cries out, I'll shoot (*them, him*).
6. None of this material is pertinent now, but (*it, they*) may be later.
7. Whoever wishes to enter a claim on this property must make (*his, their*) wishes known at once.
8. Last week our chess team lost (*its, their*) final match.
9. Some stand and wait, but (*he, they*) also serve in the higher cause.
10. I won't join community groups because (*it, they*) consume too much of my limited time.

Note: To avoid the clumsy effect of "he or she" or "his or her" use the masculine pronoun except where the antecedent is clearly feminine.

Right: Each of the students wishes to have *his* say.

Although the class roll may show the names of both boys and girls, the sentence would gain little by adding "his or her say."

Right: Every member of the mother's club prepared her own plan.

Now the antecedent, although still of common gender, suggests through the context of the sentence that a feminine pronoun should be used.

Note: Maintain consistency in person between pronoun and antecedent. Shifts in person confuse the reader because they obscure point of view.

Wrong: I enjoy photography because *you* acquire a souvenir of whatever place *we* visit.

The original pronoun *I* is shifted twice in this sentence: to *you*, and again to *we*. Thus the reader no longer knows who is telling the story. Revised, the sentence reads logically.

Right: I enjoy photography because through it I acquire a souvenir of whatever place I visit.

Exercise No. 38

Rewrite the following passage so that a consistent relationship exists between the person of the pronoun and its antecedents.

Hesitantly, I approached the darkened stairwell where you could not help feeling the gloom enclose everyone. Although I was trembling, I began to mount the worn old steps we had trod so often in the happier times of our youth. You just sensed that at the summit of those steps our whole lives would change, but I had to go on.

CASE OF PRONOUNS

The case of a pronoun depends on its use in the sentence. The pronoun agrees with its antecedent in number, person, and gender, but **not** in case. To avoid sentence errors involving case, watch for two trouble spots:

The distinct forms of the personal and relative pronouns in each of their three cases:

NOMINATIVE	OBJECTIVE	POSSESSIVE
I	me	my
he	him	his
she	her	her
we	us	our
they	them	their
who	whom	whose

The uses of the pronoun in the sentence:

Nominative

Subject of a verb: *He* marches in the parade.

Predicate Nominative: It is *they*.

Direct Address: *You*, go away!

Appositive: He who knows pain—*he* and *he* only—knows the fullness of life.

Objective

Direct object of a verb: I admire *him*, but the others in his crowd, *whom* I know too well, I despise.

Indirect object of a verb: I gave *him* a book.

Object of a preposition: I know with *whom* you went. I gave it to *him*.

Appositive: They nominated Joe for president —*him*, of all people.

Possessive

To indicate possession, source, authorship, and similar relationships:

I have read Johnson for *his* ironic wit.

I know *whose* verse that is.

Garlic has *its* own peculiar odor.

Use the nominative form when the pronoun is subject of a sentence or clause, no matter what the antecedent of the pronoun is.

Right: His family disinherited Cain because he was not a good brother.

Although *Cain*, antecedent of *he*, is in the objective case, *he* takes the nominative case because in its own clause it is the subject of the verb *was*.

Right: Cain was disinherited because his family considered him a bad brother.

Although *Cain*, antecedent of *him*, is in the nominative case, *him* remains objective because in its own clause it is the object of the verb *considered*.

After a linking verb, the pronoun usually takes the nominative case.

FORMAL: It is *I*. That is *he*. It is *they*.

INFORMAL: It's *me*. That's *him*. It's *them*.

This use of the objective case after a finite form of *to be* has become so common that it is generally considered to be acceptable.

Use the objective case when the pronoun is the direct or indirect object of a verb or preposition.

Wrong: Give that rod to Ed and I.

Ed and I is the object of the preposition *to*, but *I* is not the objective pronoun.

Right: Give that rod to Ed and me.

Wrong: He invited Jim and I to the dance.

Jim and I is the object of the verb, but *I* is not the objective case of the pronoun.

Right: He invited Jim and me to the dance.

Wrong: We resented the Shanes, both he and his wife.

He and his wife is in apposition with *Shanes*, and should be in the objective case after the verb *resented*.

Right: We resented the Shanes, both him and his wife.

Use the objective case when the pronoun acts either as subject of or as object of an infinitive.

Right: His instructors considered him to be promising.

Him is the subject of the infinitive *to be*.

Right: The investigators suspected the embezzler to be him.

Him is the object of the infinitive *to be*.

Before a gerund, the pronoun is usually in the possessive case.

Right: We fully approve of their marrying.

Marrying is a gerund, object of the preposition *of*. The error that may result is usually caused by the writer's assuming that the pronoun is also object of the preposition. Actually the pronoun is a possessive modifying the gerund. If the pronoun is used in the objective case—We fully approve of *them* marrying—the sentence sense is ambiguous, for it suggests that we like these young people, but leaves *marrying*, now a participial modifier, awkwardly modifying *them*.

Note: If the emphasis is intended to be on the person or thing, the pronoun should be in the objective case and should be modified by a participle.

Right: Often I worry about him working too hard.

The stress here is on *him* rather than on *working*.

Note: An indefinite pronoun cannot be used in the possessive case before a gerund:

Right: I know men who indulge in lying on occasion, but I cannot think of anyone indulging consistently.

Anyone is an indefinite pronoun.

Right: Many girls behave as she does, but I know of some behaving quite differently.

Some is an indefinite pronoun with no distinct form in the possessive.

Pronouns take the same case as the nouns or pronouns to which they are linked by coordinating or correlative conjunctions. Thus, if the noun or pronoun before the conjunction is in the nominative case, then the pronoun following the conjunction ought to be in the nominative case.

Wrong: Between him and I there is little to choose.

Him is object of the preposition *between*. *I*, linked to *him* by the conjunction *and*, should also be the object of the preposition and consequently in the objective case:

Right: Between him and me there is little to choose.

Wrong: Since the judges selected only one winner, neither Jim nor me won a prize.

Jim is subject of *won*. *Me*, joined to *Jim* by the correlative conjunction *nor*, should also be part of the subject and consequently in the nominative case:

Right: Since the judges selected only one winner, neither Jim nor I won a prize.

Note: *But* may act as a preposition as well as a conjunction. In its function as a preposition *but* means "except," and is followed by the objective case:

Right: Everyone fled but him.

Pronouns in apposition take the same case as the noun or pronoun of which they are appositives.

Right: All will attend the party—they and we. The subject of the verb *will attend* is *all*. *They and we* is in apposition with *all*, and therefore takes the nominative case.

Right: He murdered both of them—him and her.

The object of the verb *murdered* is *both*. *Him*

and her is in apposition with *both*, and therefore takes the objective case.

The conjunctions *than* and *as* have no effect upon the case of the pronoun which follows them.

Wrong: You can be taller than her.

Than is a conjunction introducing the clause *than she is* (understood). The writer has misused it as a preposition and made *her* the object of the preposition.

Right: You can be taller than she [is].

Wrong: I am as happy as them.

Right: I am as happy as they [are].

Avoid substituting the reflexive for the personal pronoun.

Wrong: The Johnsons have a splendid gift for Hilda and myself.

The reflexive pronoun should be used to indicate an action reflecting back upon the subject, as in *I hate myself*. In the sentence cited, no such action takes place.

Right: The Johnsons have a splendid gift for Hilda and me.

The case of the relative pronouns *who* and *whom* is determined by their use in the sentence.

Nominative: This is the agent who is responsible for the sabotage.

who acts as subject of the verb *is*.

We tried to determine who she was.

who is the complement of *was*, not the object of the infinitive *to determine*.

Objective: Give the car to whomever you wish.

whomever is the object complement of *wish*.

He learned that Pennsfield, whom he despised, was an informer.

whom is the object of *despised*.

Whom are you speaking to?

whom is the object of the preposition *to*.

Note: To decide whether the nominative or the objective case of the relative pronoun ought to be employed, substitute a personal pronoun for the relative:

who or *whom* is responsible
he or *him* is responsible

He is obviously the correct answer, and the corresponding form of *he* is the relative *who;* therefore, *who is responsible* is the correct form.

who or *whom* are you speaking to?
you are speaking to *who* or *whom?*
you are speaking to *he* or *him?*

Him is correct, and the corresponding form of *him* is the relative *whom;* therefore, *whom are you speaking to?* is the proper form.

To distinguish between *whoever* and *whomever* note that

whoever   the one *who*
whomever   the one *whom*

Note: Parenthetic expressions like *I believe, I think,* or *he says* do not affect the case of the relative pronoun.

Wrong: He is the man whom I think pilfered the sleeping pills.

I think is merely parenthetic. The subject of the verb *pilfered* is *who.* Try substituting the personal pronoun to prove that *who* is correct: *he* or *him pilfered?* Clearly, the answer is *he pilfered,* and the relative pronoun corresponding with *he* is *who.*

Right: He is the man who I think pilfered the sleeping pills.

Wrong: That irritating fellow who they say everyone tried to avoid has finally left town.

They say is parenthetic and does not influence the case of the relative pronoun. The object of the infinitive *to avoid* is *whom.* Everyone tried to avoid *him.*

Right: That irritating fellow whom they say everyone tried to avoid has finally left town.

Exercise No. 39

Select the proper case for each of the following pronouns.

1. Ed and (*I, me*) are going to the meeting.
2. Laura is a girl (*who, whom*) may make my life difficult.
3. I cannot conceive of (*he, his, him*) accepting the post.
4. Did you hear about George and (*she, her*) eating live snails?
5. The debate between his brother and (*he, him*) ended in a draw.
6. I believe they are deliberately plotting against (*we, us*) boys.
7. Do you suspect it is (*they, them*)?
8. I cannot bear the thought of (*his, him*) going away.
9. (*Who, whom*) do you wish to send this letter to?
10. The principles he preaches convince neither (*he, him*) nor (*I, me*).
11. I refuse to talk to anyone but (*he, him*).
12. We insisted that we were as intelligent as (*they, them*).
13. Bill divided the money between John and (*he, him, himself*).
14. The reporter took the names of only two people, (*he, him*) and (*I, me*).
15. (*Whoever, whomever*) assumes his statement true is foolish.
16. Here is the fellow (*who, whom*) I believe asked about your trip.
17. The hat fitted Bob better than (*I, me*).
18. Not a single one of (*us, we*) men will support that troublemaker.
19. If only that could have been (*we, us*).
20. Did you wish the winner to be (*he, him*)?

REFERENCE OF PRONOUNS

The pronoun substitutes for the noun. Unlike the noun, the pronoun does not name, but refers to the word (antecedent) that does name the person, place, or thing being discussed:

William answers the doorbell because he works nearest the locked door.

He is the pronoun which refers to the person *William.* Because it functions as a word of reference, the pronoun must be placed with extreme care so that no doubt exists about the noun to which it refers:

When Mary looked at her sister, she blushed. *She* may refer to its immediate antecedent, or to *Mary;* consequently, the reference of the pronoun *she* is ambiguous. **To avoid ambiguous reference:**

The pronoun must be placed as near as possible to its logical antecedent:

Mary blushed when she looked at her sister.

The antecedent must be supplied or repeated:

When she looked at her sister, Mary blushed.

The sentence must be recast to achieve clarity:

Looking at her sister, Mary blushed.

The sections below discuss several problems in accurate reference of pronouns.

Avoid placing the pronoun in a position where it may refer to more than one antecedent.

Wrong: Stephen followed Tommy into a corner, where he hid.

He may refer either to *Stephen* or to *Tommy,* and is, consequently, ambiguous.

Right: Stephen followed Tommy into a corner and saw him hide there.

The related nouns and pronouns are now in parallel order.

Stephen, subject of the verb *followed,* corresponds with the understood subject of the verb *saw;* Tommy, object of the verb *followed,* corresponds with the pronoun in the objective case, *him.*

Right: Tommy hid in the corner to which Stephen had followed him.

Wrong: Bill told his friend that he would soon be home.

He may refer either to *friend* or to *Bill.* The sentence needs to be recast.

Right: Bill told his friend, "I will be home soon."

Wrong: Craven asked Nevins whether his car would be safe in his garage.

This sentence represents confusion worse confounded. Four meanings are possible:

Nevins' car, Nevins' garage

Craven's car, Craven's garage

Nevins' car, Craven's garage

Craven's car, Nevins' garage

The sentence must be recast.

Right: Craven asked Nevins, "Will my car be safe in your garage?"

Note: Avoid explaining the ambiguous pronoun by placing its antecedent in parentheses:

Awkward: Craven asked Nevins whether his (Craven's) car would be safe in his (Nevins') garage.

Avoid using pronouns to stand for ideas rather than for nouns. Most errors of this kind are caused by the demonstrative pronouns (*this, that*) and the relative pronouns (*who, which, that*).

Vague: Valerie brought home from school several excellent ceramics and watercolors. This made her family extremely proud.

This has no actual antecedent in the preceding sentence. The pronoun suggests only the implied idea that all of Valerie's activities brought pleasure to her family. But pronouns do not refer to implied ideas; they refer only to specific antecedents. Therefore the sentence must be recast.

Right: When Valerie brought home from school several excellent ceramics and watercolors, her family was extremely proud.

Right: The ceramics and watercolors Valerie brought home from school made her family extremely proud.

Note: The demonstrative pronouns may on occasion be used correctly without an antecedent:

Right: He eats garlic. *That* is why he gets a seat in the subway.

That refers clearly to an idea expressed by the whole clause.

Right: This is the way we wash clothes.

Right: That is Joe at bat now.

In each of these constructions the pronoun stands for a noun which follows rather than precedes the pronoun. *This* stands for *way, that* stands for *Joe.*

Wrong: We tried to complete the book in a month, which is why we were utterly exhausted. *Which* refers only to the implied idea of the preceding clause, not to any specific antecedent.

Avoid using the pronouns *it, you,* and *they* to stand for ideas rather than nouns.

Wrong: The employer intended to wish good cheer to each of his workers. He knew it would make a splendid impression on them.

It refers to the general notion of good wishes, but has no specific antecedent.

Right: The employer intended to wish good cheer to each of his workers. He knew that such a message would make a splendid impression upon them.

A noun, *message*, has been supplied.

Right: The employer knew that sending a message of good cheer to his workers would make a splendid impression upon them.

The sentence has been recast.

Wrong: It says in my notebook that pronouns must have clear reference.

It has no specific antecedent.

Right: My notebook contains the statement that pronouns must have clear reference.

Note: Avoid repeating the same pronoun within a single sentence when the pronoun has different antecedents.

Wrong: The club was the scene of a nightly brawl; nevertheless it was patronized by men who liked participating in it.

The first *it* intends referring to *club*, the second to *brawl*. But the combination of *it's* is clumsy and confusing.

Right: Though the scene of nightly brawls, the club was patronized by men who liked participating in them.

Right: The club was the scene of a nightly brawl; nevertheless, men who liked participating in it patronized the club.

Note: *It* may on occasion be correctly used without an antecedent:

Impersonal expressions. *It is raining; it is damp.*

Constructions in which *it* stands for a noun or noun equivalent which follows rather than precedes. *It is a splendid day.* *It* stands for the noun *day* which follows.

Wrong: If you look for the pot of gold, you may find it.

Unless the pronoun *you* refers to a specific person (as "You, George," or "You, the reader"), avoid using the impersonal second person pronoun. Here *you* seems to refer generally to anybody.

Better: If one looks for the pot of gold, one (*or* he) may find it.

The impersonal pronoun *one* avoids the inaccuracy of impersonal *you*, but it is often a stiff and formal usage. A wiser procedure involves recasting the entire sentence:

Right: The man who searches for the pot of gold may find it.

Wrong: They say that the new crop of inductees is well educated.

The indefinite use of *they* seems to refer to some far removed authority or to people generally. Use a specific antecedent.

Right: Draft Officials say that the new crop of inductees is well educated.

Avoid referring to an antecedent so remote from the pronoun that the central meaning of a sentence is obscured.

Wrong: The Aztecs for centuries held great power in Mexico. The lakes were filled in and a great city developed. They brought with them many cultural patterns hitherto unknown to the natives.

They, introducing the third sentence, refers to *Aztecs*, the subject of the first sentence. But the antecedent is so remote from the pronoun that the loose reference causes obscurity.

Right: The Aztecs for centuries held great power in Mexico. They filled in the lakes, introduced cultural patterns hitherto unknown to the natives, and developed a great city.

The pronoun *they* has been brought nearer to its antecedent *Aztecs*, and the other elements of the sentence have been arranged in parallel construction.

Avoid referring to an antecedent in a subordinate construction.

Wrong: We bought copies of the magazine he was selling to earn his way through college. It was *The New Yorker.*

It refers awkwardly to *magazine*, object of the preposition *of.* The phrase, a subordinate construction in the sentence, is lifted to undue prominence, and the central meaning of the sentence is obscured.

Right: We bought copies of the magazine he

was selling to earn his way through college. He was selling *The New Yorker*.

The antecedent has been repeated to clarify the reference. The revision is still slightly awkward.

Right: We bought copies of *The New Yorker*, the magazine he was selling to earn his way through college.

Exercise No. 40

Rewrite the following sentences, correcting all faults in reference.

1. The Happy-Thought-of-the-Day Club sent a magazine to its readers which had many wholesome suggestions.
2. If your hat does not fit your head, it should be made smaller.
3. Ed's father is returning from abroad, which will make him happy.
4. They say that everything will get better next year.
5. The transit officials plan to increase the fare in order to cut down the annual deficit. This will be a hardship on commuters.
6. Chaucer wrote entertainingly about the Middle Ages. These were years in which feudalism and religion exercised profound influence on noble and serf alike. He tells of these matters in *The Canterbury Tales*.
7. Although it was a dull party for me, it was amazing how many there enjoyed it.
8. If you borrow material from another writer's work, it should be acknowledged.
9. In Franklin's *Autobiography*, it gives precepts on thrift.
10. Beethoven's later works are remarkable, more so when you consider that he was deaf when he wrote them.

VERBS

SEQUENCE OF TENSES

Logical sequence of tenses—adjusting the tense of the verb in the subordinate clause to the tense of the verb in the main clause—ought to be maintained. Violating tense sequence often effects awkward or ambiguous constructions.

Noun, adverbial, and adjective clauses present different problems.

NOUN CLAUSES If the verb in the main clause is in the past or past perfect tense, the verb in the noun clause is generally (though not invariably) in the past or past perfect tense.

MAIN CLAUSE · · · · · · SUBORDINATE CLAUSE

He $\begin{Bmatrix} believed \\ had\ believed \end{Bmatrix}$ that he $\begin{Bmatrix} trisected \\ had\ trisected \end{Bmatrix}$ angles

Using dates may clarify the principle involved:

He *believed* (in 1979) that he *trisected* angles (in 1979).

He *had believed* (in 1979, presumably before being disillusioned) that he *trisected* angles (in 1979).

He *believed* (in 1979) that he *had trisected* angles (in 1979).

He *had believed* (in 1979) that he *had trisected* angles (in 1979).

Note: The principle—that a past in the noun clause follows a past in the main clause—applies with especial force to indirect discourse:

He *said* that he *was* Napoleon.

If the verb in the main clause is in the present tense, the present perfect tense, the future tense, or the future perfect tense, the verb in the subordinate clause may be in any tense at all.

MAIN CLAUSE · · · · · · SUBORDINATE CLAUSE

He believes
He has believed
He will believe } that he
He will have
believed

trisects
trisected
will trisect
has trisected } angles
had trisected
will have
trisected

To express some universal truth (real or supposed), **a past tense in the main clause may be followed by a present tense in the subordinate clause.**

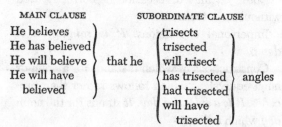

MAIN CLAUSE		SUBORDINATE CLAUSE
He *believed*	that	angles *are* trisectable
He *had believed*	that	angels *guard* us

ADVERBIAL CLAUSES If the verb in the main clause is in the past or past perfect tense, the verb in the subordinate clause is in the past or past perfect tense.

MAIN CLAUSE   SUBORDINATE CLAUSE

He $\begin{Bmatrix} \text{was} \\ \text{had been} \end{Bmatrix}$ honest although he $\begin{Bmatrix} \text{was} \\ \text{had been} \end{Bmatrix}$ rich

If the verb in the main clause is in the present, present perfect, future, or future perfect tense, the verb in the subordinate clause may be in any tense at all.

MAIN CLAUSE   SUBORDINATE CLAUSE

He $\begin{Bmatrix} \text{is} \\ \text{has been} \\ \text{will be} \\ \text{will have} \\ \text{been} \end{Bmatrix}$ honest although he $\begin{Bmatrix} \text{is} \\ \text{was} \\ \text{will be} \\ \text{has been} \\ \text{had been} \\ \text{will have} \\ \text{been} \end{Bmatrix}$ rich

Note: In an adverbial clause of *degree* (one which tells *how much* or to what extent) or of *comparison*, any tense may be used in the subordinate clause (regardless of the tense of the verb in the main clause):

He *weighed* as much as *I shall weigh* after my diet.

He *will like* you better than he *has liked* his wife.

ADJECTIVE CLAUSES In adjective clauses, the subordinate verb may express any time that the sense demands.

Freud formulated the theory which men *ignored* at first, which they *attack* now, and which they *will accept* ultimately.

INFINITIVES The present infinitive shows action taking place *at the same time as* (or *after*) the action of the main verb.

He wanted *to read* all books, *to swim* all rivers, *to love* all women.

The **perfect infinitive** shows action taking place *before* the action of the main verb.

He wanted *to have been* rich, *to have been* rich from birth, to have had the experiences of those born rich.

They are glad *to have helped,* but they expect to be paid.

PARTICIPLES The present participle shows action taking place *at the same time as* the action of the main verb.

Hating mankind, Swift nevertheless loved Tom, Dick, and Harry.

The **perfect participle** shows action taking place *before* the action of the main verb.

Having embarked for Utopia, he landed in Riverdale.

Note: More informally, the present participle may show action taking place before the action of the main verb:

Embarking for Utopia, he landed in Riverdale.

Exercise No. 41

Choose the correct form of the tense in each of the following.

1. The artist, plainly a better critic than painter, destroyed what he (*labored over, had labored over*) for ten years.
2. The man insisted that he (*had once seen, once saw*) a mermaid riding a sea-horse.
3. He declared that he (*wore, wears*) no man's collar.
4. They never saw snakes when they (*have visited, visited*) Ireland.
5. Einstein thought Newton had missed the point, that he (*neglected, had neglected*) important data.
6. He regretted (*being born, having been born*).
7. The ambitious sergeant hoped (*to be, to have been*) a general.
8. The books were infinitely dull and Gulliver had only a small capacity for boredom; consequently he wanted (*to have read, to read*) them—reading them was too painful a task.
9. (*Having been taught, Being taught*) manners by my heavy-handed father, I suppressed my yawns.
10. (*Reaching, Having reached*) for the moon, he brought down a star.

SHALL AND WILL In informal speech and writing, *will* does duty for all three persons. Formal usage, however, still insists on distinctions—though defending them becomes progressively more futile. The formal principles governing the use of *shall* and *will* follow:

Shall expresses **simple futurity** in the **first person**, singular and plural; *will* expresses **simple futurity** in the **second and third persons**, singular and plural.

SIMPLE FUTURITY

1. I shall	We shall
2. You will	You will
3. He, she, it will	They will

I *shall* drown; nobody *will* help me. Here the speaker predicts only—he does not exhibit any determination to drown. (If he did, the sentence would read: "I *will* drown; nobody *shall* help me.")

He will try to make his getaway, but perhaps we shall be too much for him.

You will leave for a vacation, but I shall stay on here working.

Will expresses **determination** in the **first person**, singular and plural; *shall* expresses **determination** in the **second and third persons**, singular and plural.

DETERMINATION

1. I will	We will
2. You shall	You shall
3. He, she, it shall	They shall

Thou *shalt* worship no other god.

The weather man says, "It *will* rain"; God says, "It *shall* rain."

We *will* keep the commandments.

In questions, the form expected in the answer is used:

Shall God be denied? (God shall not be denied.)

Shall you hop or jump? (I shall walk sedately.)

Will you take this woman? (I will.)

Contractions

INFORMALLY:

I shall or *I will* becomes *I'll.*

You will or *you shall* becomes *you'll.*

He will or *he shall* becomes *he'll.*

We shall or *we will* becomes *we'll.*

They will or *they shall* becomes *they'll.*

The negative *will not* becomes *won't.*

The negative *shall not* becomes *shan't.*

Note: *I'd, you'd, he'd,* etc. are the corresponding contractions for *should* and *would*, the past forms of *shall* and *will*.

Exercise No. 42

Choose the correct form of the verb in each of the following sentences.

1. What (*shall, will*) we do with the drunken sailor?
2. We (*shall, will*) go to the park today if the weather remains pleasant.
3. What (*shall, will*) we do now, what (*shall, will*) we ever do?
4. If I lend you my finest collection of records, (*will, shall*) you return it?
5. Yes, I promise absolutely that I (*shall, will*) return them next week.
6. "That young man," said the future president's father "(*shall, will*) be a famed man one day."
7. If I die, no soul (*shall, will*) pity me.
8. These are the principles which I know (*will, shall*) have their way, no matter how formidable the attempt to defeat them.
9. The studio posted a notice which read: "No one (*shall, will*) enter while the red light is lit."
10. Next week, I (*shall, will*) return all cigarettes I have grubbed.

TROUBLESOME MODAL AUXILIARIES Eight auxiliary verbs show the manner in which a statement is made. Since *mood* achieves the same function, these auxiliaries are called *modal auxiliaries*. The modal auxiliaries express:

1. **potentiality** (ability or possibility): *may, might, can, could.*
2. **condition**: *should, would.*
3. **obligation**: *must, ought.*

Note: The modal auxiliaries are followed by the infinitive without *to.*

Compare: Women can *play* while men *must* work.

with

Women are able to *play* while men are obliged *to work.*

Modal Auxiliaries are frequent sources of error because their meaning shifts with shifting contexts.

May implies **permission, doubt, or possibility.**

You *may* rest tomorrow.

He *may* be telling the truth.

It *may* rain tonight.

Might, though the past tense of *may*, does not necessarily represent past time. Commonly it implies **more doubt**, a greater dependence on circumstances than *may*:

If the clouds are salted, the rains *might* come. Here *might* presents a future possibility in spite of its past form.

Can implies **ability**:

We *can* still win.

You may leave if you *can* walk.

The preceding sentence might be translated: "You are permitted to leave if you are able to walk."

Note: The distinction between *can* and *may* still holds in formal speech and writing, but it is usually disregarded in informal speech and writing. The construction *can't* regularly does duty for mayn't: "We can't leave without permission."

Could, although the past tense of *can*, does not necessarily represent past time. Commonly it implies a **more uncertain condition** than *can*.

She *could* refuse, but she never does.

Note: Here *could* presents a future ability, in spite of its past form.

Should expresses futurity from the standpoint of some past time:

I said that I *should* help if called. *Should* is future with respect to *said*.

Note: Normally *should* and *would* are governed by the same rules that govern shall and will:

SIMPLE FUTURITY		DETERMINATION	
1. I should	we should	I would	we would
2. you would	you would	you should	you should
3. he, she, it would	they would	he, she, it should	they should

In reporting indirectly, *should* **may substitute for the** *shall* **of direct speech:**

Direct: "I shall return in lilac time," the poet declared.

Indirect: The poet declared that he should return in lilac time.

But either *should* or *would* is correct.

Commonly, *should* does not represent past time; rather it implies duty or fitness; doubt or hesitancy; supposition or condition. To express these meanings, *should* is used for all three persons, singular and plural.

I *should* hardly think so.

Properly, you *should* wear a black tie.

He *should* pass his examination.

If they *should* attack, they will attack in force.

If I *should* die before I wake, I pray the Lord my soul to take.

Note: *Should* is probably used most often to express duty or condition.

Would **expresses futurity from the standpoint of some past time.**

He said that he *would* help if he could.

In reporting indirectly, *would* **may stand for the** *will* **of direct speech:**

Direct: "There will be free drinks," the bartender commented.

Indirect: The bartender commented that there would be free drinks.

Commonly, *would* does not represent past time; rather, it implies habitual action, determination, or condition:

Charles Churchill *would* go to bed ossified night after night.

I *would* go, I decided, in spite of all their protests.

If she were shrewd, she *would* resist their offer.

Note: In the last sentence, note that *would* appears in the main clause. In standard English, *would* (unlike *should*) is not used in an if-clause.

Must **implies necessity or obligation:**

Night *must* fall.

You *must* see his new twelve-act play.

Must **may also express conviction, in the teeth of contradictory evidence:**

Mars *must* be inhabited.

Note: *Must*, originally a past tense, is used only in the present.

Ought **implies duty or obligation** (more strongly than *should*):

You *ought* to be more kind.

He *ought* to make the most of his small abilities.

Note: *Ought* is used with *to* plus the infinitive (unlike the other modal auxiliaries, which omit *to*).

Exercise No. 43

Choose the correct modal auxiliary in each of the following sentences.

1. We (*can, may*) still beat them if we try.
2. If a peace treaty is signed, the world (*may, might*) relax.
3. I believe that we (*can, could*) swim the channel, if it were not too rough.
4. The operator said that she (*should, would*) call us when she had reached our party.
5. Because she is my sister, I (*should, would*) attend her wedding.
6. I want no argument. You (*ought, should, must*) to listen when I am speaking.
7. If you (*can, may*) relax sufficiently tonight, you (*should, ought*) be in good shape for the hike tomorrow.
8. The captain insisted that he (*should, would*) lead his team to victory.
9. Do you think I (*can, may*) get permission from the principal to leave school early tomorrow?
10. He (*should, would*) not climb to the peak of Everest if he were really intelligent.

ADJECTIVES AND ADVERBS

Many errors result from failure to recognize similarities and dissimilarities between the functions of adjectives and adverbs.

Similarities Both modify other parts of speech.

She is a *lovely* lady.

The adjective *lovely* describes or modifies the noun *lady*.

He followed her *rapidly*.

The adverb *rapidly* describes or modifies the verb *followed*.

Certain adverbs and adjectives have identical forms.

I hold him in *high* regard.	Adjective
Send the kite *high*.	Adverb
Late guests are always welcome.	Adjective
But don't always come *late*.	Adverb
Eddie lives a *fast* (colloquial) life.	Adjective
Eddie lives too *fast* (colloquial).	Adverb

Both have degrees of comparison.

	POSITIVE	COMPARATIVE	SUPERLATIVE
ADJECTIVES	good	better	best
	bad	worse	worst
	cold	colder	coldest
ADVERBS	well	better	best
	badly	worse	worst
	coldly	colder	coldest

Dissimilarities Adjectives modify nouns or pronouns by identifying, limiting, or describing them.

Mock turtle soup is *delicious*.

Adjective *delicious* describes or modifies the noun *soup*.

He is *handsome*.

Adjective *handsome* modifies pronoun *he*.

Adverbs modify other sentence elements, generally verb, adjective, or other adverb.

The boxer *deftly* jabbed his left.

Adverb *deftly* modifies the verb *jabbed*.

This chocolate soda is *extraordinarily* sweet.

Adverb *extraordinarily* modifies adjective *sweet*.

The preacher spoke *exceedingly* well.

Adverb *exceedingly* modifies adverb *well*.

Eating *slowly* conduces to better digestion.

The adverb *slowly* modifies the gerund *eating*.

Thus:
1. Learn the conventions which govern each form.
2. Note how the word is used in the sentence before using the adjective or adverb form.

Note: Do not allow an adjective to modify a verb:

Wrong: He eats *rapidly* and *sloppy*.

The adjective *sloppy* cannot modify the verb *eats*. Substitute the adverb *sloppily*.

Note: Do not allow an adjective to modify another adjective:

Wrong: We will *sure* be glad when this book is finished.

The adjective *sure* cannot modify the adjective *glad*. Substitute the adverb *surely*.

Wrong: I'll be with you *most* any time now.

The adjective *most* cannot modify the adjective *any*. Substitute the adverb *almost*.

Wrong: He is *some* smarter than I thought he was.

The adjective *some* cannot modify the adjective *smarter*. Substitute the adverb *somewhat*.

Note: An adjective, not an adverb, is generally used to complete the meaning of the following verbs and to describe their subjects: *to be, become, seem, appear*.

Right: The story of Cyrano is *sad*.

Right: Suddenly he became *silly*.

Right: Their situation seems *desperate*.

Right: The plot increasingly appeared *absurd*.

Note: Adjectives are generally used after the sensory verbs: *feel, taste, sound, look, smell*, and after verbs like *remain, prove*, and *grow*.

Right: Edmond felt *happy* about winning his letter for football.

Happy describes (or modifies) *Edmond*, not the verb *felt*. Since it is the noun rather than the verb which is modified, an adjective rather than an adverb should be used.

The crepe suzettes we ate last night tasted *sour*.

Sour modifies the noun *crepe suzettes*, not the verb *tasted*.

Hoagy's arrangement of Orpheus sounds *good*.

Good modifies the noun *arrangement*, not the verb *sounds*.

Now that I've seen Edwina, Julie looks *beautiful*.

Beautiful modifies the noun *Julie*, not the verb *looks*.

The marinara sauce smells *sweet*.

Sweet modifies the noun *sauce*, not the verb *smells*.

Note, however, that if the *manner* of feeling, tasting, and the like is required, an adverb should be used.

Right: After his nose was broken, George smelled *badly*.

The adverb *badly* describes George's ability to smell, not his personal odor.

Right: She looked *sadly* about her.

The adverb *sadly* describes the *manner* in which the girl observed her surroundings.

Note that the distinctions between *good* and *well*, *bad* and *badly* fall within this category.

I feel *good*. Adjective suggesting good spirits, a sense of well being.

I feel *well*. Adverb suggesting good health.

I feel *bad*. Adjective suggesting poor health or poor spirits.

I feel *badly*. Adverb meaning literally that the sense of touch is impaired.

A useful device to distinguish whether adjective or adverb ought to be used is this: For the sensory verb followed by the adjective substitute a form of *to be*. If the resulting construction appears sensible, allow it to stand; otherwise substitute an adverb for the adjective.

Do you feel (dizzy, dizzily)?

For the sensory verb *feel* substitute a form of *to be* (*are*) and add the adjective.

Right: Are you dizzy?

He looked (foolish, foolishly) about the room. For the sensory verb *looked* substitute a form of *to be* (*is*) and add the adjective: He is foolish. In this example the result is obviously nonsensical; therefore the adverbial and not the adjectival form must be used:

He looked *foolishly* about the room.

Note: After a verb and its direct object, the modifier may be either an adverb or an adjective depending upon its function in the sentence. It is an adverb if it modifies the verb, an adjective if it modifies the noun or pronoun.

Right: Kerner held the rudder *steady*. Adjective *steady* is correct, for it suggests that the *rudder* is steady.

Right: Kerner held the rudder *steadily*. Adverb *steadily* is also correct, for here the implication is that Kerner *held* steadily, and so the adverb modifies the verb.

Exercise No. 44

Select the correct form and give your reason. If more than one form is correct, explain why.

1. I can't hear the actors (*good, well*) from the last row.
2. Secretariat won the race (*easy, easily*).

3. We'll arrive at Endican (*most, almost*) any time now.
4. The marlin looked (*fresh, freshly*) to the old man.
5. We thought that *Streetcar* was a (*real, really*) good play.
6. I can't read (*good, well*) with these glasses.
7. Gladioli will smell (*sweet, sweetly*) in the living room.
8. The damp air (*sure, surely*) feels (*good, well*) after that long dry spell.
9. The prospect of yet another war makes him feel (*bad, badly*).
10. She clasped the infant (*tight, tightly*) in her arms.
11. He rides his mount (*good, well*).
12. The Secretary of State stood (*firm, firmly*) in his decision.
13. The dazed victim of the accident gazed (*helpless, helplessly*) across the road.
14. Some actors speak their lines far too (*loud, loudly*).
15. Some actresses speak (*soft, softly*), but the gallery goers hear them (*clear, clearly*) nevertheless.
16. The orchestra sounded (*cacophonous, cacophonously*) at rehearsal.
17. Most (*gentle, gently*) he stroked the cat's fur.
18. The verdict of guilty made the prisoner feel (*angrily, angry*) toward the jury.
19. The crowd approved (*hearty, heartily*) of the fielder's catch.
20. The jet plane flew by too (*quick, quickly*) for me to see it, but it (*sure, surely*) sounded (*real, really*) (*noisy, nosily*).

Comparisons must be complete and logical
When two subjects are being compared, use the comparative form of the adjective or adverb.

Right: Of Orwell's two satires, I think *Animal Farm* the better.

Better is the comparative form of the *adjective,* and ought to be used here. *Best,* the superlative, would be correct if the sentence read: *Animal Farm* is the best of Orwell's works.

When the comparative degree of an adjective or adverb is used, exclude the subject of the comparison from the class with which it is compared.

Wrong: Writers are generally more neurotic than people.

Writers, the subject of the comparison, cannot logically be compared with *people,* the class or group.

Right: Writers are generally more neurotic than *other* people.

The word *other* excludes *writers* from the class with which it has been compared.

Wrong: The atom bomb is more destructive than any implement of warfare.

Right: The atom bomb is more destructive than any *other* implement of warfare.

Compare only things which can logically be compared.

Wrong: His skis are as well polished as an Olympic champion.

This sentence is absurd because it implies a comparison between *skis* and an *Olympic champion.* Skis must be compared with skis, not with people.

Right: His skis are as well polished as *those* of an Olympic champion.

Right: His skis are as well polished as an Olympic champion's.

Wrong: Whitman, undeniably our greatest poet, is undeniably prosier than any poet in American literature.

The comparison is absurd because it suggests that Whitman was more prosy than anyone, including himself.

Right: Whitman, undeniably our greatest poet, is often prosier than *any other* poet in American literature.

Complete each comparison before modifying it.

Wrong: Our Chevrolet is as old as, if not older than, Bill's.

Right: Our Chevrolet is as old as Bill's, if not older.

Wrong: Muriel is as short as, if not shorter than, her brother.

Right: Muriel is as short as her brother, if not shorter.

Some adjectives are absolute and must not be compared: *unique, round, square, perfect, empty, dead, opposite, entirely.*

Wrong: This is a very unique example of a Persian ceramic cat.

Since unique means "only one of a kind," it cannot logically be qualified. Thus, the adverb *very* must be omitted.

Note: The same principle applies to words like "rounder," "more square," and the like, for objects cannot logically be more round or square than what is already round or square. In the strictly formal sense, the framers of the Constitution had no right to aim toward a "more perfect union," since *perfect* is an absolute.

Nevertheless, **in colloquial usage, these superlatives are often qualified:** *deadest party, roundest head, more completely,* and the like.

Avoid the vague, half-finished comparison.

Wrong: It was *so* pleasant.

So may carry meaning when the person hears the enthusiasm of the speaker, but in writing, it suggests that half a sentence has been written.

Right: It was so pleasant that we must return again.

Right: It was pleasant.

Wrong: He is such a goodhearted fellow.

Right: He is a goodhearted fellow.

Right: He is such a goodhearted fellow that people can't help suspecting him.

The adverbs *but, hardly, never, only, scarcely,* **have negative meanings, and when used in sentences require no other word of negation.**

Wrong: We did not hardly have time to eat.

Since *hardly* has a negative meaning, combining it with *did not* produces a faulty double negative.

Right: We did not have time to eat.

Right: We hardly had time to eat.

Exercise No. 45

Some of the following sentences are correct; some contain errors of faulty comparison. Let those which are correct stand, but make any necessary corrections in the others.

1. Most students believe that their writing is better than their fellow students.
2. We had more rainfall in the East in 1978 than in any other year.
3. We think that our cat is almost as unique as any cat.
4. Keeping tropical fish is almost as time-consuming, if not more so, than raising cactus.
5. Lydia has more trouble taking care of Philip than anyone.
6. His collection of antiques is as valuable as that owned by the best museums.
7. Valerie can sing as well as anyone in her class.
8. Clumsiness is the worst of his faults.
9. Many soldiers have found that being in politics is not so simple as the military.
10. I have heard both his speeches, and I think yesterday's clearly the best.

PROBLEMS INVOLVING THE USE OF MODIFIERS

Modifiers are words, phrases, or clauses which alter the meaning of other sentence elements by limiting, describing, or emphasizing them.

I wear a coat of brocaded silk in the woodland house that I share with my friend.

of brocaded silk—phrase modifying *coat.*

woodland—word modifying *house.*

that I share with my friend—clause modifying *house.*

When each modifier is in its proper place, it adds depth to an otherwise simple statement: I wear a coat in my house. If, however, the modifiers are incorrectly placed, the sentence becomes confusing:

I wear a coat of brocaded silk in the house in the woodland that I share with my friend.

Does he share the *house* **or the** *woodland* **with his friend?**

Modifiers, then, must modify precisely; else they distort the meaning and blur the intention of the sentence.

DANGLING MODIFIERS—"dangling" when there is no word to which they can clearly and logically relate:

Having at last reached home, the door closed behind him.

The modifier *Having reached home* improperly modifies *door,* but fails in any way to describe the main subject or action. To eliminate the error, change the word order so that the dangling element relates to an adequate subject, or expand the sentence so that an adequate subject is provided:

Having at last reached home, he closed the door behind him.

When he reached home, he closed the door behind him.

Note: Many dangling constructions may be eliminated by using the active rather than the passive form of the verb. Instead of the passive *The door closed behind him,* use the active *He closed the door.*

Dangling modifiers occur in various forms which are discussed below.

Dangling Participles—at the beginning of the sentence:

Dangling: Dancing and drinking every night, her reputation in the community suffered.
The modifying phrase *Dancing and drinking* modifies, illogically, (*her*) *reputation.*

Right: Dancing and drinking every night, she lost her reputation in the community.
The participial phrase has been made to relate to an adequate subject.

Right: Because she danced and drank every night, her reputation suffered.
The participial phrase has been expanded to a subordinate clause.

Dangling participles at the end of the sentence:

Dangling: Our vacation passed happily, swimming and playing tennis.
Our vacation did not swim or play; we did.

Right: We passed our vacation happily, swimming and playing tennis.

Right: Our vacation passed happily, for we swam and played tennis.

Note: The expressions *thus* and *thereby* often introduce loose verbal phrases:

Loose: The boys quibbled throughout their trip, thereby ruining their vacation.

Loose: I took a cabin amidships, thus making my voyage more comfortable.

These sentences are illogical ("upside down" constructions) because the main idea is in the subordinate phrase and seems to dangle.

Right: The boys ruined their vacation by quibbling throughout their trip.

Right: By taking a cabin amidships, I made my voyage more comfortable.

Exercise No. 46

Correct the following sentences which contain dangling participles.

1. Hanging from the bell tower, crowds watched as the fanatic prepared to leap.
2. Having entered his car, the windows were immediately rolled down.
3. Gingerly walking barefooted on the cobblestones, his eyes caught sight of a silver coin.
4. Listening to the concert with rapt attention, Beethoven seemed more than ever a magnificent composer.
5. Working too hard and earning too little, my ulcer is starting to bother me again.
6. Tonight I'll not work, already tired and indisposed.
7. Leaving his apartment in a violent temper, her fury mounted higher as she thought of his insolence.
8. Hanging round her neck, he saw her diamond necklace.
9. Dante spilled gravy on Beatrice's gown, thereby spoiling their evening together.
10. Entering the drug store, his cigarette hung limply between his lips.

Dangling Infinitives

Dangling: To prepare for an examination, solitude and concentration are essential.
A person to study for the examination is the primary essential. Only then are solitude and concentration important.

Right: To prepare for the examination, *a man* needs solitude and concentration.

Right: Solitude and concentration are necessary when *one* prepares for an examination.

Dangling: To have a successful party, good conversation and food are always useful.
Good conversation and food do not give parties.

Right: To have a successful party, *one* ought to provide good conversation and food.

Right: Good conversation and food always help to make a party successful.

Exercise No. 47

Correct the following sentences which contain dangling infinitives.

1. To travel in comfort, money is a prerequisite.
2. To smoke safely, filters ought to be used.
3. To row all afternoon without getting blisters, gloves should be worn.
4. To get ten miles to the gallon, moderate speed must be maintained.
5. To work as a pianist, constant practice is of great importance.

Dangling Gerunds

Dangling: After seeing the dentist, his teeth stopped aching.

His *teeth* did not see the dentist.

Right: After he saw the dentist, his teeth stopped aching.

Right: After seeing the dentist, he thought that his teeth stopped aching.

Dangling: In planning an Arctic expedition, careful preparations are needed.

Careful preparations do not plan Arctic expeditions.

Right: In planning an Arctic expedition, explorers need to make careful preparations.

Right: Explorers need to make careful preparations when planning an Arctic expedition.

Exercise No. 48

Correct the following sentences which contain dangling gerunds.

1. Before leaving for Europe, reservations must be made.
2. After attacking my lateness, I was fired.
3. On his first attempt at flycasting, the trout took the bait.
4. When entering the theater, the clothes of the audience surprised me.
5. While turning the page, the ashtray spilled on his book.

Dangling Elliptical Clauses

Elliptical constructions from which a subject or predicate has been omitted are generally acceptable if the subject corresponds with the subject of the main clause and if the predicate is clear:

Right: When (I am) hunting, I always keep my gun loaded.

However, when the omitted subject does not correspond with the subject of the main clause, the elliptical clause dangles:

Wrong: While asleep in the subway, a thief picked my pocket.

The omitted subject of the elliptical clause, *I was,* does not correspond with the subject of the main clause, *thief,* and therefore the elliptical construction dangles, suggesting that it was the thief who slept.

Right: While I was asleep, a thief picked my pocket.

The elliptical clause has been supplied with subject and predicate.

Right: While sleeping, I had my pocket picked by a thief.

The main clause has been recast so that its subject and that of the elliptical clause correspond.

Exercise No. 49

Correct the following sentences which contain dangling elliptical clauses.

1. When three years old, John's mother taught him archery.
2. While visiting in Concord, the weather was excellent.
3. Once relaxed, Hilda's back felt better.
4. Stephen kept watching the light till green.
5. Although famished, caviar was not his dish.

MISPLACED MODIFIERS—are "misplaced" when they are not clearly connected with the word they modify. Misplaced modifiers occur in the various forms discussed below.

Misplaced Modifying Words

Such adverbs as: *only, nearly, almost, hardly, scarcely, just, even, quite,* should be placed next to the words they modify.

Wrong: I only told the jury what I had seen. The adverb *only* "squints," looking in three directions at once. Does the writer mean: *I and no one else told the jury?* If so, then the sentence must be recast so that *only* acts as an adjective modifying the pronoun *I:*

Right: Only I told the jury what I had seen. *I told the jury what I had seen and nothing else?* If so, then *only* must be so placed that it modifies the noun clause *what I had seen:*

Right: I told the jury only what I had seen. *I told only the jury and no one else?* If so—and this sentence arrangement warrants the use of *only* as an adverb—*only* must be so placed that it modifies the verb *told:*

Right: I told only the jury what I had seen. Thus, the modifier must be placed near the word it modifies in order to avoid ambiguity.

Any other adverb may "squint" if it is placed so that it **refers ambiguously to both the preceding and succeeding word.**

Wrong: People who teach rarely get rich. Does *rarely* modify *teach* or *get rich?* A major difference in meaning attaches to each choice.

Right: Teachers rarely get rich.

Right: Rarely do people who teach get rich.

Note: Frequently, the difficulties caused by misplaced modifiers may be eliminated by placing them at the beginning of the sentence.

Wrong: Drivers who speed often have accidents.

Right: Often, drivers who speed have accidents.

Exercise No. 50

Revise the following sentences so that the misplaced modifying words are correctly placed.

1. Those who listen to Dr. Sermione's lectures, even the most intellectual, will be confused.
2. Vivien only reads the best in Irish literature.
3. The baby nearly walked across his playpen.
4. Eating candy frequently ruins teeth.
5. I scarcely opened the door when his dog leaped at me.

Misplaced Modifying Phrases

Misplaced **terminal** phrases.

Wrong: Harold kept the child who misbehaved in the corner.

In the corner should modify *kept,* not *misbehaved.*

Right: Because the child misbehaved, Harold kept him in the corner.

Wrong: Stephen fed his tropical fish shrimp-eggs with eagerness at bedtime.

Two phrases are grouped erroneously at the end of this sentence to produce an absurd result.

Right: At bedtime, Stephen eagerly fed his tropical fish shrimp-eggs.

Misplaced **medial** phrases.

Wrong: I asked him the next time to invite more lively people.

The next time squints toward both *asked* and *to invite.*

Right: I asked him to invite more lively people the next time.

Wrong: The commander promised as soon as possible to send the soldier overseas.

As soon as possible squints toward both *promised* and *to send.*

Right: As soon as possible, the commander promised to send the soldier overseas.

Right: The commander promised to send the soldier overseas as soon as possible.

Exercise No. 51

Rewrite the following sentences so that the modifiers are in proper position.

1. A scream tore through the house, waking the girl in bed with a cry.
2. In eastern Mexico there is a village inhabited by Indians called Patzcuaro.
3. Columbus vowed as soon as he landed to claim the New World for Ferdinand and Isabella.
4. No cathedral have I ever seen like that one in all my travels.
5. I located the trouble with my television set in the laboratory.

Misplaced Modifying Clauses

Relative clauses.

Wrong: The face of the man looking through the window which was cruel and sardonic startled Sweeney.

Which was cruel and sardonic has as its antecedent *window* instead of its logical antecedent *face.*

Right: Looking through the window, the man's face, which was cruel and sardonic, startled Sweeney.

To avoid confusion place the relative clause immediately after its antecedent.

Right: The cruel and sardonic face of the man looking through the window startled Sweeney.

Recast the Sentence

Wrong: I heard the bees near the flowers that were buzzing.

Right: I heard the bees that were buzzing near the flowers.

Parallel Modifying Clauses

Wrong: After Oedipus, our cat, has crouched behind the chair, he leaps at our ankles, as soon as he has decided we no longer suspect him.

The two subordinate clauses are parallel in form, and should therefore be combined and placed either before or after the main clause.

Right: After Oedipus, our cat, has crouched behind the chair and has decided that we no longer suspect him, he leaps at our ankles.

Right: Oedipus, our cat, leaps at our ankles after he has crouched behind the chair and decided that we no longer suspect him.

Squinting Clauses

Wrong: Because food spoils when not in use it should always be refrigerated.

The elliptical clause *when not in use* squints toward *spoils* and *should always be refrigerated.*

Right: Because food spoils, it should always be refrigerated when not in use.

Exercise No. 52

Revise the following sentences so that the modifying clauses are correctly placed.

1. We set out for the city beyond the rainbow in which we lived.
2. When we visited foreign lands, we tried to learn their folkways when we spoke with inhabitants.
3. He examined the specimen in the microscope that was in a glass slide.
4. He promised to visit us as we were leaving.
5. Letters can win friends that show personality and spirit.

Split Constructions Parts of the sentence that are closely related should not be needlessly separated.

Split Subject and Verb

Wrong: David, after deceiving Uriah and sending him to the battlefield to die, repented. Unless a good reason exists for separating them, subject and verb should remain together.

Right: After deceiving Uriah and sending him to the battlefield to die, David repented.

Split Verb and Complement

Wrong: The teacher suggested, since so many students had failed to do the lesson which had been assigned two weeks before, that they remain after school.

Although it is wrong to separate verb and complement to achieve emphasis, an extended modifier may, as here, destroy the clarity of the sentence.

Right: Since so many students had failed to do the lesson which had been assigned two weeks before, the teacher suggested that they remain after school.

Split Infinitive Normally, the infinitive is considered to be a unit consisting of the sign of the infinitive (*to*) and the infinitive (which corresponds to the first person singular, present indicative form of the verb). **To separate *to* from the infinitive may result in distortion of meaning or loss of emphasis:**

Awkward: The editor intended to closely and painstakingly scrutinize the manuscript.

Better: The editor intended to scrutinize the manuscript closely and painstakingly.

Sometimes, however, clarity and emphasis are improved by separating *to* from the infinitive:

Right: The audience was asked to kindly take its seats.

To place *kindly* elsewhere in this sentence would result in a "squinting" construction: The audience was asked kindly to take its seats.

Right: With a lowering of the draft age, the army expects to more than treble its forces.

Thus, **to attain clarity or to achieve emphasis, the infinitive may be split.** However, it ought not to be split without some sufficient reason:

To without reason split an infinitive disappoints the reader's sense of proper diction.

Split Comparison

Wrong: Greek ruins are as interesting, if not more interesting than, Roman ruins.

Because the modifying phrase *if not more interesting* is wrongly placed, the main clause is illogical: Greek ruins are as interesting than Roman ruins.

Complete each comparison before introducing a modifying phrase:

Right: Greek ruins are as interesting as Roman ruins, if not more interesting.

Correct, but stilted: Greek ruins are as interesting as, if not more interesting than, Roman ruins.

Exercise No. 53

Revise the following sentences whenever the split construction damages their effectiveness.

1. Dr. Johnson, although he befriended Boswell and spent many pleasant hours with his Scottish biographer, despised the Scots.
2. I warned him that, even though we had spent many years together and had shared experiences neither of us would ever forget, I would take no more of his nonsense.
3. The preacher asked his flock please to contribute to the establishment of a new community center.
4. He tried to suddenly and violently swerve his car away from the oncoming truck.
5. The view from the waterfront in New Orleans is as dismal, if not more so, than that from the New Jersey docks.

SHIFTS IN POINT OF VIEW

A foolish consistency may be the hobgoblin of little minds, but stylistic consistency is not foolish. An easy mastery of varied writing techniques characterizes the mature writer; to sustain it, his writing must be resolutely consistent. Shifts in person, in number, in voice dismay the reader and consequently damn the writer.

MAINTAIN CONSISTENCY OF NUMBER AND PERSON

Wrong: We were frightened during our drive across the Sierra Madre Mountains, for one saw everywhere wreckage from previous automobile accidents.

Shift from first person plural *we* to third person singular *one*.

Right: We were frightened during our drive across the Sierra Madre Mountains, for we saw everywhere wreckage from previous automobile accidents.

Wrong: After I held the job of masseur in a Turkish bath for six months, you never knew one body from the next.

Shift from first person *I* to second, *you*.

Right: After I held the job of masseur in a Turkish bath for six months, I never knew one body from the next.

Wrong: Root canal therapy is a standard technique to save teeth. All dentists use them.

Shift from singular *therapy* to plural *them*.

Right: Root canal therapy is a standard technique to save teeth. All dentists use it.

MAINTAIN CONSISTENCY OF TENSE

Wrong: We hurried to the door, but nobody is there.

Shift from past tense *hurried* to present *is*.

Right: We hurried to the door, but nobody was there.

Wrong: *Limbo* tells about the horrors of a cybernetic world. The novel described how a brain surgeon who was lost on a tropical island during World War III returned to what was left of America and tried to find meaning in the new order.

Shift from present tense *tells* to past tense for the rest of the passage.

Use the present tense when writing about a work of literature, music, or art.

Right: *Limbo* tells about the horrors of a cybernetic world. The novel describes how a brain surgeon who is lost on a tropical island during World War III returns to what is left of America and tries to find meaning in the new order.

Right: *Othello* is one of Shakespeare's great tragedies.

Right: *The Birth of Venus*, Botticelli's masterpiece, distinguishes itself among any collection of art works.

Right: Mozart's *Don Giovanni* has exquisite lyrical passages.

MAINTAIN CONSISTENCY OF MOOD

Wrong: Address the chairman first and then you will be recognized.

Shift from imperative mood *address* to indicative *will be recognized*.

Right: If you will first address the chairman, you will then be recognized.

MAINTAIN CONSISTENCY OF VOICE AND SUBJECT

Wrong: He abhorred prejudice, and all people were considered equal by him.

Subject shifts from *he* to *people;* voice shifts from active *abhorred* to passive *were considered*.

Right: He abhorred prejudice and considered all people equal.

Wrong: He visited churches in Rome, went skiing in Les Rousses, and night clubs were his haunts in Paris.

Subject shifts from *he* to *night clubs;* voice shifts from active *visited* and *went* to passive *were*.

Right: He visited churches in Rome, went skiing in Les Rousses, and haunted night clubs in Paris.

Note: Sometimes it is necessary to shift from active to passive to avoid a clumsier shift in subject:

The thief twisted through heavy traffic to elude the police. He was almost trapped between a trailer truck and a bus, but squeezed through and sped on. Although he managed to hide safely for ten minutes in a darkened hallway, he was finally cornered and arrested by three detectives.

Active: Thief *twisted, squeezed, managed*

Passive: was trapped, was cornered and *arrested*

Thus, the *thief,* central subject of the passage, sometimes acts, sometimes is acted upon. Although the principle of consistency is violated, it is wiser to shift from active to passive than to lose the center of attention by sharing the *thief* with a *trolley car, a truck,* and *three detectives*.

MAINTAIN CONSISTENCY OF TONE

Wrong: When studying for an examination, try to achieve flexibility in handling your material: aim at insight rather than sheer memory.

What you must memorize will then benefit from a reserve of reflective thought.

By this time you've probably knocked yourself out and won't be able to pass anyhow, but just in case, let's go on to some other advice. Try to anticipate the questions you may be asked. . . .

Shift from serious, factual discussion to dubious humor disrupts rather than enhances the tone of the communication. The second paragraph would be better in this way:

Another useful technique involves trying to anticipate the questions you may be asked. . . .

Exercise No. 54

Correct all violations of consistency in number, person, tense, mood, voice, subject, or tone.

1. One should listen carefully to his employer if you want promotions.
2. Lorelei was a cold-hearted girl and diamonds were to her the best friends a girl could have.
3. Beethoven's *Fifth Symphony* was a famous musical achievement.
4. If he were to take an old friend's advice, he will leave his job.
5. I know that I wouldn't go out with that gang unless you want to get into trouble.
6. A true democrat accepts the opinion of the majority even if they disagree with it.
7. When Job heard the Voice from the Whirlwind, he knows that his moment of reckoning has come.
8. Everyone has some favorite recipe that they concoct for their friends.
9. Tom and Huck entered the cemetery and the tomb stones were enough to frighten anybody at night.
10. A smart wrestler knows how to feign agony, and you could always tell they were not really hurt.
11. Giving directions to a stranger is not always easy but you must try to be simple and specific. So what if he gets lost a little; he'll see more of the town. But in any event, it is only courteous to try to guide him as well as possible.
12. The Indians defeated Custer, and all his men were exterminated by them.
13. If I allow him enough rope, you'll hang yourself.
14. Go West, young man, and there you will find California.
15. One must continue to practice if you wish to succeed.

PARALLELISM

To master parallelism is to control one of the principal techniques of English prose. No other single device helps more to clarify relationships between kindred ideas. **Parallelism signifies the grammatical balance of two or more logically related sentence elements:**

NOUN	ADJECTIVE	VERB	PARTICIPLE
Socrates had ability, knowledge, honesty, and courage.	Socrates was intelligent, able, honest, and courageous.	Socrates analyzed, discussed, questioned, and generalized.	Socrates faced his trial fearlessly, insisting on the truth as he saw it, and rejecting expedient compromises.

GERUND	INFINITIVE	PHRASE	CLAUSE
Socrates won fame by asking embarrassing questions and by giving ironic replies.	Socrates loved to trap his friends into seemingly innocent statements and then to expose their errors in logic.	Socrates confronted his accusers with complete assurance and with unabashed candor.	Socrates believed that the ideal state should be governed by intellectual aristocrats and that democracy was a dangerous creed.

Study the parallel constructions in these passages by professional writers:

"What another would have done as well as you, do not do it. What another would have said as well as you, do not say it; written as well, do not write it." (Gide)

"A great nose indicates a great man—
Genial, courteous, intellectual,
Virile, courageous." (Rostand)

"Men reject their prophets and slay them, but they love their martyrs and honor those whom they have slain." (Dostoevsky)

Like any rhetorical device, parallelism may be abused (see section on Style). But the amateur writer, once he learns to avoid the pitfalls described below, will find parallelism indispensable to mature prose.

Parallel sentence elements linked by a coordinating conjunction **must be parallel in form:** noun must parallel noun, adjective must parallel adjective, phrase must parallel phrase, etc.

Nouns

Wrong: A good scholar must be precise and possess originality.

Precise is an adjective, *originality* a noun.

Right: A good scholar must be precise and original. (Adjectives)

Right: A good scholar needs precision and originality. (Nouns)

Wrong: Consider the origins of man and how he has developed.

Origins is a noun, *how he has developed* a clause.

Right: Consider the origins and development of man. (Nouns)

Right: Consider how man originated and how he developed. (Verbs)

Adjectives

Wrong: Give me the aggressive fellow and who has initiative.

Aggressive is an adjective, *who has initiative* is a clause.

Right: Give me the fellow who is aggressive and who has initiative. (Clauses)

Verbs

Wrong: This morning I went to a brunch party, shopping at the supermarket, and lunching at the diner.

Went is a verb, *shopping* and *lunching* are participles.

Right: This morning I went to a brunch party, shopped at the supermarket, and lunched at the diner. (Verbs)

Participles

Wrong: Nero was flattered by the courtiers, praised by the soldiers, but the people hated him.

Flattered and *praised* are participles, *but the people hated him* is a clause.

Right: Nero was flattered by the courtiers, praised by the soldiers, but hated by the people. (Participles)

Right: The courtiers flattered Nero and the soldiers praised him, but the people hated him. (Verbs)

Gerunds

Wrong: Playing croquet is delightful, but to box is barbaric.

Playing is a gerund, *to box* is an infinitive.

Right: Playing croquet is delightful, but *boxing* is barbaric.

Right: To play croquet is delightful, but to box is barbaric. (Infinitives)

Infinitives

Wrong: The pilot received orders to bomb the target and that he would then return home.

To bomb is an infinitive, *that he would then return home* is a clause.

Right: The pilot received orders to bomb the target and then to return home. (Infinitives)

Phrases

Wrong: He hoped for an increase in salary and to get a longer vacation.

For an increase in salary is a phrase, *to get* is an infinitive.

Right: He hoped for an increase in salary and for a longer vacation. (Phrases)

Right: He hoped to get an increase in salary and a longer vacation. (Nouns)

Clauses

Wrong: The prophet warned his people of oncoming disaster and that the Assyrians would conquer them.

Main clause made parallel with subordinate clause.

Right: The prophet warned his people that disaster lay ahead and that the Assyrians would conquer them. (Subordinate clauses)

Right: The prophet warned his people of oncoming disaster and predicted the Assyrian conquest. (Main clauses)

Note: The second element in the parallel construction need not immediately follow the coordinating conjunction, but it must remain parallel in form:

Right: She carried herself with poise and, when engaged in conversation, spoke with animation.

Carried and *spoke* are separated by a clause, yet they are parallel.

Right: Jojo is a clown, winsome, hilarious, and sentimental, but more than that he is a satirist, incisive, critical, and penetrating.

Clown and *satirist* remain parallel although separated by a series of parallel adjectives and a phrase.

Exercise No. 55

Revise the following sentences so that the related sentence elements are parallel in form.

1. Some public officials are always investigating dead scandals or usually publicity hounds.
2. He believes that having courage is better than fearing and that faith is truer than doubt.
3. I want stouthearted men and who are fighters when necessary.
4. The Indian Summer of life should be sunny and sad, like the season, and an infinity of wealth and deepness of tone.
5. The school commission voted for improved building facilities and to enlarge the teaching staff.
6. Find time to learn goodness and giving up laziness.
7. The child eagerly awaited the hour of his birthday and that he would soon have all his new presents.
8. Saying is one thing; but to do is another.
9. What Charles needs is a doctor and a rest.
10. We studied the life of the ant and how it operates a social community.

Parallel sentence elements linked by correlative conjunctions (either . . . or, neither . . . nor, not only . . . but also, whether . . . or) **must be parallel in form.** If an adjective follows the first conjunction, an adjective must follow the second; if a verb follows the first conjunction, a verb must follow the second, etc.

Wrong: The witness not only accused the defendant but also his entire family.

Not only is followed by *accused*, a verb; *but also* is followed by *his entire family*, a noun phrase.

Right: The witness accused not only the defendant but also his entire family.

Two nouns, *defendant* and *family* follow the correlatives.

Wrong: We know truth either by learning to reason or by the heart.

Either is followed by *learning to reason*, a gerund phrase; *or* is followed by *heart*, a noun.

Right: We know truth either by mind or by heart.

Exercise No. 56

Revise the following sentences so that the related sentence elements are parallel in form.

1. They couldn't decide whether they should leave the theater or to hiss the performance.
2. Bill either stops mimicking me or I will bang his head.
3. Franklin was not only a skillful politician but also had a genius for inventions.
4. He neither can do as he is told, nor his parents hope to change him.
5. When Billy grows up, either he wants to be a business tycoon or an actor.

A series of two or more parallel sentence elements must be parallel in form.

Wrong: My colleague is a distinguished yachtsman, gourmet, and is also interested in entomology.

Yachtsman and *gourmet* are parallel, but the third element, a clause, is not.

Right: My colleague is a distinguished yachtsman, gourmet, and entomologist.

Wrong: Emma Lazarus wrote a novel, two plays, and the Statue of Liberty has one of her poems.

Novel and *plays* are parallel; the third element, a clause, is not.

Right: Emma Lazarus wrote a novel, two plays, and many poems, one of which appears in part on the base of the Statue of Liberty.

Note: The succeeding elements in a parallel series need not immediately follow the first element, but they must remain parallel in form:

His experiences abroad taught him patience—which he learned by watching the controlled emotions of war-agonized people suffering pain and anguish—humility, and deep compassion. The parallel series consists of *patience, humility,* and *compassion.* The first element is followed by a clause, the second stands alone, and the third has a single modifier. Nevertheless, the structure remains parallel throughout.

To assure parallel form, repeat, where necessary, the word that introduces the parallel constructions. The words usually involved are prepositions, relative pronouns, and the sign of the infinitive: *to.*

Weak: We had to advise Edwards that to accept his offer was out of the question, to leave our homestead was impossible, and to move our ailing father was dangerous.

Omission of *that* in the second and third parallel clauses confuses the meaning of the sentence.

Right: We had to advise Edwards that to accept his offer was out of the question, that to leave our homestead was impossible, and that to move our ailing father was dangerous.

Weak: Electrical contractors face involved problems in estimating costs and particularly maintaining stock supplies.

Omission of the preposition *in* before the second element obscures the meaning of the sentence.

Right: Electrical contractors face involved problems in estimating costs and particularly in maintaining stock supplies.

Weak: The draftsman had to adjust the drawing board, which had tilted too sharply, and replace the worn tracing paper.

Omission of the sign of the infinitive, *to,* before the second element obscures the meaning of the sentence.

Right: The draftsman had to adjust the drawing board, which had tilted too sharply, and to replace the worn tracing paper.

Note: If the infinitives appear close together, repetition of *to* is generally unnecessary:

Right: He refused to listen, understand, or compromise.

Note: If the objects of the prepositions appear close together, repetition of the preposition is generally unnecessary:

Right: Their organization stands for liberty, equality, and fraternity.

Note: Change the word that introduces a series of parallel elements, if doing so is necessary to maintain correct idiomatic expression:

Wrong: He is awed and courteous to high ranking officials.

Although *courteous* and *awed* are parallel, the preposition *to* is unidiomatic and illogical when used with *awed.*

Right: He is awed by and courteous to high ranking officials.

Right: He is awed by politicians and courteous to them.

Note: Change any word in a series of parellel elements if doing so is necessary to maintain correct grammatical form:

Wrong: Men have always and will continue to try improving their standard of living.

Have and *will continue* are parallel, but in seeking a short cut, the writer has neglected to complete each verb properly.

Right: Men have always tried and will continue trying to improve their standard of living.

Exercise No. 57

Revise the following sentences so that the related sentence elements are parallel in form.

1. Henry Adams wrote history, fiction, and the cathedrals at Chartres and Mt. St. Michel turned him to architecture.
2. Dumas always has and will continue to excite readers young and old.
3. The yokels were attentive then swindled by the huckster.
4. The artist decided to exhibit his paintings, which hardly deserved public attention, and give lectures.
5. The doctors warned Jones that to work would prove fatal, to travel might help, but to rest would effect a complete recovery.

Sentence elements must be parallel in meaning as well as in form: action must parallel action, generalization must parallel generalization, description must parallel description, etc. If the elements are not parallel in meaning, the parallel construction must be eliminated and the sentence recast.

Wrong: The commissioner suggested that the parking dilemma could be solved and that automobiles must not park in the streets.

The two main clauses are parallel in form, but not in meaning. The first clause, *The commissioner suggested*, generalizes; the second clause, *that automobiles must not park*, specifies.

Right: The commissioner suggested that the parking dilemma could be solved, adding that part of the solution might be to prohibit automobiles from parking in the streets.

Note that to preserve the sense of the sentence, the parallel construction has been excised.

Wrong: Entering the room and being good natured, Tom genially welcomed his guests.

The two participial phrases are parallel in form, but not in meaning. *Entering the room* describes an action; *being good natured* describes a quality.

Right: Being genial and good natured, Tom welcomed his guests as soon as he entered the room.

Right: Tom, a genial and good-natured host, welcomed his guests as he entered the room.

Wrong: The passenger complained of the steward's insolence and of his refusal to answer when called.

The phrases *of the steward's insolence* and *of his refusal to answer* are parallel in form but not in meaning. The first phrase describes a quality, the second an action.

Right: The passenger complained of the insolent steward's refusal to answer when called.

Exercise No. 58

Where necessary revise the following sentences to assure logical relationships in meaning as well as in form.

1. The president warned about relaxing vigilance and about the Martian invasion of Oregon.
2. Opening the refrigerator, and being extremely hungry, he grabbed the chicken leg.
3. He promised them that walruses would be delightful to watch, and that two of the largest specimens were in the city zoo.
4. If he takes the time to study French, and if he tries hard, he will surely succeed.
5. Timid and infuriated by his attacks on her intelligence, she fled from the room.

OMISSIONS AND MIXED CONSTRUCTIONS

In the interest of economy, good usage accepts the omission of certain words from the sentence pattern. Legitimate omissions are called *ellipses:*

"Didn't you hear what happened?"

"No. What [happened]?"

"[What happened] To Ole?"

"Well, tell me."

"The killers took him for a ride."

"Where [did they take him] to?"

"[They took him] To the cabin where the Indian and the gambler live with Nick and Maria. [Do you] Want to hear the rest?"

"Yes. I do [want to hear the rest]."

However, words necessary for clear meaning or complete grammatical construction must never be omitted.

Avoid omitting articles, possessives, or connectives necessary for clearness or completeness.

Wrong: The heiress bought a gold and silver urn.

Did she buy one gold and one silver urn, or one made in part of each metal?

Right: The heiress bought a gold and a silver urn.

Right: The heiress bought a gold-and-silver urn.

Wrong: He left his money to his wife and aunt.

Right: He left his money to his wife and to his aunt.

Wrong: The class bell rang the same time as always.

Right: The class bell rang at the same time as always.

Avoid omitting any forms of main or auxiliary verbs necessary for clearness or completeness.

Wrong: Edwards is intelligent, but all the others stupid.

The elliptical construction *all the others stupid* assumes a verb, but the verb must be *is* to conform with the verb in the first clause. The number of *all the others*, however, is plural.

Right: Edwards is intelligent, but all the others are stupid.

Wrong: We work as diligently as they have or are working.

As they have what? *Work? Working?* Neither of the verb forms provided in the sentence fits.

Right: We work as diligently as they have worked or are working.

Note: Avoid using a single form of *to be* as both main and auxiliary verb.

Wrong: The violinist was in superb form and applauded by the entire audience.

Was is understood before *applauded*, but its use as an auxiliary differs from the use of *was* as the main verb in the opening clause, *The violinist was in superb form.* Therefore, the auxiliary verb must be repeated:

Right: The violinist was in superb form and was applauded by the entire audience.

Note: Only one auxiliary verb need be used to serve as predicate for two parallel subjects:

Right: I can speak as well as he (can).

Avoid omitting subordinate conjunctions or relative pronouns before clauses used as subject, object, or predicate complement.

Wrong: Caligula noted Lazarus laughed even at pain.

It is possible to mistake the noun *Lazarus* as the object of *noted* whereas it is the subject of the subordinate clause. The entire clause is object of the verb *noted*.

Right: Caligula noted that Lazarus laughed even at pain.

Wrong: The reason he failed was he refused to study.

He refused to study is an awkward predicate complement after *was*.

Right: The reason he failed was that he refused to study.

Right: He failed because he refused to study.

Note: If there is no likelihood of mistaking the subject of the subordinate clause for the object of the verb in the main clause, the subordinating conjunction may be omitted:

Right: All knew he was a drunkard. (*that* omitted after *knew*)

We assured him we agreed with his argument. (*that* omitted after *him*)

This is the portfolio I bought. (*which* omitted after *portfolio*)

Avoid omitting words that leave comparisons ambiguous.

Wrong: He likes Miami as well as Alice.

Does he like Miami and Alice, or do he and Alice like Miami equally?

Right: He likes Miami as well as Alice does.

Wrong: He dislikes visitors as much as his wife.

Does he dislike visitors and his wife, or do he and his wife dislike visitors?

Right: He dislikes visitors as much as his wife does.

Avoid omitting words necessary to complete the meaning of a sentence.

Wrong: One of the problems in administering the Marshall Plan was that some nations complained that they failed to receive enough.

Failed to receive enough what? Enough problems? Enough plans? Or is it that some nations believed that they had not received sufficient benefits from the Plan? The gaps in thought must be filled in.

Right: One of the problems in administering the Marshall Plan was that some nations complained that they had received insufficient benefits from it.

Wrong: Gertrude Stein studied psychology at Radcliffe with William James and did research on automatic writing. Then she went to Paris and wrote a novel.

Right: After Gertrude Stein had studied at Radcliffe with William James, she went to Paris where she wrote a novel that made good use of her earlier studies in psychology and automatic writing.

Avoid shifting from one construction to another before the first construction has been completed.

Wrong: By shifting into first, it changes the gear ratio of the differential, you put the car into low speed.

The writer has begun with a phrase *By shifting into first;* then, without logically completing his construction, shifted to main clauses. As a result, *it* has no antecedent and *puts* has no subject.

Right: By shifting into first and changing the gear ratio of the differential, you put the car into low speed.

Right: Shifting into first changes the gear ratio of the differential and puts the car into low speed.

Wrong: As far as his lecture goes, often it was difficult to follow him.

The writer has confused two patterns without completing either. Both remain illogical.

Right: His lecture was often difficult to follow.

Right: As far as his lecture goes, I must admit that he was often difficult to follow.

Avoid omitting prepositions which are needed to complete the meaning of a sentence.

Wrong: No one, but no one, can be more desirous or eager for customers than Gombil's.

Desirous or eager for is not an acceptable idiomatic usage, but it is the only preposition provided in this sentence.

Right: No one, but no one, can be more desirous of customers or more eager for them than Gombil's.

Wrong: The shape of his head is different yet reminiscent of a ripe cantaloupe.

The preposition needed to complete *different* has been omitted.

Right: The shape of his head is different from, yet reminiscent of, a ripe cantaloupe.

Exercise No. 59

Fill in any omissions in the following sentences, or recast the sentence if the constructions are mixed.

1. The house was burned, but the children saved.
2. I remember Al Capone better than Vincent Coll.
3. I have six calculators but he two.
4. The teacher which I referred would not write a letter for me.
5. My dog and girl friend are going with me on my vacation.
6. He has bought as many books as any man has or can buy.
7. Our only chance was Johnson might send out an alarm.
8. The patient moaned, perspired, and other symptoms of delirium.
9. The major problem is she is not at all interested.
10. We were more familiar with the Smiths than the Joneses.
11. His recitation was highly effective and admired by all.
12. The fact is that tornadoes and typhoons are becoming more frequent, and possibly because rainmakers are "seeding" too many clouds.
13. So far as his writing is concerned, sometimes pointless in its thinking.
14. His vision at night was almost as good as a cat.
15. Harold collected relics as well as read about New England.

PARAGRAPHS AND PARAGRAPHING

IMPROVING THE PARAGRAPH

THE FUNCTION OF THE PARAGRAPH The paragraph links several related sentences, sentences that focus on the same topic, that amplify it, explain it, defend it.

THE LENGTH OF THE PARAGRAPH Since the paragraph is a unit of a larger whole, a stage in total development, it may be one word long—or a thousand words long. If the point of the paragraph has been adequately made, the paragraph is long enough no matter how few words it contains. Today paragraphs generally average from 100 to 300 words; but the average is not the norm. The nineteenth-century paragraph was much longer, much more uniform. One scholar traces the "decline of the paragraph" to mass production: "When newspapers, and then magazines, began to be published for the millions, writers soon found that their readers were short-winded. They would hold their brains together for three or four sentences, not more." But even the relatively short paragraphs now prevailing observe certain principles—clarity, vigor and variety, the same principles which apply to the sentence.

DEVELOPING THE PARAGRAPH Though the size of the paragraph has decreased, many writers still find it too long. They find it difficult to create sturdy, full-blooded paragraphs. Commonly theirs suffer from an illness which has been diagnosed as "paragraph anemia."

The cure depends on an intelligent regimen: the writer must know something about the care and feeding of paragraphs. Suppose, for example, he believes that soldiers make good presidents. First he must articulate the thought, discover how boldly he wants to state it, with what modifications he wants to hedge it. Does he mean all soldiers, or officers only? All officers, or only those who have had commands requiring administrative ability? Would they make good presidents at any time, or only in time of war or rumors of war?

Assume his winnowed thought to be: **Good generals who have commanded troops in combat make good presidents.** Then he can develop it in several ways:

By Illustration and Example What good combat generals have made good presidents?

By Comparison What are the capacities and qualities which both good combat generals and good presidents require?

By Cause and Effect What causes (education, training, habit of mind, intelligence, and the like) make a good combat general a good president?

There are other ways too, of developing the paragraph about the central statement concerning generals and presidents; but those cited seem the most likely. For a reverse thesis—combat generals do not make good presidents—a different technique of development might be enlisted: **contrast:** what qualities and capacities of good combat generals and good presidents are inimical? And other methods of paragraph development are appropriate to other topics, especially topics which do not require a supporting argument. One might, for example, develop a paragraph on the pleasant topic of love by the method of **definition** or of **elimination**—explaining what love is or what it is not; or conceivably by the method of **analogy**—explaining how it is like something apparently very different (perhaps a bowl of cherries or a lighted cigarette).

OUTLINING Paragraphs link sentences and are themselves linked to one another. To establish a logical union of paragraphs and to ensure proportionate development of each, most experienced writers outline their projected work. If it is a long and complex one, they will probably prefer a formal outline. Thus, an essay on the outline might be formally outlined in the following way:

I. The Outline
  A. Advantages
    1. coherence
    2. proportion
    3. order
  B. Dangers
    1. straitjacketing
      a. tendency to adhere rigidly
      b. tendency to stifle initiative
    2. mechanistic

Of course, the headings and subheadings may require more elaboration: instead of words or phrases, the writer may need sentences or even paragraphs in constructing his outline.

On the other hand, for a short and relatively simple work, he may need to jot down only a few points:

    1. definition
    2. advantages
    3. dangers

At any rate, it enables him to see what his starting point and what his terminal point will be and what route he will take from the one to the other.

CLARITY

THE TOPIC SENTENCE You should construct a clearly defined topic sentence for each paragraph. **A topic sentence is one that states or summarizes the theme of the paragraph**; it forms the base of the well-built paragraph. Though generally the first or second sentence in the paragraph, it may be the last (particularly when the paragraph consists of details which require summary). Bacon's essay "Of Studies" begins with a model topic sentence: "Studies serve for delight, for ornament, and for ability." Every other sentence in the long paragraph which follows radiates from the topic sentence like spokes from a hub.

COHERENCE You should interrelate the sentences of your paragraph. Each sentence ought to follow naturally from the impetus of the preceding one. Each ought to give the reader a "sense of the uninterrupted flow of the mind." Ultimately, the harmony and sequence of parts must proceed from an organic idea, a unit concept; and mechanical devices for attaining coherence are of secondary importance.

Yet they may not be wholly discounted. The following paragraph shows why:

"Fortune, we are told, is a blind and fickle foster-mother, who showers her gifts at random upon her nurslings. But we do her a grave injustice if we believe such an accusation. Trace a man's career from his cradle to his grave and mark how Fortune has treated him. You will find that when he is once dead she can for the most part be vindicated from the charge of any but the most superficial fickleness. Her blindness is the merest fable; she can espy her favorites long before they are born. We are as days and have had her parents for our yesterdays, but through all the fair weather of clear parental sky the eye of Fortune can discern the coming storm and she laughs as she places her favorites it may be in a London alley or those whom she is resolved to ruin in kings' palaces. Seldom does she relent towards those whom she has suckled unkindly and seldom does she completely fail a favored nursling."   (Samuel Butler)

Hardly a perfect paragraph; but certainly an exceedingly crafty one.

Note: (1) The organizing idea, the analogy governing the disposition of sentences in the paragraph: *Fortune* is similar to a foster-mother who favors some of her children, bears animus toward others of them.

(2) The repetition of *Fortune*—personified for the sake of immediacy.

(3) The judicious ordering of pronouns—the personal (*he, she, you, his, her, they*) especially, but also the demonstrative (*those*) and the indefinite (*such, all*)—which link with nouns in other sentences.

(4) The neat introduction of the topic sentence (the second sentence) through contrast and the concise summation in the final sentence.

The author might also have employed one or more of the conjunctive adverbs (*however, therefore, consequently, on the contrary, on the whole,* and the like). However, though they are important words for establishing the relation of ideas, they are likely to clutter prose when used too often; in any case, the *buts* serve the same connective purpose.

In addition to the other merits of the paragraph, it flows smoothly into the next:

"Was George Pontifex one of Fortune's favored nurslings or not? On the whole I should say he was not, for he did not consider himself so; he was too religious to consider Fortune a deity at all; he took whatever she gave and never thanked her, being firmly convinced that whatever he got to his own advantage was of his own getting. And so it was, after Fortune had made him able to get it."

Note here the use of the conjunctive adverb *on the whole* as well as of the conjunctions *for* and *and.* (The latter word, incidentally, often expedites sentence flow.)

FORCE AND VIGOR

POSITION You should place your important idea at the beginning or at the end of the paragraph, or else (rarely) isolate it in a one-sentence paragraph. Advertising men know the impact of the strategically placed sentence. In an airline advertisement, for example, one paragraph begins: "Monday through Friday departures offer you the only direct one-carrier service to busy Tokyo." Another ends: "Call your Travel Agent or 246-0600." And the lead paragraph might consist of one sentence only: "Now Pan American flies 7 superb services a week across the sunny Pacific—and on to exotic Japan, where you will find modern comforts in deluxe hotels . . . at the lowest prices."

FOCUS You should concentrate on one dominant idea in each paragraph. Avoid discussing anything which does not continue or exemplify your central thought: if it is worth saying, there are other paragraphs to say it in. If the central thought is a comprehensive one, of course, the paragraph may properly range in time or space:

"The Romantic Period is customarily dated from the publication of the *Lyrical Ballads* by Coleridge and Wordsworth in 1798 to the accession of Victoria in 1837. Since dates are convenient, these will do: but the tissue of tendencies called romanticism had its genesis more than half a century before the publication of the *Lyrical Ballads* and has endured up to the present day—in fact, one or another 'romanticism' has never been totally absent from English literature, or from any other literature."

VARIETY

LENGTH AND STRUCTURE You should vary the length and structure of your paragraphs. Variety spices discourse; and sometimes it is a subtle spice. Consider the two paragraphs quoted below, the first containing sixty-nine words, the second twenty-seven: they illustrate the principle of variety not merely because they differ in length or in the structure of their sentences (in fact the sentences have an apparent—not real—structural likeness). The pace and the pauses, the shifting rhythms, diverse stresses, changing cadence of the paragraph—these, rather, give them variety:

"Ours is essentially a tragic age, so we refuse to take it tragically. The cataclysm has happened, we are among its ruins, we start to build up new little habitats, to have new little hopes. It is rather hard work: there is now no smooth road into the future: but we go round, or scramble over the obstacles. We've got to live no matter how many skies have fallen.

This was more or less Constance Chatterley's

position. The war had brought the roof down over her head. And she realized that one must live and learn." (D. H. Lawrence)

CONCRETENESS You should illustrate your thought concretely. "All true merit consists in the specific concrete," one critic writes: at any rate much true merit does. Just as it is better to say, "They punish by hanging, burning, and torturing" than to say, "The regulations of their penal code are severe," it is better to describe a man's nose, ears, eyes, and skin than to call him ugly or handsome. One is definite, evokes a picture; the other is vague, evokes a blur.

Note that the author of the following paragraph does not say "everything was in a turmoil" or "everybody was making feverish preparations." She specifies concretely:

I found London agog. Scaffolds were building all along the line of march. Light horse were told off to patrol the streets. Foot guards to the number of 2800 were assigned posts about the court. In Bow Street the magistrates issued orders for keeping the peace by day and by night. In Westminster Hall the Lord High Steward perfected a mannerly horse in the art of backing out of the Royal presence. At St. James's the young King wedded and bedded his new Queen. (Lillian de la Torre)

Exercise No. 60

Rearrange the following sentences so that they constitute well-ordered paragraphs. Underline the topic sentence of each paragraph.

1. (a) His death in 1916 left the matter of his preferences as to nationality still inconclusive. (b) In 1915, unhappy over American neutrality, he severed the last formal tie binding him to the country of his birth, and adopted British citizenship. (c) The migratory childhood of Henry and William James was the result of their father's attempt to keep them from taking premature root. (d) He directed that after cremation his ashes be taken to Mount Auburn Cemetery in Cambridge, Massachusetts. (e) Even though he permanently settled in England in 1875, he became, as he confessed to Hamlin Garland a quarter of a century afterward, "a man who is neither American nor European." (f) He succeeded perhaps too well with Henry, for the latter remained rootless all his days.

2. (a) "My next letter shall refute you," said Lady G. (b) George Selwyn once affirmed in company that no woman ever wrote a letter without a postscript. (c) And after her signature stood: "P.S. Who is right now, you or I?" (d) Selwyn soon after received a letter from her.

3. (a) The free people of the world look to us for support in maintaining their freedoms. (b) The seeds of totalitarian regimes are nurtured by misery and want. (c) They reach their full growth when the hope of a people for a better life has died. (d) They spread and grow in the evil soil of poverty and strife. (e) We must keep that hope alive.

4. (a) I [G. Bernard Shaw] claim that from the first upper cut with which Cashel Byron stops his opponent's lead-off and draws his cork (I here use the accredited terminology of pugilism) to the cross-buttock with which he finally disables him, there is not a single incident which can be enjoyed on any ground other than that on which the admittedly brutalized frequenter of prize fights enjoys his favorite sport. (b) I guarantee to every purchaser of *Cashel Byron's Profession* a first class fight for his money. (c) At the same time he will not be depraved by any attempt to persuade him that his relish for blood and violence is the sympathy of a generous soul for virtue in its eternal struggle with vice. (d) Out of the savagery of your tastes you delight in it.

5. (a) Believe me, mankind has been doing nothing else ever since it began to pay some attention to ideas. (b) It has been said that a benevolent despotism is the best possible form of government. (c) You seek to impose your ideas on others, ostracizing those who reject them. (d) I do not believe that saying, because I believe another one to the effect that hell is paved with benevolence, which most people the proverb being too deep for them, misinterpret as unfulfilled intentions. (e) Excuse my rambling. (f) I meant to say, in short, that though you are benevolent and judicious you are none the less a despot. (g) As if a benevolent despot might not by any error or judgment destroy his kingdom and then say, like Romeo when he got his friend killed, "I thought all for the best!"

PUNCTUATION

TRENDS IN PUNCTUATION

Punctuation more and more rejects formal rules, becomes less and less hospitable to the commands "thou shalt" and "thou shalt not." Rules found in the standard textbooks are necessarily conservative: they generally memorialize past practice; they do not often report prevailing current usage.

Today magazines and newspapers—the media influencing the practice of punctuation basically —employ about half as many points (marks of punctuation) as they did fifty years ago. Since today the average sentence is shorter and less involved than the sentence of 1900, it requires fewer points, fewer guides through its mazes. Moreover, sentence structure, diction, and grammar have also progressed toward simplicity, and that evolution has further decreased the need for an elaborate system of pointing.

"The general principles governing the use of punctuation," declares the Government Printing Office *Style Manual*, "are (1) that if it does not clarify the text it should be omitted and (2) that in the choice and placing of punctuation marks the sole aim should be to bring out more clearly the author's thought." Most modern style manuals essentially agree: punctuation must be bound to communication, not to rules. If violating any rule enhances the sense or even the grace of a sentence, one ought to violate the rule; otherwise he violates both the sentence and the reason for the rules.

Two kinds of pointing practice are in vogue: conservative, close, or formal punctuation, which prefers to use all marks not expressly forbidden; and liberal, open, or informal punctuation, which prefers to omit all marks not definitely required. Actually, most experienced writers strike a medium: they try to punctuate flexibly—less formally than Lord Chesterfield and less informally than others. In the following sections, formal usages will be systematically described, since they are valid for formal contexts. However, the informal options will be regularly cited, since they are the ones most people exercise.

END PUNCTUATION

End marks of punctuation point out that a sentence has come to a full stop. (The end or sentence marks of punctuation are sometimes called full stops.)

THE PERIOD—is used to mark the end of a declarative sentence, or of an imperative sentence that issues its command mildly rather than forcefully.

"If a man holds up a mirror to your nature and shows you that it needs washing—not whitewashing—it is no use breaking the mirror. Go for soap and water." (G. B. Shaw)

THE QUESTION MARK—(or *interrogation point*) is used to mark the end of an interrogative sentence.

"Why does the blind man's wife paint herself?" (Benjamin Franklin)
Who can refute a sneer?

Note: One or more question marks may sometimes be used within the body of a single sentence. Such sentence interrupters (a) may show the close-linked nature of the questions; or (b) emphasize each of the separate questions.

"How then was Abraham's faith reckoned? when in circumcision, or in uncircumcision?" (Romans)

"Canst thou draw out leviathan with a hook? or his tongue with a cord which thou lettest down?" (Job)

Will Stella marry John? or will Jane? or will anyone?

To show uncertainty or—sparingly—to warn of humorous intention. (For either indication, place the question mark in parentheses.)

William Dunbar, who was born in 1465 (?) and who died in 1530 (?), ranks next to Robert Burns in Scotland's literary history.

His humor (?) nauseates.

Do **not** use the question mark:

To mark the end of an indirect question— one implying rather than expressing a question.

Right: Poor Richard wants to know why the blind man's wife paints herself.

To mark the end of a polite or formal question.

Right: May we hear from you shortly.

Note: The interrogative force of "courtesy questions" has diminished through frequent use, and general practice tends to omit the question mark after them. However, you may properly use it if you want to.

Option: May we hear from you shortly?

THE EXCLAMATION POINT—is used to mark the end of an exclamatory sentence, phrase, or clause.

How the mighty have fallen!

What a mess!

For crying out loud!

Note: A single exclamation point suffices.

To point a vigorous interjection, or a nominative of address when strong feeling is present.

Curses! here come Captain Jinks and the horse marines!

"Father! father! it is I! Alice! thy own Elsie!" (James Fenimore Cooper)

"But hark! what notes of discord are these which disturb the general joy, and silence the acclamations of victory? They are the notes of John Hook, hoarsely bawling through the American camp, beef beef! beef!" (Patrick Henry)

Note: The exclamation point, like the question mark, may be used within the body of a sentence. Such a sentence interrupter (a) may show strong feeling bursting through the sentence bounds; or (b) may emphasize each exclamation.

Do **not** use the exclamation point to mark mild exclamations.

Well, we have come through.

Note: The exclamation point ought to be used purposefully, not loosely. Overuse of the exclamation point characterizes "the schoolgirl style." When hesitating between the exclamation point and another mark, generally prefer the other mark.

Exercise No. 61

Insert the appropriate mark of end punctuation.

1. Never I would rather die
2. Die you shall
3. Jason asked why Luster had turned left
4. He exclaimed angrily that he welcomed opposition
5. "Never" did you say
6. Well played
7. May I suggest that you reply with a certified check, not later than June 1, 1981
8. O Scotia my dear, my native soil
9. "Heigh-ho" he exclaimed
10. Bah he's never met his deadline

INTERNAL PUNCTUATION

Internal (or medial) marks of punctuation are used within the body of the sentence to point out that the flow of thought in the sentence is being interrupted. They warn the reader to go slow because something is added to the communication, or subtracted from it; or because the communication is making a detour or taking a shortcut.

THE COMMA—separates sentence elements; it is the most frequent, and the least emphatic, of the internal marks of punctuation.

Use the comma:

To separate two independent clauses joined by a coordinating conjunction (*and, but, or, nor; for, so, yet, either . . . or, neither . . . nor*).

"A rabbit's foot may bring good luck to you, but it brought little to the rabbit."

(Ambrose Bierce)

Note: If the independent clauses joined by the coordinating conjunction are short and closely related, omit the comma.

Right: "They laid Jesse James in his grave and Dante Gabriel Rossetti died immediately."

(Thomas Beer)

Note: If the connection between two independent clauses joined by *so, yet,* or *for* is intimate, prefer the semicolon to the comma; if the connection is loose—if the communications are relatively separate—prefer the comma to the semicolon.

"The objects which I perceive are not the cause of my perceptions; for they are my perceptions."

(W. E. Hocking)

"Discovering truths and winning arguments are different matters, for one depends on logic and the other on rhetoric."

(Arthur Schopenhauer)

To separate words, phrases, or clauses in a series (that is, three or more items).

"On taking thought it seemed to me that I must aim at lucidity, simplicity and euphony."

(Somerset Maugham)

Trollope has a thoroughly conventional mind, no discernible relevance to our times, a style with all the grace and flexibility of the Albert Memorial.

Trollope's commonplace vehicles carry us to an impossible province, where no shadow of ethical doubt glooms, where right and wrong are palpable as a clergyman's gown or a barrister's wig, where every deserving Jack ultimately gets his Jill.

Note: Dominant modern practice is to omit the comma before the *and* or *or* connecting the last two items of a series. Formal writers, however, still retain the comma in such a context. Either retain it or omit it, as you choose, but be consistent in your practice.

Option: A, B, C, and *D* or: *A, B, C* and *D.*

To separate two adjectives each of which modifies the noun individually.

He was a brilliant, forthright speaker.

Here the adjectives are coordinate modifiers of the noun: they may be linked by *and* instead of the comma:

He was a brilliant and forthright speaker.

If the conjunction *and* may be logically set between the adjectives modifying the noun, the comma is in order. However, the adjectives are not always coordinate; often the noun and the adjective next to it form a single unit, one thought:

He is a brilliant military analyst.

Here, the conjunction *and* may not be logically set between the adjectives. Consequently, no comma is required. Compare the following phrases.

An old, broken-down tramp.

A broken-down old tramp.

A large, spacious house.

A large brick house.

A cold, dark night.

A cold spring night.

To set off a long adverbial clause or phrase coming before the main clause.

"When a book about the literature of the eighteen-nineties was given by Mr. Holbrook Jackson to the world, I looked eagerly in the index for Soames, Enoch." (Max Beerbohm)

"By resolute malice and unblinking devotion to the letter rather than to the spirit of the law, he managed to bring in another conviction."

(H. H. Grote)

Note: The tendency in modern punctuation, however, is to omit the comma after such clauses and phrases unless misunderstanding will result. The commas are optional, therefore, even in the sentences cited above.

To set off an introductory verbal phrase (a participial, gerund, or infinitive phrase).

Having dexterously evaded the large questions, the genteel writers trifled engagingly with a multiplicity of small ones.

To see infinity in a grain of sand, one needs vision rather than eyesight.

After riddling an opponent, you may discover that his argument is still whole.

Note: Many modern writers omit the comma after the verbal phrase, except where misreading may ensue.

Option: To credit many columnists it is necessary to discredit the laws of evidence.

To set off an absolute phrase in any part of the sentence—beginning, middle, or end.

Perhaps we waste our energies, *sunshine being more general than showers,* by preparing so diligently for rainy days.

Note: If the phrase in italics came at the beginning of the sentence it would be followed by a comma; if at the end it would be preceded by a comma.

To prevent misreading—even temporary misreading.

When I want to dance, well women grow sick.

In brief, dresses will be shorter.

Should you wish to swim, the ocean lies at your doorstep.

Although there were jobs for a hundred, thousands applied.

The soldier dropped, a bullet in his leg.

To separate the year from any of its divisions:

December 25, 1979.

Christmas, 1979.

December, 1979.

Note: The comma between month and year is often omitted.

Option: December 1979.

To separate the parts of geographical names, addresses, zones, and the like.

The Bronx, New York.

1820 Loring Place, The Bronx, New York.

New York, NY 10453.

To set off nouns in direct address.

Friends, Romans, countrymen, lend me your ears.

To indicate the omission of one or more words.

He eats no fat; his wife, no lean.

Note: Unless some misreading might ensue, current usage generally omits the comma in such a context.

Option: He eats no fat; his wife no lean. (Here, too, the comma may replace the semicolon.)

To set off a short or informal quotation, for the purpose of distinguishing between the speaker and what he says.

"Stupid people," said Michael Arlen, "have an uncanny way of hitting the right nail on the head with the wrong hammer."

To set off two or more contrasting statements.

"Millions for defence, but not one cent for tribute." (Charles Pinkney)

"Millions for defence, not a damned penny for tribute." (Charles Pinkney)

To set off non-restrictive phrases and clauses —elements which break the continuity of the sentence.

Buicks, *which have four wheels,* are more expensive than Fords, *which likewise have four wheels.*

Note: A comma precedes each of the italicized clauses because they merely offer incidental information concerning the nouns they modify. Compare:

Buicks *that have three wheels* are not so expensive as Fords *that have four wheels.*

Here the italicized clauses offer essential information concerning the nouns they modify. They are called *restrictive* clauses because they restrict or limit *Buicks* and *Fords:* three-wheeled Buicks are cheaper than four-wheeled Fords. (Presumably—though the sentence does not explicitly say so—four-wheeled Buicks are more expensive than four-wheeled Fords.)

Phrases, too, may be restrictive:

Buicks *with three wheels* are cheaper than Fords *with four wheels.*

If a clause or phrase restricts (or limits or defines), it is not set off by commas. **If it does not restrict,** if it merely offers information not essential to the main communication, **it is set off** by commas. To test for restrictiveness, simply blot out the clause: if the essential communication remains clear, the clause is non-restrictive; if, however, blotting out the clause blots out the intended meaning as well, the clause is restrictive.

Compare the following:

Restrictive: The man *who smiles* is the man worth while. (The clause is a necessary part of the communication: the intent of the sentence is not that any man is worth while, but specifically that the man who smiles is.)

Non-restrictive: My smiling uncle, *whom everybody trusts,* cheerfully cuts salaries. (The italicized clause is non-restrictive: the essential communication is that my smiling uncle cuts salaries; that everybody trusts him is incidental information. In the former sentence the clause identifies; in this, presumably, no identification is necessary.)

Restrictive: Women *who eat garlic* need to be beautiful.

Non-restrictive: Women, who generally possess educated taste-buds, rarely eat too much garlic.

Restrictive: The girl on the calendar was Hyacinthine Horlick.

Non-restrictive: The calendar girl, in spite of her manager's discreet silence, was Hyacinthine Horlick.

Restrictive: He will speak *if you do not.*

Non-restrictive: He will speak, *whether you do or not.* (The dependent clause in the first sentence may not be omitted without changing the communication basically; the clause is restrictive, therefore, and commas are superfluous. The dependent clause in the second sentence may be omitted, however, without radically altering the communication; the clause is non-restrictive, therefore, and commas are in order.)

Restrictive: He proved *that any part of the doughnut* is greater than the hole.

Non-restrictive: The doughnut, which is a Dutch confection, is a weak sister of the bagel.

Note: Noun clauses are always restrictive. Adjective and adverbial clauses may be either restrictive or non-restrictive, depending on whether they are essential or unessential to the sense of the communication.

To set off parenthetical expressions, mild interjections, words or phrases in apposition, sentence modifiers.

Parenthetical Expression: The world, *it seemed to him once,* was his oyster, but later he discovered, *as many before him had,* that the oyster was inedible and contained no pearls.

Mild Interjection: *Why,* this shirt has three sleeves!

Appositive: "Ice-Box" Murphy, *box-car tripper, amateur yegg,* and *one-time running mate of "A No. 1," the world-famed hobo,* was taken on by Soapy Smith as a booster.

Note: The last phrase in italics is in apposition with "A No. 1," the others with "Ice-Box" Murphy.

Sentence Modifier: His position, nevertheless, seems shaky.

Note: The sentence elements listed above are all essentially non-restrictive: they are not fundamentally necessary for the central communication.

Do not use the comma:

To separate the subject or complement from the verb (unless a non-restrictive element comes between).

"*Life is* the *art* of drawing sufficient conclusions from insufficient premises."

(Samuel Butler)

"Our *opinions follow* our *inclinations.*"

(Goethe)

To precede the first or to follow the last item of a series.

Who believes that beans, butter, bread build biceps?

Who believes that beans, butter, and bread build biceps?

Note: The comma is optional after *butter* in the second sentence cited.

To set off an adverb or adjective from the adjacent word it modifies.

Poverty is like rain: it drops down *ceaselessly,* disintegrating the finer tissues of man, his recent, *delicate* adjustments, and leaves nothing but the bleak and *gaunt* framework.

To separate words, phrases, or dependent clauses joined by a coordinating conjunction (unless some purpose like contrast is to be served).

He proved ready and willing [, but not able].

He proved to be ready and to be willing.

He proved that he was ready and that he was able.

To set off restrictive elements.

A prude is *one who blushes modestly at the indelicacy of her thoughts.* (Ambrose Bierce)

To break up any logically close or structurally smooth group of words.

Indeed I did.

I did indeed.

The theorem is thus proved.

Note: Whether to insert commas or not to insert them in such contexts depends on the experience and tact of the writer. If the construction without commas meets his meaning better or achieves a rhythm more consonant with his thought, he ought to employ it regardless of rules.

Exercise No. 62

Insert commas where necessary in the following passages.

1. Just as the procedure of a collection department must be clear-cut and definite the steps being taken with the sureness of a skilled chess player so the various paragraphs of a collection letter must show clear organization giving evidence of a mind that from the beginning has had a specific end in view.

2. In some jobs it is necessary to understand interpret and apply rules and principles. In others it is necessary also to discover principles from available data or information. These types of reasoning ability can be tested by different kinds of tests—for example questions on the relationship of words understanding of paragraphs or solving of numerical problems.

3. A plane figure consists of a square ten inches on a side and an isosceles triangle whose base is the left edge of a square and whose altitude dropped from the vertex opposite the ten-inch base of the triangle common to the square is six inches.

4. Few people take the trouble of trying to find out what democracy really is. Yet this would be of great help for it is our lawless and uncertain thoughts it is the indefiniteness of our impressions that fill darkness whether mental or physical with spectres and hobgoblins. Democracy is nothing more than an experiment in government more likely to succeed in a new soil but likely to be tried in all soils which must stand or fall on its own merits as others have done before it. For there is no trick of perpetual motion in politics any more than in mechanics. President Lincoln defined democracy to be "the government of the people by the people for the people."

5. I went to the woods because I wished to live deliberately to front only the essential facts of life and to see if I could not learn what it had to teach and not when I came to die discover that I had not lived.

6. In all my lectures I have taught one doctrine namely the infinitude of the private man. This the people accept readily enough and even with loud acclamation as long as I call the lecture Art or Politics or Literature or the Household; but the moment I call it Religion they are shocked though it be only the application of the same truth which they receive everywhere else to a new class of facts.

7. When Melville died on September 28, 1891 he left in manuscript a novelette *Billy Budd* which was not published until 1924 though written about 1888–1891.

8. Man was not made for any useful purpose for the reason that he hasn't served any; he was most likely not even made intentionally and his working himself up out of the oyster bed to his present position was probably a matter of surprise and regret to the Creator.

9. Fitzgerald said "The very rich are different from you and me." "Yes" Hemingway replied "they have more money."

10. To see how this was so let us ask ourselves why the spheres were ever supposed to exist. They were not seen or directly observed in any way; why then were they believed to be there.

11. We keep one eye open however safe we feel. Indeed some of us keep both eyes open others of us moreover wish for a third eye.

12. For him to think meant to act.

13. To die bravely fighting at first seemed good, later retreat seemed better.

14. Dear Jojo

    I received your last letter. At least I hope it was your last letter.

    Sincerely
    Butch Butcher

15. The title role of *Elmer Gantry* (which Rebecca West the English critic has termed "a sequence of sermons and seductions") is played by a profligate clergyman a ponderous monster

bleater of platitudes ankle-snatcher and arch hypocrite whom we meet first as an "eloquently drunk" student at Terwilliger College in Cato Missouri.

16. He had forgotten his wallet which reposed in his green trousers; the money which he had in the purple pair that he was wearing didn't equal the amount of the bill.

THE SEMICOLON—functions in the area between comma and period—rather closer to the period. It separates more definitely than the comma, but not so decisively as the period. A formal mark of punctuation, it fills a diminished need in most contemporary writing, especially informal writing.

Use the semicolon:

To separate two or more independent clauses not linked by a coordinating conjunction.

"Man can have only a certain number of teeth, hair, and ideas; there comes a time when he necessarily loses his teeth, hair, ideas."

(Voltaire)

Note: Even though a coordinating conjunction links the independent clauses, a semicolon may be used to separate them more emphatically.

The 7:19 is my regular train; but I seldom make it.

"Shaw said that Socialism had made him a man; and so he endeavored to make men socialists."   (Maurice Elson)

To separate clauses or phrases already containing commas.

He saw Nicholas Scratch, president of the Diabolist Society; Harry Clootie, professor of moral philosophy; Lucifer Poker, public censor; and Mephisto Mammon, sales manager of the Lost Souls Merchandising Company.

"As Caesar loved me, I weep for him; as he was fortunate, I rejoice at it; as he was valiant, I honor him; but as he was ambitious, I slew him."

(Shakespeare)

To set off a conjunctive adverb joining two independent clauses. (The conjunctive adverbs most commonly employed are *therefore, nevertheless, hence, however, moreover, consequently, thus, besides, furthermore, otherwise, accordingly*.)

There are certain and invariable deductions; consequently, the science of logic is possible.

Note: When the conjunctive adverb stands first in its clause, it is customarily followed by a comma; however, modern usage tends increasingly to omit it.

Option: All power corrupts; moreover absolute power corrupts absolutely.

When the conjunctive adverb is not the first word in the clause it modifies, it is preceded by a comma.

No great writer formed better sentences than Emerson; no great writer, *likewise,* constructed worse paragraphs. Thoreau was Emerson's friend; he did not especially like Emerson, however.

Note: Mistaking the conjunctive adverb for the subordinating or coordinating conjunction leads to many errors in punctuation.

To set off such introductory specifying words as *for example, e.g.* (the abbreviation of Latin *exemplum gratia,* "for the sake of example"), *that is, i.e.* (*id est,* "that is"), *in other words, namely, viz.* (*videlicet,* "namely"), *to wit, sc.* or *scil.* (*scilicet,* "to wit"). **These words introduce explanations and enumerations.**

"He was a behaviorist; that is, one who extracts habits from a rat."

(William York Tindall)

" 'A Cooking Egg' (by T. S. Eliot) demands first of all that we recognize the meaning of its title; namely, the kind of egg used when the strictly fresh is not required."

(George Williamson)

Note: The semicolon after such introductory words ought to be employed sparingly; in fact, the words themselves ought to be employed sparingly. However, the semicolon legitimately precedes them when an independent clause follows them, or when the sentence is long or formal. Otherwise, prefer the comma.

Do not use the semicolon:

To set off dependent sentence elements.

Right: "I think that common sense, in a rough,

dogged way, is technically sounder than the special schools of philosophy, each of which squints and overlooks half the facts and half the difficulties in its eagerness to find in some detail the key to the whole." (W. James)

Note: The semicolon seems especially appealing before subordinate clauses and participial phrases in long sentences. Resist its appeal. The semicolon sets off elements of equal rank.

To follow the salutation or the complimentary close of a letter.

Wrong: Dear Sir;

Right: Dear Sir:

Wrong: Sincerely yours;

Right: Sincerely yours,

Exercise No. 63

In the following sentences, replace the inappropriate commas with semicolons. (For the purpose of this exercise, prefer the semicolon to an alternate mark of punctuation.)

1. Courtship in animals is the outcome of four major steps in evolution: first, the development of sexuality, secondly, the separation of sexes, thirdly, internal fertilization, or at least the approximation of males and females, and finally, the development of efficient sense-organs and brains. (Julian Huxley)
2. They [anthropologists] wanted to know "how modern man got this way": why some people are ruled by a king, some by old men, others by warriors, and none by women anymore, why some people pass on property in the male line, others in the female, still others equally to heirs of both sexes, why some people fall sick and die when they think they are bewitched, and others laugh at the idea.
3. He is a man, hence, he is fallible. She is a woman, therefore she will fool him.
4. It is hard to form just ideas, wayward notions, however, come without being called.
5. A small group of people arrive: I recognize Jean Negulesco, the director, Wolfgang Reinhardt, the supervising producer, and George Amy, the cutter.

THE COLON—signals that a statement or an explanation or an enumeration follows: it is "a mark of anticipation" primarily. It points a break in the communication greater than that pointed by the full stop.

Use the colon:

To introduce a series.

There are three kinds of women: the beautiful, the intellectual, and the majority.

A salad needs three things: a miser for the vinegar, a spendthrift for the oil, and a madman for the tossing.

To stress a word, phrase or clause that follows.

Intelligently enough, he attributed his error to a single cause: stupidity.

Note: A colon may be followed by a capital letter, particularly when it introduces an independent clause:

"Some people praise art because it can improve the individual: That is like admiring roses because an eye wash can be distilled from them." (Remy deGourmont)

To introduce a long or formal quotation.

Thoreau wrote: "The mass of men lead lives of quiet desperation. What is called resignation is confirmed desperation."

To separate clauses when the second explains or amplifies or contrasts with the first.

"She needed him just as any idol needs worshippers in order to become a god: in the empty chapel it is only a piece of carved wood, but let even one devotee enter, prostrate himself and pray, and the piece of wood is transformed into a god equal to Allah or Brahma."

(Guy deMaupassant)

"When angry, count four: when very angry, swear." (Mark Twain)

To follow the salutation of a letter.

Dear Sir:

To separate the parts of titles, biblical and other citations, clock times, bibliographical references.

Accent: A Quarterly of New Literature

The Double Agent: Essays in Craft and Elucidation by R. P. Blackmur

Luke 4:3

5:55 P.M.

Bertholle, Louisette: *French Cuisine for All,*

Garden City, N.Y.: Doubleday & Company, Inc., 1980.

Note: There are a variety of options for bibliographical entries, but most style manuals prefer the colon between the place of publication and the name of the publisher.

Do not use the colon:

To supplement a word or words that adequately introduce a list or an explanation.

Wrong: He honored: the wise, the witty, and the wealthy.

Right: He honored the wise, the witty, and the wealthy.

Exercise No. 64

In the following sentences, replace the *inappropriate* semicolons and commas with colons. (For the purpose of this exercise, prefer the colon to an alternative mark of punctuation.)

1. Dear Sir;
   I have read your letter, a courtesy you apparently did not vouchsafe mine.
                                    Yours truly,
                                    Jojo Jones
2. There are two methods of curing the mischiefs of faction; the one, by removing its causes; the other, by controlling its effects.
3. Dr. Jucovy, a noted psychiatrist, writes: "The statement, 'People are stout because they eat more and consume more calories' no longer suffices. Now we ask, '*Why* do some individuals eat more?' "
4. All will be well; God is silent; he is not indifferent.
5. In *The Short Bible; An American Translation,* Professor Smith translated Psalms 19:1 thus; "The heavens are telling the glory of God, And the sky shows forth the work of his hands."

THE DASH—in typing, made by striking the hyphen key twice—has **the force of a strong comma.** But it ought not to be used as a loose substitute for the comma, since it marks sharper breaks in the continuity and achieves more definite effects of suspense and abruptness than the comma.

Use the dash:

To mark a sharp or sudden turn in the thought or structure of a sentence, or an afterthought tacked to the main thought.

"Women who write always have one eye on the page and the other on some man—except the Countess Haan-Haan, who has only one eye."   (Heine)

In printing, the dash here described—the one customarily employed—is called the *em* dash, to distinguish it from the *hyphen* or *en* dash and the *double dash* or 2-em dash.

"He seemed to have a notion that there was some sort of esoteric cookery book, full of literary recipes, which you had only to follow attentively to become a Dickens, a Henry James, a Flaubert—'according to taste,' as the authors of recipes say."   (Aldous Huxley)

To separate a parenthetical expression from the main communication.

"Bacon believed—rightly, as we now know—that science could provide a more powerful magician's wand than any that had been dreamed of by necromancers of former ages."

                              (Bertrand Russell)

Note: Commas or parentheses may also set off a parenthetical expression. How choose among the three? If the parenthetical expression is relatively distant from the center of the communication, prefer the parentheses; if relatively near, the comma; if intermediate, the dash. But the choice depends on individual tact, finally.

To set off a word or words in apposition or amplification, especially when several words intervene.

"I feel that this award (the Nobel Prize for Literature) was not made to me as a man but to my work—a life's work in the agony and sweat of the human spirit, not for glory and least of all for profit, but to create out of the materials of the human spirit something which did not exist before."   (William Faulkner)

To set off the word or words gathering or summarizing a preceding series.

"Amos on the Tekoan hills, the Great Isaiah by the waters of Shiloah and the Second Isaiah by those of Babylon, Job in the dust with his sententious friends, "physicians of no value" to him, St. John on the island of Patmos, Daniel by the river Ulai—these were men of dreams and of visions who struggled with the questions that beset us all." (Mary Ellen Chase)

To set off a word or words intended to effect suspense, climax, or anticlimax.

"He who laughs—lasts." (*Reader's Digest*)

Freshman themes generally have an introduction, a body, a climax—and an anticlimax.

To mark an unfinished sentence.

"Heroes do not write epics. Heroes—"

"What do they do?"

"They die." (Frederick Karinthy)

Note: To mark an unfinished sentence, use the double or 2-em dash (four strokes of the hyphen key in typing).

Do not use the dash:

To serve, casually, the functions of a comma or other mark of punctuation.

Breathless style: There was a certain magnificence in the high-up day—a certain eagle-like royalty—so different from the equally pure—equally pristine and lovely—morning of Australia—which is so soft—so utterly pure in its softness—and betrayed by green parrots flying.

D. H. Lawrence: "There was a certain magnificence in the high-up day, a certain eagle-like royalty, so different from the equally pure, equally pristine and lovely morning of Australia, which is so soft, so utterly pure in its softness, and betrayed by green parrots flying."

Note: The luxuriant dashes in the first specimen distract the reader: he can focus only on discrete impressions, not on the essential integrity of the sentence. The dashed sentence is not "wrong"; it is irritating and ineffective.

Exercise No. 65

In the following sentences, replace the inappropriate commas with dashes. (For the purpose of this exercise, prefer the dash to an alternative mark of punctuation.)

1. Persuasiveness of argument, apt examples from history and experience, inner logic, and perhaps our simple need to have a part of our experience given satisfactory meaning, these have played a far greater role in the history of theories in the social sciences than strict canons of evidence and proof.

2. Why haven't I a butler named Fish, who makes a cocktail of three parts gin to one part lime juice, honey, vermouth, and apricot brandy in equal portions, a cocktail so delicious that people like Mrs. Harrison Williams and Mrs. Goodhue Livingston seek him out to get the formula?

3. More than thirty-five million women, about 40 per cent of the nation's labor force, are in paid employment.

4. My expectations were not high, no deathless prose, merely a sturdy no-nonsense report of explorers into the wilderness of statistics and half-known fact.

5. Henry's genius, if that's the word, was sometimes indistinguishable from another man's pig-headedness.

6. To be a scientist, it is not just a different job, so that a man should choose between being a scientist and being an explorer or a bond-salesman or a physician or a king or a farmer.

7. In the country there are a few chances of sudden rejuvenation, a shift in the weather, perhaps, or something arriving in the mail.

8. Why they are called comics, when people who read them, both young and old, almost always look like undertakers, eludes me.

9. Restraint, Repression, Respectability, those are the three R's that made him [Sinclair Lewis] see Red.

10. And we, well, we shut our eyes, then say, "We can't see a thing wrong."

THE PARENTHESES—(or *curves*) enclose supplementary or explanatory matter of smaller relevance to the communication than that set off by the comma or dash. The parenthetical matter is structurally separate from the sentence: the sentence ought to read as well without it, and any mark of punctuation that would be needed without parentheses is needed with them too.

Use the parentheses:

To enclose supplementary or explanatory material relatively distant from the center of communication.

"Most birds are monogamous, however, at least for the season (or sometimes only for a single brood—like the American wren, which as bird-banding experiments have shown, usually changes partners between the first and second broods of a single year)."

(Julian Huxley)

"Perhaps the first adumbration of courtship is seen in the nuptial dances of certain marine bristle-worms (*Polychaetes*), in which at certain seasons of the year and phases of the moon the creatures swim up out of their crannies in the rocks and gather in groups, excited males wriggling round the females."

(Julian Huxley)

Note: The period at the end of the first sentence quoted and the comma after *Polychaetes* in the second would be proper even if the parenthetical matter were omitted. The sentence is punctuated always as if it contained no parentheses; the words in parentheses are punctuated independently of the rest of the sentence. A whole sentence, or several sentences, may be in parentheses:

The road seemed endless. (It was ten miles long, actually. But we were in no mood for statistics.)

Do not use the parentheses to substitute loosely for commas or to enclose words necessary to the sense of the communication.

Ineffective: The writing of a dictionary (therefore) is not a task of setting up authoritative statements about the "true meanings" of words, but a task of recording (to the best of one's abilities) what various words have meant to authors in the distant or immediate past.

Improved: "The writing of a dictionary, therefore, is not a task of setting up authoritative statements about the "true meanings" of words, but a task of recording, to the best of one's abilities, what various words have meant to authors in the distant or immediate past."

(S. I. Hayakawa)

Note: If commas seem to do as well as the parentheses in realizing your meaning, prefer the commas. Not only can an excessively parenthetical style become irritating, but also it can obscure important features of your argument. Handle parentheses with care.

Exercise No. 66

In the following sentences, replace the inappropriate dashes and commas with parentheses. (For the purpose of the exercise, prefer the parentheses to alternative marks of punctuation.)

1. In the days that followed, happy days of renewed vigor and reawakened interest, I studied the magazines and lived, in their pages, the gracious life of the characters in the ever-moving drama of society and fashion.
2. As the Hebrews saw their history—Genesis to Judges—it fell into several discrete sections, writes H. H. Watts; and the author—authors?—of only the first sections, Genesis 1–11, made no distinction between Hebrew and non-Hebrew fate.
3. Winchell, according to H. L. Mencken, invented *pash,* for passion, *lohengrined,* for married, and *Reno-vated,* for divorced.
4. If the rise over the continent of North America should amount to a hundred feet, and there is more than enough water now frozen in land ice to provide such a rise, most of the Atlantic seaboard, with its cities and towns, would be submerged.
5. Mr. W. M. Thackeray has published—under the Cockney name of "Michael Angelo Titmarsh"—various graphs and entertaining works: *The Paris Sketch-Book,* London, 1840, *Comic Tales and Sketches,* London, 1841, and *The Irish Sketch-Book,* London, 1842.

THE BRACKETS—enclose matter entirely independent of the sentence—usually comments, queries, corrections, criticisms, or directions inserted by someone other than the original writer.

Use the brackets:

To correct or call attention to an error in the text.

A thing has it's [sic] law.

Note: The *sic* ("thus") in brackets indicates that the word to which it refers was misspelled by the original writer, not by the present writer, who is merely citing what he sees.

"Shakespeare was born in 1563 [1564 is the correct date] and died in 1616."

To mark an editorial comment or addition or explanation.

"The trouble with Harry [Henry James] seems to be that he has learned to swim without ever going near the water." (John LaFarge)

To enclose parentheses within parentheses.

"No less a personage than Winston Churchill (once, with T. S. Eliot, Santayana and Charles deGaulle, a member of the [International] Mark Twain Society) has testified that Tom Sawyer and Huck Finn 'represent America' to him."   (Philip Young)

Note: Punctuation following the brackets disregards their existence: any mark correct without them is correct with them; any mark incorrect without them is incorrect with them.

Exercise No. 67

In the following exercise, strike out those brackets that you think are incorrectly placed.

1. "He died on February 30 [28], 1880."
2. "I will [applause from the Conservative benches] not [applause from the Liberal benches] say [silence]."
3. "American poets [generally speaking] have abandoned Whitman's way of writing."
4. "They are divid'd [sic] and deject'd [sic]."
5. Though his first book (anonymously published [London, 1830]) fell flat, he refused to be defeated [and the reception of his second book justified his optimism].

THE QUOTATION MARKS—always in pairs, break sharply the continuity of the writer's thought. They are a shorthand way of saying *quote—unquote*.

Use the quotation marks:

To enclose a direct quotation—the actual words used by a speaker or writer.

Sidney Smith remarked, "It is impossible to feel affection beyond 78° or below 20° Fahrenheit."

Note: (a) The period and the comma go *inside* the closing quotation mark:

"It is impossible," Sidney Smith remarked, "to feel affection beyond 78° or below 20° Fahrenheit."

All other marks of punctuation go *outside* the quotation marks, save when they belong to the quotation. Compare the following sentences:

He asked, "Who has seen eternity?"

Did he say, "I saw eternity the other night"?

End marks of punctuation are not duplicated: the question mark in each of the sentences cited serves alone. Logically a period, too, should be used to mark the end of the declarative part of each sentence; but usage and logic are at odds here, and, as always in punctuation, usage is the guide.

(b) The semicolon presents a special difficulty in punctuating quotations. Compare:

"He can talk for five minutes on anything," she commented, "but indefinitely on nothing."

"He can talk for five minutes on anything," she commented; "however, he can talk indefinitely on nothing."

In the first of the sentences instanced, the full quotation would read: "He can talk for five minutes on anything, but indefinitely on nothing." Since the quotation demands no semicolon, none belongs after the interrupting words *she commented*.

In the second of the sentences, though, the full quotation would read: "He can talk for five minutes on anything; however, he can talk indefinitely on nothing." Here the quotation is punctuated internally by a semicolon, and therefore it must be reproduced after the interrupting words *she commented*. Logically, perhaps the semicolon belongs after *anything*; but again logic yields to usage.

(c) A quotation may be restrictive and consequently require no punctuation:

Bryan declared that he was "more interested in the Rock of Ages than in the age of rocks."

To enclose provincialisms, slang expressions, and technical terms that seem out of harmony with the general tone of the writing.

He went "plumb loco."

The "objective correlative" has a diminished application to the art of the dance.

It dwells mainly, we at once see, in the depths of Milly Theale's "case."   (Henry James)

Note: The last citation may represent another function of the quotation marks, one of which many authors are excessively fond (Henry James most notably): to enclose tongue-in-cheek expressions—those intended ironically.

To enclose titles of poems, stories, chapters, essays, or articles appearing in a larger work.

"The Whiteness of the Whale" is a key chapter in Herman Melville's *Moby Dick*.

Note: The usage described here—quotation marks for the part, italics for the whole—is that of most publishing companies. However, some still retain quotation marks for the entire work as well as for its divisions.

To enclose the beginning and the end of a quotation extending over several paragraphs.

Note: Each paragraph in an extensive quotation begins with a quotation mark, but the closing quotation mark is placed at the end of the last paragraph only. The eccentric paragraphs which follow are from D. H. Lawrence's *Studies in Classic American Literature:*

"What do you think of the ship Pequod, the ship of the soul of an American?

"Many races, many people, many nations, under the Stars and Stripes. Beaten with many stripes.

"Seeing stars sometimes.

"And in a mad ship, under a mad captain, in a mad, fanatic's hunt.

"For what?

"For Moby Dick, the great white whale."

A preferable method of quoting extended material is single spacing it (an indication to the printer that it is to be set in smaller type).

To enclose a quotation within a quotation. Here, however, single quotation marks are employed:

"To the demonstration of a curate who wished to hold two livings that the towns were only twenty miles apart 'as the crow flies,' [Bishop] Thirlwall briefly replied, 'Mr. Brown, are you a crow?'"   (J. C. Thirlwall, Jr.)

For quotations further complicated—a quotation within a quotation within a quotation and so on—simply alternate single and double quotation marks as often as necessary:

"In his summation, Lord Thurlow said, 'I quote the legal maxim of Sir Edward Coke: "Corporations cannot commit treason, nor be outlawed nor excommunicated, for they have no souls." '"   (James Welch)

Do **not** use the quotation marks:

To head an essay, story, or other composition of your own authorship—unless it is a quotation.

To enclose popularly accepted nicknames or slang expressions, technical terms that have been assimilated into the main body of the language, folk sayings or proverbs, and the like.

Right: Rocky Marciano, Ike Eisenhower
Right: bolo punch, pop-up, gripe, shenanigans
Right: shaman, syncope, Gothic bold, colloid
Right: right as rain, a stitch in time, cart before the horse

Note: Many popular saws have become worn out with overuse. They are no less trite because enclosed in quotation marks.

Exercise No. 68

In the following passages, place quotation marks around those words requiring them.

1. Bentley, the publisher of *Bentley's Miscellany,* said to Jerrold, I had some doubts about the name I should give the magazine; I thought at one time of calling it *Wits' Miscellany.* Well, was the rejoinder, you needn't have gone to the opposite extreme.
2. One of the old philosophers, Lord Bacon tells us, used to say that life and death were just the same to him. Why, then, said an objector, do you not kill yourself? Because it is just the same.
3. The American Scholar, Emerson's address to the Phi Beta Kappa Society at Cambridge in 1837, was termed our intellectual Declaration of Independence by Oliver Wendell Holmes.
4. The so-called race between population and food supply has again come forward as an absorbing topic of conversation, M. K. Bennett notes.
5. William Keddie, in his *Anecdotes Literary and Scientific,* tells this anecdote: A friend of the poet Campbell once remarked: It is well known that Campbell's own favorite poem was his Gertrude. I once heard him say, I never like to see my name before the Pleasures of Hope; why, I cannot tell you, unless it was that, when young, I was always greeted among my friends as Mr. Campbell, author of the Pleasures of Hope. Good morning to you, Mr. Campbell, author of the Pleasures of Hope.

THE ELLIPSIS—three spaced periods is a mark of omission. It is used to let the reader know that a word or group of words has been omitted as irrelevant.

Use the ellipsis:

To mark the omission of one or more quoted words not required for the immediate purpose.

Ellipsis Allan Devoe writes, "The wild creatures of the earth have reacted in a variety of fashions to the coming of that unique two-legged animal . . . who made his startling appearance on their earth a few millenniums ago."

Full Quotation "The wild creatures of the earth have reacted in a variety of fashions to the coming of that unique two-legged animal, gifted with a convoluted cortex and a devious will, who made his startling appearance on their earth a few millenniums ago."

Note: If the omitted word or group of words comes at the end of a declarative sentence, the period marking the end of the sentence *and* the ellipsis are employed.

C. S. Lewis writes: "Now what interests me about all these remarks [the remarks made by a man quarrelling with another] is that the man who makes them isn't just saying that the other man's behaviour doesn't happen to please him. . . . Quarrelling means trying to show that the other man's in the wrong."

To mark a thought expressed hesitantly, or one interrupted or left unfinished. (Such an ellipsis is employed in fiction more frequently than elsewhere.)

He paused. "If . . . if I should confess, what then?" he asked.

"I thought that no girl so young and beautiful could put, you know . . . put the passion and terror into it, do you understand? . . . Sol and I were out front for that scene in the last act."

(John Dos Passos)

Do not use the ellipsis to substitute loosely for more specific marks. And use only three periods—neither fewer nor more—to mark a word or words omitted.

WORD PUNCTUATION

Several marks of punctuation are used to set apart or distinguish a word or words—particular units of speech. Word punctuation may show that two or more words are to be taken as a unit (a compound word); that a word or group of words is to be given special emphasis; that a word or group of words is to be construed possessively; that a word or group of words is to be read in a particular way (as a title, as an abbreviation, as one of several similar units).

THE HYPHEN—is essentially a **combining** mark. It fuses parts into a new whole, expresses a unit idea. When a combination becomes familiar, the tendency is to omit the hyphen and to write the word as a solid unit. But the hyphen is itself a halfway mark. For when words first become associated, they are generally (not always) written separately. For example, the name of the game was early written *basket ball*, later *basket-ball*, and now (invariably) *basketball*. Since the hyphen is a transitional mark, its use varies. Dictionaries regularly warn that authorities disagree as to which compounds ought to be written solid, which separate, and which hyphenated. The best principle seems to be: When in doubt consult the current edition of a good dictionary.

Use the hyphen:

To join two or more words used as a single adjective and preceding their noun.

most-favored-nation clause
out-of-date notions
iron-clad principles
never-to-be-forgotten experience
salt-water fishing

To join two or more words used as a single part of speech.

ne'er-do-well
hero-worship
forget-me-nots
go-between
goof-off

Note: Words like those listed are particularly troublesome, because of their instability. Many once hyphenated are now written solid (*today, tomorrow, tonight*). Others may now be written either solid or hyphenated or separately (*war monger, war-monger,* or *warmonger; folk-lore, folklore; tax-payer* or *taxpayer; man-power* or *manpower*). When in doubt (and without dictionary), write solid.

To join two or more words when the last is a participle.

shallow-thinking columnist
worm-eaten apple
ready-made clothing
hard-working woman
V-shaped head

Note: Some such compounds, long in the language, are written solid (*sunburnt, easygoing, widespread*).

To join an adjective or noun to a noun ending in *d* or *ed*.

blue-eyed Minerva
bull-necked wrestler
bird-brained politician

To separate compound numbers, fractions used as adjectives, and compound fractions.

twenty-one years
twenty-first year
two-thirds majority (*but* two thirds of the men)
twenty-one twenty-fifths of those voting

To avoid ambiguity or confusion.

A woman-hating man needs a gun.
(*Compare:* A woman hating man needs a gun.)
re-form, re-creation, re-cover
(*Compare:* reform, recreation, recover)

To prevent three identical consonants or two identical vowels or a lower-case letter and a capital letter from coming together.

hall-lamp	shell-like	grass-seed
re-echo	pre-eminent	semi-invalid
anti-Semitism	pro-Germanic	un-American

Note: *Coordinate* and *cooperate* (and the words derived from them) may be written solid.

To separate the prefixes *self* and *ex* (meaning "former") from the rest of the compound.

self-reliance	self-hate	self-starter
ex-president	ex-professor	

To join fanciful, coined, or duplicating words.

a come-up-and-see-me-sometime glance
a know-it-all delusion
an ever-never choice
the clomp-clomp-clomp of heavy boots

To separate two or more compounds with a common base.

2- or 3-em dashes
bright, -er, -est
1- and 2-inch nails.

To divide a word at the end of a line.

mid-dle	mid-summer
mi-cro-scope	mi-cro-scop-ic

Note: A one-syllable word ought never to be divided: *wrong, died, spared.*

A word ought never to be divided after a single letter. Avoid: a-broad, E-zekiel.

Words are divided by syllables, and pronunciation is the clue to syllabification. But when in doubt consult your dictionary.

Do not use the hyphen:

To join two or more words used as an adjective when they follow the word modified.

His notions were out of date years ago.
His principles are iron clad.
It was an experience never to be forgotten.

To join a group of words acting as a unit modifier when it is enclosed by quotation marks.

"good neighbor" policy
"most favored nation" clause
"all for love" attitude

Note: If any word or group of words was originally hyphenated, the hyphen is retained: *"blue-pencil" habit, "actor-manager" duties.*

To join two words comprising a proper noun when they act as a unit modifier.

New York life
South American music

Note: If two proper nouns act as a unit modifier they are properly joined by the hyphen: *Latin-American music, Austro-Hungarian Empire.*

To join a prefix or suffix and a root.

antislavery	tenfold
extracurricular	spoonful
neoclassic	clockwise
misspell	kingdom
ultraviolet	womanhood

Exercise No. 69

Place the hyphen between the words requiring hyphenation.

1. He was a science fiction devotee; he had the American mania for reading about space travel, time travel, martian maidens, and extragalactic supermen.
2. After the four mile torchlight parade, General Clark served as best man at the wedding of his only son, Major William Clark, 28, a thrice wounded Korean veteran and 25 year old fashion model Audrey Loflin.
3. All cargo air transport offers direct, dependable deliveries to many countries and cities on all six continents. By lighter packing, lower insurance rates, less transshipment, they compete with other shipping media.
4. The mop up over, the victorious leader of the opposition pledged that his government would adopt a pro United States middle road government.
5. His anti vivisectionism alienated the one focused fanatics.
6. Land rich but money poor, he walked unhappily through the fields of thriving, knee high corn.

THE APOSTROPHE—is a mark of omission: it indicates that a word has been contracted; that a letter or letters which belong to it (or which belonged to it at some earlier period in the history of the language) have been intentionally left out.

Use the apostrophe:

To indicate a contraction.

it's (for *it is* only)

mornin' (in colloquial speech, for *morning*)

B'klyn (for *Brooklyn*)

don't (for *do not*)

'tis (for *it is*)

'tisn't (for *it is not*)

ne'er (for *never*)

won't (for *will not*)

To form the possessive case of a noun.

POSSESSIVE SINGULAR	POSSESSIVE PLURAL	GROUP POSSESSIVE
John's medicine	Joneses' marriage	William and Mary's reign
Dr. John's tonic	teachers' tasks	man of straw's backbone
Boston *American's* columns	gods' laughter	Tom and Tilly's candy
Holmes's *Autocrat*	gentlemen's preference	men and women's approval
razor's edge	children's play	Arthur Wellesley, Duke of Wellington, the Field Marshal's death.

Note: (a) To form the possessive singular of a noun, add *apostrophe s* to its simple form. Add only the *apostrophe* if another *s* would cause an awkward combination of *s*-sounds.

Holmes's novel, but *Holmes' sonnet*.

(b) To form the possessive plural of a noun, add only the *apostrophe* to the simple plural form of the noun; but if the simple plural form does not end in *s*, add *apostrophe s: boys' books*, but *men's books*.

(c) To form the possessive of a group of words containing a single idea, add *apostrophe s* to the last word: William and Mary's reign (they reigned jointly), but Henry's and Elizabeth's reign (they reigned separately).

To form coined plurals, as well as standard plurals of letters, numbers, symbols, and of words referred to as words.

W.C.T.U.'s or their equivalents have sprung up.

The *x*'s equal the *y*'s.

The 1940's have been called the "Aspirin Age."

There are not three *two*'s in English.

Do not use the apostrophe:

To form possessive pronouns.

its (not *it's*)

hers (not *her's*)

ours (not *our's*)

theirs (not *their's*)

yours (not *your's*)

To form the possessive of nouns that stand for inanimate objects, save in a few idiomatic constructions.

the value of the picture (*not* the picture's value)

the location of the comma (*not* the comma's location)

the trees of the wood (not the wood's trees)

But: duty's call, sun's beams, wit's end (all idiomatic)

Exercise No. 70

Place the *apostrophe*, or the *apostrophe s*, wherever required. (Below are given the nominative forms of those nouns to be converted into the possessive.)

1. Smith Brothers Cough Drops
2. Newton Law
3. earth surface
4. geese cackling
5. hero welcome
6. Prince of Wales horse
7. James novels
8. Queen Elizabeth II coronation
9. Achilles heel
10. anybody else word
11. princess gown
12. princesses gowns
13. Xerxes triumph
14. heres how
15. at 6s and 7s
16. *Mississippi* has four *s* s
17. six o clock
18. youll
19. theyd
20. whos

THE PERIOD FOR ABBREVIATIONS The period may mark a shortened word, an abbreviation. Abbreviations are perfectly appropriate to material requiring condensation—catalogues, for example. But in more formal contexts only conventional abbreviations ought to be employed (*Mr., Mrs., Dr., Jr., St.*). Avoid abbreviations not sanctioned by general usage.

Use the period to mark abbreviations.

Rev. Hiram Wilbur	(formal: the Reverend
or	Hiram Wilbur, *not*
Rev. H. Wilbur	Rev. Wilbur)

Prof. R. C. Dickson	(formal: Professor R. C. Dickson or Professor Dickson, *not* Prof. Dickson)
Dr. Jucovy	Milton Jucovy, M.D.
Thomas Connop Thirlwall, Jr.	
St. Francis	

etc. (*et cetera*), "and so forth."

e.g. (*exempli gratia*), "for example."

et al. (*et alii*), "and others."

Note: Avoid abbreviations of titles when they are not followed by a proper name and abbreviate proper names sparingly.

Do not use the period to mark abbreviations when the period is not part of the official name or when the period has been popularly discarded.

FBI	OPA
NBC	TNT (trinitrotoluol)
WNYC (radio station)	US 40
NATO (North Atlantic Treaty Organization)	*NED* (*New English Dictionary*)
	TVA

Exercise No. 71

Abbreviate the following words.

1. *anno domini*
2. bachelor of arts
3. *ante meridiem*
4. doctor
5. logarithm
6. private first class
7. radio aircraft discovery and recognition
8. tuberculosis
9. South Dakota
10. *videlicet*
11. square inch
12. gill
13. barrel
14. Puerto Rico
15. hundredweight
16. ton
17. January
18. Monday
19. northwest (compass direction)
20. Celsius

ITALICS—(in handwriting and typewriting indicated by underlining with a single straight line) call attention to a word or words as being distinct from other words.

Use italics:

To emphasize or contrast.

Consider what he *is*, not what he *was*.

To set forth words in a foreign language.

We arrived, *enfin* [finally].

The latter grunted, *"C'est defender."* ["It is forbidden."]

Note: If the foreign word has become naturalized—absorbed into English—italics are unnecessary:

Latin: bona fide, et cetera, dramatis personae

French: café, elite, ensemble

German: delicatessen, Weltanschauung, Gesundheit

To set forth titles of separately published works—plays, novels, symphonies, pamphlets, magazines, newspapers, and the like.

Hamlet (play)

Gone with the Wind (novel)

Lohengrin (opera)

The Crisis (pamphlet)

The New York *Times*

Note: Style books differ as to italicization of newspaper titles. Some omit the city; others omit the definite article; others include the full title as it appears on the newspaper masthead: either The New York *Times*, The *New York Times*, or *The New York Times*.

Titles of parts of published works are in quotation marks: "I Begin a Pilgrimage" in e e cummings' *The Enormous Room*.

To set forth names of ships or planes.

Airforce One

The *Titanic*

The *Sacred Cow*

To indicate a word, letter, or number as such.

The antonym of *part* is *whole*.

He knows a *p* from a *q*.

Primitive people think *7* has a magical significance.

Do not use italics to gain emphatic effects in a mechanical way. Excessive use of italics is one of the symptoms of the schoolgirl style.

Exercise No. 72

Italicize (underline) those words that require italicization.

1. Charles W. Morton, associate editor of the Atlantic, had been collecting examples of periphrasis, the use of three words where one would do. In the Atlantic Bulletin, a monthly promotion letter, he cited these horrible examples: The New York Herald Tribune called the beaver a "furry, paddle-tailed mammal"; and Lincoln Sunday Journal-Star termed milk "the vitamin-laden liquid" issuing from "a bovine milk factory"; Travel magazine said skiers slid down the slopes on the "beautiful barrel staves."
2. He sailed to Europe on the America; he flew back on the Antipodes.
3. "Sally Bowles," perhaps the best story in Christopher Isherwood's Goodbye to Berlin, was adapted into a mediocre play, I Am a Camera, by John van Druten.
4. The pull of -or is so strong that the pedagogues, who began calling themselves educationists a decade or so ago, have now gone back to educator, which appeared as a rival for the homely teacher in Shakespeare's time.
5. I saw the motion picture Come Back, Little Sheba in France, with French voices dubbed in. It seemed odd to hear Shirley Booth refer to "la petite Sheba."

CAPITAL LETTERS Capitalization is a conventional device intended to ease the reader's way, but faulty capitalization impedes it. The initial capital signifies that a word is a proper noun or adjective (or to be considered as one), or that a new sentence or line of verse succeeds a former.

Use an initial capital letter:

To mark a proper noun or adjective, a title of distinction, a common noun personified, a reference to Deity.

Proper names: Andrew Jackson, Texas, England, Oxford

Proper adjectives: Jacksonian, Texan, English, Oxfordian

Races, ethnic groups, religions (and the people who belong to them): Caucasian, Judaism, Catholicism, Black, Jew, Protestant, Buddhist

Deity: God, Jehovah, Jove, Brahma, His word

Wars and battles: World War II, Battle of the Bulge

Days and months: Monday, October

Companies, organizations, clubs: Associated Press, General Motors Corporation, Young Men's Christian Association, Rotary Club

Geographical divisions: the Hudson River, the West, Pike's Peak, the North Pole, the East Side, Fifth Avenue, Piccadilly, Main Street

Official bodies: the United States Senate and House of Representatives

Titles of distinction: Bishop of New York, Duke of York, Superintendent of Documents

Personifications: There, Honor battled Ease. The Chair recognizes nobody

Specific courses: Economics 10, Mathematics 21

To mark the first word of every sentence, line of verse, and full quotation.

A man must eat.

"Hope springs eternal in the human breast,
Man never *is*, but always *to be*, blest."

(Pope)

"In a republic," wrote Calvin Coolidge, "the law reflects rather than makes the standard of conduct and the state of popular opinion."

To mark the pronoun *I* and the interjection *O*.

It was I.

"Who could have thought such starkness lay concealed

Within thy beams, O Sun!" (Blanco White)

To mark a word signifying family relationship when used as a name.

Yes, Father said he would.

(But: My father said he would.)

Do not use the initial capital letter:

To mark general or class names.

Every child wants to be president.

President Eisenhower was once a five-star general.

Though he was a democrat in principle, he did not belong to the Democratic Party.

To mark point of the compass, save where it refers to a recognized geographical division.

Lars Porsena sent his men north, south, east, and west to summon his array.

(But: The South has become an industrial area.)

To mark the seasons of the year.

spring, summer, autumn, fall.

Exercise No. 73

Use an initial capital letter for the words requiring capitalization.

1. the anglo-saxon language was the language of our saxon forefathers in england, though they never gave it that name. they called it english. thus king alfred speaks of translating "from book-latin into english"; abbot aelfric was requested by aethelward "to translate the book of genesis from latin into english"; and bishop leofric, speaking of the manuscript (the "exeter manuscript") he gave to exeter cathedral, calls it "a great english book."

2. the city of nome, alaska, acquired its name through error. there was a small prospectors' settlement known as anvil city on the seward peninsula in alaska. a washington clerk, in drawing a map, did not know its name, and wrote "name?" at that place on the map. one of his superiors took the word for "nome" and that name still stands.

3. *stories in the modern manner,* edited by philip rahv and william phillips, was published by avon books. perhaps the best story in it is gide's "theseus."

4. the lion is a kingly beast.
he likes a hindu for a feast.

5. it is the grace of god that urges missionaries to suffer the most disheartening privations for their faith. this grace moved saint isaac jogues to say (when he came to canada), "i felt as if it were a christmas day for me, and that I was to be born again to a new life, to a life in him."

SPELLING

THE DILEMMA

Weak spellers lose prestige socially and professionally. They may be intelligent and even educated, but their errors in spelling cause others (often erroneously) to consider them a trifle backward. Although good intelligence and good spelling do not correlate, the weak speller can profit from the snob-appeal attached to spelling correctly by heeding the principles of spelling. Until he faces the reality of his problem, the weak speller depends upon a poor compromise. Afraid to try spelling the effective word, he uses the one he knows how to spell and hopes that it means almost the same thing. The dangers of this method are clear:

STUNTED VOCABULARY:

The girl in the bright red suit *walked* across the street.

INSTEAD OF *slithered, undulated, jiggled, strutted.*

INCORRECT USAGE:

That boy xylophonist is a *progeny*.

INSTEAD OF *prodigy*.

THE CAUSES

In part the spelling problem results from **illogical relationships between the sound and the spelling of English words.** These inconsistencies are due to:

Changes in pronunciation without changes in spelling.

EXAMPLE: In the Middle Ages *meat* rhymed with *neat*, but *sweet* did not rhyme with *eat*.

Changes in spelling without changes in pronunciation.

EXAMPLE: The Old English word *bough* remains today as a noun; but the verb exists as *bow*.

Changes in both spelling and pronunciation.

EXAMPLE: Old English *skip* has become modern *ship*; yet Old English *skipper* remains unchanged.

Thus, in modern English spelling, we have troublesome sounds like:

oo (a.) m*oo*n, d*o*, cr*ui*se, (b.) g*oo*d, l*oo*k, r*oo*f.
rendezv*ou*s, Hind*u*, (c.) d*oo*r, fl*oo*r.
rag*ou*t, s*ue*. (d.) z*oo*logy.

k (a.) li*k*e, *q*uery (d.) anti*q*ue
(b.) li*q*uor (e.) hibis*c*us
(c.) ex*c*ept (f.) ac*c*umulate

ough r*ough* thor*ough* hicc*ough* c*ough*
silent letters kil*n* autum*n* *w*riter *p*neumonic

Because of such phonetic confusion, absurdities like the following may easily be constructed:

We had *ghoti* on *phraideigh*.
ghoti = fish gh as in *cough*
o as in *women*
ti as in *vacation*
phraideigh = Friday ph as in *philosophy*
ai as in *aisle*
eigh as in *neighbor*

With certain sounds in English, no rules are effective. One has no choice but to learn the word.

Other causes for poor spelling lie with **the individual.**

He has not learned **to read** carefully.
He has not learned **to listen** carefully.
He has not learned **to memorize.**
He has not learned **to work** in order **to learn.**

THE DILEMMA SOLVED

The **ideal solution** is to reform English spelling. In Spanish and Italian, words are spelled as they sound—each letter has its fixed correspondent in sound. Although attempts have been made to modernize English spelling, the weak speller ought not to await the outcome of these experiments before solving his spelling problem.

Thus, the best **practical** solutions may be summarized:

Analyze the Difficulty—does it stem from:
1. Carelessness in writing, reading, listening?
2. Groups of similar words differently spelled?
3. Varied sorts of "special" complexities?

Eliminate the Difficulty—by:
1. Learning the "Rules."
2. Using Mnemonic Devices.
3. Using the Dictionary.
4. Drilling on words over and over until they are absolutely learned.

Copy each word neatly, carefully, using the dictionary as a double check for accuracy.

Limit the spelling list to *twenty words* at a time. It is easier to learn smaller groups of words.

LEARNING THE RULES Memorizing the spelling of a word is better than memorizing the "rule" for spelling. But rules do help: To explain how certain groups of words are spelled; To indicate what exceptions to the rules must be learned. Thus, a few rules and the words which illustrate them will help the weak speller to conquer almost all of his difficulties.

Note: Only those rules which are most helpful have been included in this section. Exceptions to almost every rule are frequent. One has no recourse save to learn them. Where there have been too many exceptions to make a rule practical, that rule has been omitted.

Learn each rule before proceeding to the next.

IE and EI

Rule: When pronounced as *ee* (as in *week* or *meek*), *i* is followed by *e*, except after *c*.

> Place I before E
> Except after C

EXAMPLES:

IE pronounced as EE

ach*ie*ve	cash*ie*r	gr*ie*f	shr*ie*k
ap*ie*ce	ch*ie*f	n*ie*ce	s*ie*ge
bel*ie*f	f*ie*ld	p*ie*ce	th*ie*f
bel*ie*ve	f*ie*nd	p*ie*rce	t*ie*r
b*ie*r	f*ie*rce	repr*ie*ve	w*ie*ld
br*ie*f	fr*ie*ze	sh*ie*ld	y*ie*ld

Typical exceptions:

> *ei*ther, n*ei*ther, s*ei*zure, sh*ei*k, l*ei*sure, w*ei*rd

EI (pronounced as ee) after c

c*ei*ling	dec*ei*ve	rec*ei*ve	rec*ei*pt
conc*ei*ve	conc*ei*t	perc*ei*ve	dec*ei*t

Typical exceptions:

> financ*ie*r, spec*ie*, spec*ie*s

EI is generally used:

If sounded as *ā* (as in *neighbor* or *weigh*)

f*ei*nt	r*ei*gn	w*ei*ght
fr*ei*ght	sk*ei*n	v*ei*l

If sounded as *ĭ* (as in *hĭt*)

counterf*ei*t	forf*ei*t	sovcr*ei*gn
for*ei*gn	surf*ei*t	

Exceptions:

> s*ie*ve, misch*ie*f, misch*ie*vous

If sounded as *ī* (as in *īce*)

*ei*der	h*ei*ght	sl*ei*ght

Except for the variations above, the order is **IE** in almost all other sound combinations:

> fr*ie*nd, l*ie*utenant.

Note: If *i* and *e* do not form a **digraph** (two letters used to represent a single sound), the rules discussed have no effect.

cloth*ie*r	d*ei*ty	hyg*ie*nic
f*ie*ry	glac*ie*r	sc*ie*nce

EXPLANATION: *fiery* breaks into *fi ery*. Since the *i* and *e* have independent sound values, they cannot be considered a digraph. The same principle applies to other words in this group. Thus, such words must simply be memorized.

Do not proceed to the next rule before completing the exercise below.

Exercise No. 74

Complete the spelling of the following words by filling in *ie* or *ei* in the blank spaces:

1. w—rd	4. s—ge	7. f—nt
2. glac—r	5. l—utenant	8. anc—nt
3. fr—nd	6. financ—r	9. conc—ve

10. for—gn   12. p—rce   14. d—ty
11. cash—r   13. w—ld   15. hyg—ne

Silent *e*

Dropping the silent *e*

Rule: Final silent *e* is usually dropped before an ending (suffix) beginning with a vowel.

EXAMPLES:

argue	arguing	grieve	grievance
become	becoming	judge	judging
change	changing	shine	shining
conceive	conceivable		

Retaining the silent *e*

Rule: Final silent *e* is usually retained before an ending beginning with a consonant.

EXAMPLES:

achieve	achievement	like	likely
bare	barely	live	liveliness
definite	definitely	love	lovely

Note: There are several exceptions to the rules governing final silent *e*, especially those about *dropping* the vowel.

1. Final silent *e* is retained after SOFT *c* and SOFT *g* before endings (suffixes) beginning with *a* or *o*.

EXPLANATION:

Soft *c* as in fan*c*y

Hard *c* as in *c*ome

Soft *g* as in ran*g*e, *g*ist

Hard *g* as in *g*amble, *g*ut

Thus, C and G are generally SOFT before *e*, *i*, and *y*, but HARD before *a*, *o*, and *u*.

So, to keep the soft sound of *c* and *g* before *a* and *o*, the final silent *e* is retained. If the *e* were not retained, *peacable* (to rhyme with *peekable*) would be the result, instead of *peaceable*.

EXAMPLES:

notice	noticing	noticeable
change	changing	changeable
manage	managing	manageable

2. Final silent *e* is retained in some words before the suffix *-ing* to prevent mispronunciation or ambiguity.

EXAMPLES:

singe   singeing = to scorch
    BUT
sing   singing = to chant
dye   dyeing = to color

BUT

die   dying   = to cease to live
tinge   tingeing = to color
ting   tinging   = to make a high-pitched sound

3. Final silent *e* is retained when the endings *ye*, *oe*, *ee* precede the suffix *-ing*.

EXAMPLES:

hoe	hoeing	eye	eyeing
agree	agreeing	see	seeing
decree	decreeing	shoe	shoeing

Do not proceed to the next rule before completing the exercise below.

Exercise No. 75

Complete the spelling of the following words by filling in *e* where necessary. If no *e* is needed, leave the space blank.

1. judg—ment   6. manag—ing
2. ey—ing   7. lov—ly
3. peac—able   8. chang—able
4. din—ing   9. sens—ible
5. courag—ous   10. ho—ing

Final Y

Changing final *y* to *i*.

Rule: When preceded by a consonant and followed by a suffix (other than one beginning with *i*), final *y* changes to *i*.

EXAMPLES:

beauty	beautiful	lonely	loneliness
busy	business	marry	marriage
easy	easily	mercy	merciful
envy	envious	rely	reliance
	BUT		
carry	carrying	occupy	occupying
	carried		occupied
ply	plying	try	trying
	plies		tries

EXPLANATION:

Since the suffix *-ing* appears in the present participles *carry*, *ply*, *occupy*, and *try*, the *y* is retained—the initial letter in the suffix is *i*.

Retaining final *y*.

Rule: If it is preceded by a vowel, the final *y* is usually retained.

EXAMPLES:

attorney	attorneys	monkey	monkeys
boy	boys	play	plays
chimney	chimneys	trolley	trolleys

Typical Exceptions:

day	daily
lay	laid
pay	paid
say	said
slay	slain

Note: Before several suffixes the final *y* is retained.

EXAMPLES:

dry—dryness	joy—joyous
employ—employment	sly—slyness
enjoy—enjoyment	play—playful

Before the suffix *-ly*, the final *y* of monosyllables is sometimes dropped and sometimes retained. Either form is permissible.

EXAMPLES:

dry	drily	shy	shily
	dryly		shyly

Do not proceed to the next rule before completing the exercise below.

Exercise No. 76

Complete the spelling of the following words by filling in the blank space with *y* or *i* (or *ie*).

1. occup—ing
2. lonel—ness
3. trolle—s
4. dr—ness
5. turke—s
6. tr—s
7. ke—s
8. bus—ness
9. rel—ance
10. occup—d

Final Consonants

Rule: A final single consonant is doubled when:

It is preceded by a single vowel (b*a*t).

It is followed by a suffix beginning with a vowel (s*i*tting).

It appears in a monosyllabic word (*hit, run*).

OR

It appears in a word accented on the last syllable (*o mit'*).

EXAMPLE AND EXPLANATION:

1. lop   lopping

Final single consonant *p* is preceded by single vowel *o*.

Final single consonant *p* is followed by suffix beginning with vowel *i* (-ing).

lop is a monosyllabic word.

THUS, final single consonant is doubled—lopping.

Note that the doubled consonant keeps the preceding vowel short. Compare *lopping* with *lōping*.

2. omit   omitted

Final single consonant *t* is preceded by single vowel *i*.

Final single consonant *t* is followed by suffix beginning with vowel *e* (-ed).

Accent is on the second syllable—o mit'.

THUS, final single consonant is doubled—omi*tt*ed. Other words whose final consonants are doubled include:

MONOSYLLABLES		POLYSYLLABLES	
beg	ship	acquit	equip
drop	stop	allot	forget
quit	swim	begin	occur
quiz		commit	permit
(Note: *qu: u* after *q* is		compel	transfer
not a vowel, but has the		confer	
consonant sound of *w*.)			

The final single consonant is NOT doubled when:

1. The accent is shifted to a preceding syllable when the suffix is added.

EXAMPLES: confer' conferr'ing BUT *con'*ference
           prefer' preferr'ing BUT *pref'*erence

EXPLANATION:

Conferring and *preferring* fulfill the provisions of the rule for doubling the final consonant. *Con'ference* and *pref'erence* shift their accents to the first syllable, and so do not meet the rule that accent must be on the final syllable.

MORE EXAMPLES:

refer	reference	benefit	benefited
counsel	counseled	conquer	conquerable

2. The final consonant is already doubled.

EXAMPLES:

start started

relax relaxing (*x* is equivalent to the double consonant *ks*)

3. The final consonant is preceded by two vowels.

EXAMPLES:

beat   beating   boil   boiling

REVIEW TEST ON RULES INVOLVING:

ie or *ei*, final *e*, final *y*, final consonants.

Exercise No. 77

Complete the spelling of the following words according to one of the four rules.

1. bugs on the c—ling.
2. no more worr—s.
3. f—ld of dais—s.
4. circus monk—s.
5. hop—ng to see you.
6. angry arg—ment.
7. sun is shin—ng.
8. nin—y years old.
9. he rec—ved a letter.
10. refer—ng to you.
11. unbel—vable story.
12. s—zed the gun.
13. what's your prefer—nce?
14. what occur—d?
15. th—ves in the night.
16. notic—able gap.
17. merc—less enemy.
18. s—ge of the fort.
19. dark, narrow all—s.
20. stud—ous scholar.
21. stud—ng all night.
22. benefit—d from rules.
23. rel—f from hunger.
24. I perc—ve.
25. very tru—y yours.

K Added to Words Ending in C

Rule: Words ending in *c* add *k* before an ending (suffix) beginning with *e*, *i*, or *y*, to preserve the hard sound of *c*.

EXAMPLES:

frolic	frolicked	frolicking
mimic	mimicked	mimicking
picnic	picnicked	picnicking
traffic	trafficked	trafficking

-cede, -ceed, and -sede

Rule: Learn the four words and eliminate the innumerable errors.

THE FOUR WORDS:

SUPERSEDE—the only word in English that ends in *-sede*.

EXCEED
PROCEED } these three are the only words in
SUCCEED } English that end in *-ceed*.

Thus, all other words having this sound end in *-cede*.

EXAMPLES:

accede	intercede	recede
concede	precede	secede

Plurals

Regular plurals.

Rule: Nouns form plurals by adding *-s* to the singular.

EXAMPLES:

boys	girls	homes
books	Greeks	lemons

Irregular plurals.

The plural of some nouns ending in *o* preceded by a consonant is formed by adding *-es*.

EXAMPLES:

echoes	tomatoes	Negroes
heroes	tornadoes	torpedoes
innuendoes	mosquitoes	vetoes
potatoes		

TYPICAL EXCEPTIONS:

albinos	gauchos	provisos
altos	halos	quartos
banjos	lassos	solos
cantos	pianos	tobaccos
dynamos	piccolos	zeros

For plurals of nouns ending in *y*, see Rule on Final *y*.

If noun ends in *y* preceded by consonant, change *y* to *i* and add suffix *-es: sky—skies; enemy—enemies.*

If noun ends in *y* preceded by a vowel, add *s: chimney—chimneys; day—days; play—plays; monkey—monkeys.*

Foreign plurals.

Most of these words, having entered the English language late, do not fall into the usual categories and must simply be learned.

EXAMPLES:

addendum	addenda
alumnus	alumni (masc.)
alumna	alumnae (fem.)
axis	axes
basis	bases
datum	data
ellipsis	ellipses
erratum	errata
memorandum	memoranda
synopsis	synopses

Note: Some nouns in English retain archaic forms in their plural:

ox—oxen; deer—deer; child—children. Such words must be checked in a dictionary.

Exercise No. 78

Underline the one correctly spelled word in each of the following groups:

1. froliced, frolicked, froleced, frollicked
2. addenda, adenda, adendda, addinda
3. pimentos, pimmientos, pimientoes, pimientos
4. synopsus, synoppsis, synopsis, synoppsus

5. innuendo, inuendo, inuenddo, innuindo
6. superside, supercede, superceed, supersede
7. succeed, succede, suceed, sucsede
8. mosquitoes, mosuito, mosquitos, mosquittoes
9. interceed, intersede, intercede, interseed
10. mimiced, mimmiced, mimicked, mimmicked
11. seceed, sesede, secede, seseed
12. Negros, Negroes, Neggros, Nigras
13. excede, ecsede, exceed, exseed
14. enemmys, enemys, enemmies, enemies
15. dynamos, dynamoes, dymanos, dymanoes

Possessives Don't confuse contractions with the possessive forms of pronouns. Possessive pronouns do not take an apostrophe.

EXAMPLES:

Possessive Pronouns	Contractions
its (The door has its knob)	it's (it is)
Note: *its'* does *not* exist	
their (They went their way)	they're (they are)
your (Have your supper?)	you're (you are)
whose (Whose book is this?)	who's (who is)

Note: No apostrophes are used with the other possessive and relative pronouns either: *his, hers, ours, yours, theirs.*

If the singular or plural noun does not end in *s*, form the possessive by adding *apostrophe s* to the simple (nominative) form of the noun.

SINGULAR: Bill's book   boy's game   Joan's hat
PLURAL: oxen's yokes   men's clothes   children's games

Note: Only the apostrophe is added if another *s* would cause sibilants (*s*-sounds) to pile up: rather than *Burns's poetry, Jones's joys,* prefer *Burns' poetry, Jones' joys.*

To form the possessive plural of nouns ending in *s*, add only the apostrophe: *ladies' coats, soldiers' guns, hostesses' etiquette, princes' privileges.*

In compounds, the last word uses the sign of the possessive.

EXAMPLES:

mother-in-law's house
attorney general's office
brother-in-law's car
commander-in-chief's army

Indicate joint possession by placing the sign of the possessive on the last item in the series; indicate individual possession by placing the sign of the possessive on each item.

EXAMPLES:

Joint	Single
Bill and Ed's house (they own it together)	Bill's and Ed's trials (each has undergone a trial)
Joint Chiefs-of-Staff's opinion	Army's and Navy's opinion.

Apostrophes are often omitted in well-known firm names, geographic names, names of organizations.

EXAMPLES: United Nations Secretariat
United States Air Force
Harpers Ferry

Homonyms—are words similar (although not necessarily exactly alike) in sound but different in meaning and often in spelling. To eliminate the innumerable errors in spelling which result from confusion about homonyms, learn the meanings of each member of the related group of words, create sentences using each word correctly, and repeat until all confusion has disappeared.

access	way of approach; admission
excess	superabundance
advice	noun (pronounce as *ice*)
advise	verb (pronounce -*ise* as *eyes*, or -*ize*)
aisle	a passageway or Avenue
isle	an Island
all ready	everything is ready
already	previously
all together	everyone in company
altogether	completely, without exception
allusion	a reference, as "an *allusion* to the Bible"
illusion	a false impression or deception
altar	place of worship (noun)
alter	to change (verb)
brake	a device to arrest motion by friction
break	to separate violently into parts
bridal	pertaining to a bride (*bride* + *al*)
bridle	headgear used to control a horse
capitol	the central place of government
capital	used for all other purposes of spelling

cite	to quote or refer
sight	noun: a view; verb: to see, aim
site	location or *situation*
coarse	gross, unrefined
course	used for all other purposes of spelling
council	group of people organized to consider affairs
consul	government official handling affairs of his nation in an alien country
counsel	noun: advice; verb: to advise
dessert'	a sweet served after the main course of a meal (accent on last syllable)
desert	used as noun and verb for all other purposes of spelling (noun has accent on first syllable: des'ert; verb has accent on last syllable: desert')
device	noun (pronounce as *ice*)
devise	verb (pronounce -*ise* as *ayes* or *ize*)
dīning	eating (pronounce first *i* as *eye*)
dĭnning	making a loud noise (din) (pronounce first *i* as *i* in *hit*)
formally	in a formal manner
formerly	previously
forth	onward
fourth	number after third; one of four equal parts
foul	ugly, evil
fowl	a winged bird
idle	lazy, doing nothing
idol	a pagan god
idyll	a poem or prose work describing joys of country life
ingenious	clever (pronounce *e* as in *eat*)
ingenuous	naive, forthright, simple, as in "the ingénue's ingenuous belief that the villain meant her no harm" (Pronounce *e* as in *hen*. Note *u*, which is pronounced as *you*.)
its	possessive pronoun of *it*
it's	contraction of *it is*
lead	noun: a metal (rhymes with *head*); verb: to conduct (rhymes with *bead*)
led	verb: the past tense of verb *lead*
loose	adjective: not tightly fastened; verb: to make loose
lose	verb: to suffer loss of
passed	past tense of verb to pass, as "We *passed* her school"
past	adjective, as "This *past* week was ended too soon"
peace	freedom from disturbance
piece	a portion
personal	belonging to a particular person. Pronounced per'sonal
personnel	people engaged in a service. Pronounced per son nel'
persecute	to oppress or injure
prosecute	to try by law
principal	chief, as in "the principal of a school," or "principal source of income"
principle	a general truth or rule. See MNEMONICS
prophecy	noun. See also *advice* and *device*
prophesy	verb
quiet	calm, still. Note two syllables: *qui*+*et*
quite	entirely, truly. Note one syllable
rain	water
rein	device used to guide horses
reign	the rule of a government
stationary	fixed position, as "A ship in drydock is *stationary*"
stationery	writing materials
than	conjunction used to introduce second item in a comparison, as "John is taller *than* his sister"
then	at that time, "*Then* he knew the truth"
to	preposition, as "He went to the store"; or sign of the infinitive, as "to sing"
too	adverb meaning more than enough, as "too long," "too soft"
two	the number after one
weather	climate
whether	conjunction introducing an alternative, as "He did not know whether or not to go"

Exercise No. 79

Underline the correct word in each of the following sentences.

1. I want your (advice, advise) in a legal matter.

2. Will the truce have any (affect, effect) on food prices?

3. I want you here (all together, altogether), not one at a time.

4. Please sit (beside, besides) me at the dinner table.

5. His manners are too (coarse, course) to allow him to play with refined children.

6. Shall we have (desert, dessert) in the (dinning, dining) room?

7. I asked our foreign (council, consul) to get me a visa.

8. I (cited, sited) him the place on the blueprint where I had selected the (site, sight, cite) for our home.

9. We must (device, devise) a new plan to capture Mary's affection.

10. Every dollar invested returns (its, it's) value in gold.

11. He (lead, led) his horse to water, and it drank.

12. During the (past, passed) six months, her life has been miserable.

13. I should prefer that you leave rather (then, than) have you insult my guests.

14. Why do you continue to (persecute, prosecute) that poor kitten?

15. If you will remain (quiet, quite) still, you will hear the echo from Forest Mountain.

Summary of Spelling Rules

	RULE	EXAMPLES	EXCEPTIONS
IE AND EI	I before E, except after C.	ach*ie*ve, but c*ei*ling	1. Use *EI* when: a. Sounded as $\bar{a}$: n*ei*ghbor, w*ei*gh b. Sounded as *ĭ*: counterf*ei*t c. Sounded as *ī*: h*ei*ght 2. Use *IE* for almost all other sounds: fr*ie*nd, l*ie*utenant. 3. If *i* and *e* do not form a digraph, rules do not apply: f*ie*ry, d*ei*ty.
FINAL SILENT E	1. **Drop** before suffix beginning with a vowel. 2. **Retain** before suffix beginning with a consonant.	grieve—grievance absolute—absolutely	1. Retain *e* after soft *c* and soft *g* before suffixes beginning with *a* or *o*: peaceable, manageable.
FINAL Y	1. **Change** final *y* to *i* if *y* is **preceded** by a **consonant** and **followed** by any suffix except one beginning with *i*. 2. **Retain** final *y* if it is preceded by a **vowel**.	beauty—beautiful BUT carry—carrying boys—boys; valley—valleys	dry—dryness; sly—slyness. day—daily; pay—paid
FINAL CONSONANTS	**Double** final consonants when: 1. Preceded by a single vowel. 2. Followed by a suffix beginning with a vowel. 3. The consonant terminates a monosyllabic word. 4. The consonant terminates a polysyllabic word accented on the last syllable.	1. drop—dropped; beg—beggar 2. quit—quitting; swim—swimmer 3. hit—hitter; run—running 4. omit—omitted; transfer—transferred	Final consonant is not doubled if: 1. Accent shifts to preceding syllable when suffix is added: confer'—confer'ring BUT con'ference. 2. Final consonant is already doubled: start—started. 3. Final consonant is preceded by two vowels: beat—beating; boil—boiling.
к added to words ending in c	**Add** *k* to words ending in *c* before a suffix beginning with *e, i, y*.	frolic—frolicking—frolicked; picnic—picnicking—picnicked	
-CEDE -CEED -SEDE	Except for super*sede*, ex*ceed*, pro*ceed*, suc*ceed*, all words having this sound end in -*cede*.	accede, precede, recede, concede	

Summary of Spelling Rules (continued)

	RULE	EXAMPLES	EXCEPTIONS
PLURALS	1. Regular noun plurals add *-s* to the singular.	boy—boys; book—books	
	2. Irregular plurals:		
	a. Add *-es* if noun ends in *o* preceded by consonant.	a. echo—echoes; Negro—Negroes	a. piano—pianos; zero—zeros; solo—solos.
	b. Change *y* to *i* and add *-es* if noun ends in *y* preceded by consonant.	b. sky—skies; enemy—enemies	
	c. Add *-s* if noun ends in *y* preceded by vowel.	c. play—plays; day—days	
POSSESSIVES	1. Don't confuse contractions with possessive pronouns.	*Contraction Posses-* *sive* 1. *Pronoun* it's (it is) its they're their (they are)	
	2. Use no apostrophes with possessive or relative pronouns.	2. *his, hers, ours, yours, theirs, whose*	
	3. If singular or plural noun does **not** end in *s*, add apostrophe and s.	3. prince—prince's (Sing.), princes' (Plur.); soldier—soldier's (Sing.), soldiers' (Plur.)	
	4. If singular or plural noun does end in *s*, add apostrophe.	4. hostess—hostess' (Sing.), hostesses' (Plur.); Jones—Jones' (Sing.), Joneses' (Plur.)	

MNEMONICS (pronounced nemon'iks)—the art of developing the memory (Greek, to remember).

In addition to the rules of spelling, the student has at his disposal mnemonic devices. These techniques of memory association can and do help so long as the student never forgets that the word to be spelled is more important than the mnemonic device.

The best methods may be grouped as SIGHT SPELLING and SOUND SPELLING.

Sight Spelling Repetition of associated visual images aids memory.

Wherever possible, reduce the troublesome word to simple words.

  sergeant = *sarge* + *ant*

  battalion = *batta* (atta boy) + *lion*

    or

  battle and battalion have double *t* + single *l*

  business = *sin* in bu*sin*ess

  separate = *pa* + *rate* or *a rat*

Group words which are spelled alike. (See HOMONYMS)

useful	earful
hopeful	cupful
careful	handful

No adjective ends in FULL (except full itself)

man-*woman*	All right
men-*women*	All wrong
	All night

Sheer trickery

cemetery	We get there with ease (E's)
experience	These are
existence	*Easy* words.
deve*lop*	*lop* off the final e.
grammar	Write *gram*, then spell it backwards, but drop the g.

indispensable	That which one is not *able to dispense* with.
principle	A princip**LE** is a ru**LE**.

Sound Spelling Repetition of associated auditory images aids memory.

Many words are spelled exactly as they sound. *Therefore, break the word into syllables, carefully pronounce each syllable, and write the word as you say it.*

op po nent	crit i cism	tem per a ture
o mit ted	oc ca sion	ev er y bod y
prom i nent	dis ap point ed	

Do not omit vowels.

bound *a* ries	in *ter* ested
soph *o* more	su p*er* in tend ent

Do not omit consonants.

rec og nize	prob a *b*ly
part ner	gov er*n* ment
can *d*i date	

Do not transpose letters.

vil l*ai*n	gua*r*d
mar r*ia*ge	we*i*rd
p*er* spi ra tion	tra ge d*y*

Work out your own mnemonic devices for the following words:

stretched	opinion	led
until	immediately	appearance
together	existence	forty

Learn the following list of words often misspelled because mispronounced. The source of error in pronunciation is italicized.

abom*i*nable	crit*ic*ism	interesting
accident*al*ly	cru*el*ty	ir*rele*vant
arc*t*ic	every	laboratory
a*th*lete	extra*or*dinary	N*iag*ara
bellig*er*ent	February	percola*t*or
benev*o*lent	gr*iev*ous	p*im*iento
chocolate	heigh*t*	re*cog*nize
charac*t*eristic		

THE DICTIONARY

A good dictionary is an invaluable tool. Even a small desk edition gives the spelling, pronunciation, usage, and meaning of thousands of words.

For each entry, the dictionary provides the correct spelling, variant spellings (when more than one is acceptable), spellings or irregular inflected forms, and syllabication. The principal parts of verbs, plurals of nouns, and the comparative and superlative forms of irregular adjectives and adverbs are often listed.

Pronunciations are given for each entry and for difficult inflected forms. The pronunciation key at the front of the dictionary explains the letter symbols and letters with diacritical marks that are used in the pronunciations.

Definitions, etymologies (origins of words), synonyms, and antonyms give a clear picture of a word's meaning.

In addition, usage notes and illustrative sentences show how a word should be used: whether it is in general use or a colloquial term, whether it is archaic or current, correct for formal writing or slang, what its position and function in a sentence are, and more.

Study the sample pages from the *Thorndike-Barnhart Comprehensive Desk Dictionary* on pages 110–11. When you know how and where to locate information in a dictionary, use your own dictionary to do these exercises.

1. Syllabify the following words:

illustration	geography	pronunciation
dictionary	poliomyelitis	dream
equivocate	definition	plateau
privilege	question	transference
collegiate	board	language

2. Pronounce the following words:

literature	rapine	singing
scallop	hauteur	fuselage
dirigible	drama	machination
phthisis	benign	vitiate
plethora	tomato	gladioli

3. Give the correct spellings of the principal parts of the following verbs:

sit	fly	sting
set	bleed	slay
lie	fight	dwell
lay	wring	cleave
drink	write	thrive

4. Which of the following words ought to be capitalized:

history	negro	kingdom
english	indian	chaucer
french		fascism

5. Study the definitions of the following words and discriminate between:

   a. satire, sarcasm, irony, parody.

   b. wit, humor.

c. town, village, hamlet.
d. flaunt, flout.
e. claim, assert.

6. Learn the etymology of the following words:
epidermis   ubiquitous   eliminate
demagogue   curfew   pajama

7. Give at least one *synonym* and one *antonym* for each of the following words:
talkative   benevolent

abhor   consent
able   narrow

8. Indicate the correct "label" (provincial, archaic, etc.) for each of the following words:

bobbysoxer	yore	saloon
shark	adobe	goner
gobbledygook	Plexiglas	androgen
billabong	swain	garçon

SPELLING LISTS

List of Words Most Frequently Misspelled by High School Seniors.

The list of words below* contains 149 words most frequently misspelled by high school seniors. These words and word-groups (those which are variants of the same word, as *acquaint* and *acquaintance*), were compiled by Dean Thomas Clark Pollock of New York University from 14,651 examples of misspelling submitted by 297 teachers in the United States and Canada. Each of the words represented was reported misspelled twenty times or more; these words, comprising fewer than three percent of the original list of 3,811 words, account for thirty percent of the total misspellings.

Note: The trouble spots in each word are italicized. Numbers beside the words indicate how frequently each word was misspelled.

their	179	occasion	54	convenience	5
receive	163	occasionally	8	convenient	33
too	152	succeed	25	difference	15
writer	11	success	22	different	23
writing	81	successful	12		
written	13	interest	56	than	38
all right	91	beginning	55	athletic	37
separate	91	immediate	3	to	37
until	88	immedi-		business	36
privilege	82	ately	51	equipped	21
definite	78	coming	53	equipment	14
there	78	embarrass	48	principal	18
believe	77	grammar	47	principle	18
its	52	humor	2	prophecy	35
it's	22	humorous	45	prophesy	35

occur	9	exist	3	benefit	16
occurred	52	existence	43	beneficial	5
occurrence	10	lose	28	benefited	11
occurring	2	losing	15	benefiting	1
describe	28	disappoint	42	develop	34
description	38	rhythm	41	environment	34
tragedy	64	study	1	recommend	34
		studied	3	fascinate	33
decide	48	studies	3	finally	33
decision	15	studying	34	necessary	24
probably	33	experience	28	necessity	9
speech	33	government	27		
argument	32	laboratory	27	during	22
		tried	27	forty	22
image	3			woman	22
imagine	7	acquaint	17	certain	21
imaginary	5	acquaintance	9		
imagination	17			commit	4
		affect	26	committed	12
quiet	32	accept	25	committing	5
then	32	accommodate	25	criticism	21
prejudice	30	excellent	25	disappear	21
sense	30	opportunity	25	exaggerate	21
similar	30			familiar	21
		marry	4	escape	21
your	2	marries	6	meant	21
you're	28	marriage	15	where	21
appearance	29	character	24	chief	20
conscious	29	complete	24		
pleasant	29	friend	24	hero	10
		truly	24	heroes	9
stop	1	accidentally	23	heroine	1
stopped	24	doesn't	23		
stopping	4			lonely	20
		foreign	14	opinion	20
surprise	29	foreigners	9	parliament	20
		performance	23	possess	20
excite	1	together	23	professor	20
excited	7	descend	13	restaurant	20
excitement	13	descendant	9	villain	20
exciting	7				

* The list compiled by Dr. Pollock appeared in the *Teachers Service Bulletin in English* (Macmillan, November, 1952).

GUIDE WORDS
are shown in large type at the top of each page and indicate the first and last entries on that page.

slip·per·y (slip′ər·ē) *adj.* ·per·i·er, ·per·i·est 1 Having a surface so smooth that bodies slip or slide easily on it. 2 That evades one's grasp; elusive. 3 Unreliable; tricky. —**slip′per·i·ness** *n.*

slippery elm 1 A species of small elm with mucilaginous inner bark. 2 Its wood or inner bark.

slip·shod (slip′shod′) *adj.* 1 Wearing shoes or slippers down at the heels. 2 Slovenly; sloppy. 3 Performed carelessly: *slipshod* work.

SYLLABICATION
is indicated by syllabic dots dividing main entry words.

slip·stream (slip′strēm′) *n. Aeron.* The stream of air driven backwards by the propeller of an aircraft.

slip·up (slip′up′) *n. Informal* A mistake; error.

slit (slit) *n.* A relatively straight cut or a long, narrow opening. —*v.t.* **slit**, **slit·ting** 1 To make a long incision in; slash. 2 To cut lengthwise into strips. 3 To sever. [ME *slitten*] —**slit′ter** *n.*

slith·er (slith′ər) *v.i.* 1 To slide; slip, as on a loose surface. 2 To glide, as a snake. —*v.t.* 3 To cause to slither. —*n.* A sinuous, gliding movement. [<OE *slidrian*] —**slith′er·y** *adj.*

MAIN ENTRY
is shown in boldface type and consists of words, phrases or abbreviations, prefixes, suffixes and combining forms.

sliv·er (sliv′ər) *n.* 1 A slender piece, as of wood, cut or torn off lengthwise; a splinter. 2 Corded textile fibers drawn into a fleecy strand. —*v.t. & v.i.* To cut or be split into long thin pieces. [<ME *sliven* to cleave] —**sliv′er·er** *n.*

slob (slob) *n.* 1 Mud; mire. 2 *Slang* A careless or unclean person. [<Ir. *slab*]

PRONUNCIATION
is shown in parenthesis and follows the main entry in phonetic equivalent.

slob·ber (slob′ər) *v.t.* 1 To wet with liquids oozing from the mouth. 2 To shed or spill, as liquid food, in eating. —*v.i.* 3 To drivel; slaver. 4 To talk or act gushingly. —*n.* 1 Liquid spilled as from the mouth. 2 Gushing, sentimental talk. [ME *sloberen*] —**slob′ber·er** *n.* —**slob′ber·y** *adj.*

sloe (slō) *n.* 1 A small, plumlike, astringent fruit. 2 The shrub that bears it; the blackthorn. [<OE *slā*]

sloe gin A cordial with a gin base, flavored with sloes.

INFLECTED FORMS
are given when there is an irregularity of form, and present participle of verbs, the plural of nouns, and the comparative and superlative of adjectives and adverbs.

slog (slog) *v.t. & v.i.* **slogged**, **slog·ging** 1 To slug, as a pugilist. 2 To plod (one's way). —*n.* A heavy blow. [?] —**slog′ger** *n.*

slo·gan (slō′gən) *n.* 1 A catchword or motto adopted by a political party, advertiser, etc. 2 A battle or rallying cry. [<Scot. Gael. *sluagh* army + *gairm* yell]

USAGE
information is included when an integral part of definition follows a colon after the particular meaning to which it applies.

slo·gan·eer (slō′gə·nir′) *Informal n.* One who coins or uses slogans. —*v.i.* To coin or use slogans.

sloop (sloōp) *n.* A small sailboat with a single mast and at least one jib. [<Du. *sloep*]

HOMOGRAPH
is a word identical in spelling, having different meanings and origins and, sometimes, pronunciation. It is differentiated by a superior figure such as slop¹ and slop².

slop¹ (slop) *v.* **slopped**, **slop·ping** *v.i.* 1 To splash or spill. 2 To walk or move through slush. —*v.t.* 3 To cause (a liquid) to spill or splash. 4 To feed (a domestic animal) with slops. —**slop over** 1 To overflow and splash. 2 *Slang* To show too much zeal, emotion, etc. —*n.* 1 Slush or watery mud. 2 An unappetizing liquid or watery food. 3 *pl.* Refuse liquid. 4 *pl.* Waste food or swill. [<ME *sloppe* mud]

Sloop

slop² (slop) 1 A loose outer garment, as a smock. 2 *pl.* Articles of clothing and other merchandise sold to sailors on shipboard. [ME *sloppe*]

an organization, or a place in a sequence. —*v.t.* **slot·ted**, **slot·ting** To cut a slot or slots in. [<OF *esclot* the hollow between the breasts]

sloth (slōth, slôth, sloth) *n.* ① Disinclination to exertion; laziness. ② Any of several slow-moving, arboreal mammals of South America. [<SLOW]

sloth·ful (slôth'fəl, slôth'-, sloth'-) *adj.* Inclined to or characterized by sloth. —**sloth'ful·ly** *adv.* —**sloth'ful·ness** *n.* —Syn. lazy, indolent, sluggish, shiftless.

slot machine A vending machine or gambling machine having a slot in which a coin is dropped to cause operation.

Three-toed sloth

slouch (slouch) *v.i.* **1** To have a downcast or drooping gait, look, or posture. **2** To hang or droop carelessly. —*n.* **1** A drooping movement or appearance caused by depression or carelessness. **2** An awkward or incompetent person. [?] —**slouch'y** *adj.* (**·i·er**, **·i·est**) — **slouch'i·ly** *adv.* —**slouch'i·ness** *n.*

slough¹ (slou; slōō *esp. for def.* 2) *n.* **1** A place of deep mud or mire. **2** A stagnant swamp, backwater, etc. **3** A state of great despair or degradation. [<OE *slōh*] —**slough'y** *adj.*

slough² (sluf) *n.* **1** Dead tissue separated and thrown off from living tissue. **2** The skin of a serpent that has been or is about to be shed. —*v.t.* **1** To cast off; shed. **2** To discard; shed, as a habit or a growth. —*v.i.* **3** To be cast off. **4** To cast off a slough or tissue. (ME *slouh*) —**slough'y** *adj.*

Slo·vak (slō'väk, slō'vak) *n.* **1** One of a Slavic people of NW Hungary and parts of Moravia. **2** The language spoken by the Slovaks. —*adj.* Of or pertaining to the Slovaks or to their language. Also **Slo·vak'i·an.**

slov·en (sluv'ən) *n.* One who is habitually untidy, careless, or dirty. [ME *sloveyn*]

Slo·vene (slō'vēn, slō·vēn') *n.* One of a group of s Slavs now living in NW Yugoslavia. —*adj.* Of or pertaining to the Slovenes or to their language. —**Slo·ve'ni·an** *(adj., n.)*

slov·en·ly (sluv'ən·lē) *(adj.)* **·li·er**, **·li·est** Untidy and careless in appearance, work, habits, etc. —*(adv.)* In a slovenly manner. —**slov·en·li·ness** *n.*

slow (slō) *adj.* **1** Taking a long time to move, perform, or occur. **2** Behind the standard time: said of a timepiece. **3** Not hasty: *slow* to anger. **4** Dull in comprehending: a *slow* student. **5** Uninteresting; tedious: a *slow* drama. **6** Denoting a condition of a racetrack that retards the horses' speed. **7** Heating or burning slowly; low: a *slow* flame. **8** Not brisk; slack: Business is *slow.* —*v.t.* & *v.i.* To make or become slow or slower: often with *up* or *down.* —*adv.* In a slow manner. [<OE *slāw*] —**slow'ly** *adv.* —**slow'ness** *n.*

slow-mo·tion (slō'mō'shən) *adj.* **1** Moving or acting at less than normal speed. **2** Denoting a television or motion picture filmed at greater than standard speed so that the action appears slow in normal projection.

sludge (sluj) *n.* **1** Soft, water-soaked mud. **2** A slush of snow or broken or half-formed ice. **3** Muddy or pasty refuse, sediment, etc. [?] —**sludg'y** *adj.* (**·i·er**, **·i·est**)

slue¹ (slōō) *v.* **slued**, **slu·ing** *v.t.* **1** To cause to swing, slide, or skid to the side. **2** To cause to twist or turn. —*v.i.* **3** To

---

DEFINITION
is the meaning. The order in which the different senses of the word are listed is based on frequency of usage.

ILLUSTRATION
to clarify the definitions.

RUN-ON ENTRY
is a word derived from other words by addition or replacement of a suffix, syllabified and stressed where needed.

ETYMOLOGY
is indicated in brackets following the definition giving the origin of the word when it came into the English language.

PART OF SPEECH
follow the pronunciation, and the labels in italics are abbreviated as follows: n. (noun), v. (verb-transitive), v.i. (verb-intransitive), adj. (adjective), adv. (adverb), prep. (preposition), conj. (conjunction), and interj. (interjection).

List of 100 Words Most Frequently Misspelled by College Freshmen

absence	don't	o'clock
accidentally	effect	omitted
across	eighth	parallel
aggravate	embarrassed	perhaps
all right	environment	principal
amateur	exercise	principles
argument	February	privilege
around	forth	proceed
athletic	forty	pronunciation
believed	fourth	quiet
benefited	friend	quite
business	government	received
busy	grammar	recommend
capital	grievance	referred
cemetery	hadn't	relieve
choose	height	rhythm
chosen	indispensable	schedule
coming	interested	seize
committee	its	separate
competition	it's	shining
conscientious	knowledge	stationery
conscious	laboratory	strength
coolly	latter	succeed
council	literature	superintendent
counsel	loose	supersede
criticism	lose	tragedy
deceive	losing	tries
definite	maintenance	truly
desert	marriage	villain
dessert	mischievous	Wednesday
dining	noticeable	weird
disappointed	occasion	whether
doesn't	occurred	woman
	occurrence	

List of Words Frequently Misspelled on Civil Service Examinations

accident	municipal	society
all right	principal	simplified
auxiliary	principle	technicality
athletic	promotional	tendency
buoyant	president	their
catalogue	precede	thousandth
career	proceed	transferred
comptroller	promissory	transient
criticise	recommend	truly
dividend	personnel	villain
embarrass	purchasable	Wednesday
expedient	responsibility	writ
government	received	whether
inveigle	regrettable	yield
monetary	supersede	

Exercise No. 80

Fill in the missing letters to complete the spelling.

1. wearing new cl....s.　　2. soph....more at high school.　　3. army serg....nt.　　4. suffered no ill ....fects.　　5. will not rec....mend his friend.　　6. super....tendent of the apartment house.　　7. old law omit....ed too much.　　8. new law super....edes it.　　9. legal proc....dure.　　10. buy a new diction....ry. 11. was ....fected by the climate.　　12. added money to his princip....　　13. the prophe....y did not come true.　　14. an inter....ting play. 15. shows bad judg....ment.　　16. sadness and lon....liness.　　17. correct pron....ciation. 18. easy consc....nce.　　19. cold in the Ar....tic. 20. cold in the w....rd cem....t....y.

Exercise No. 81

Spell correctly such of the following words as are misspelled below (ignore words spelled correctly).

innocuous	nemonic	accessible
inoculate	morgenatic	agrandize
embarassed	cemetary	plagiarize
harassed	hypocracy	transferrable
inuendo	questionaire	repellant
dessicate	manoeuver	scurrulous
mimicing	tranquility	

Exercise No. 82

Following is a list of nouns. Supply the adjective derived from the same root as the given noun.

a. opacity, inchoation.
b. satiety, abrasion.
c. cacophony, calumny, condignity.
d. acerbity, anomaly, assiduity.
e. contiguity, contumacy, garrulity.
f. misogyny, poignancy.
g. recalcitration, viscosity.
h. viscidity, salubrity, peccancy.
i. onus, parabola, plethora.

Exercise No. 83

Indicate the correct spelling by inserting the vowel or vowels necessary:

invulner....ble	forc....ble
aberr....nt	portent....s
irrefrag....ble	domin....nce
collaps....ble	malf....sance
confection....ry	enforc....ble
invid....s	adapt....ble
hymen....l	adjust....ble
concommit....nt	admiss....ble
coher....nce	dut....s
feas....ble	instantan....sly

BUILDING A VOCABULARY

THE IMPORTANCE OF A GOOD VOCABULARY

In Goethe's *Faust*, Mephistopheles gives this advice to a student:

> To words hold fast!
> Then the safest gate securely pass'd,
> You'll reach the halls of certainty at last.

At least this once we ought to listen to the Devil's counsel. Without in any way trying to raise the devil, psychologists have reached the same conclusions about vocabulary. Research carried out at such institutions as Stanford University and Dr. Johnson O'Connor's Human Engineering Laboratory verified that size and accuracy of vocabulary provide two of the most reliable guides to a man's **general ability** and, consequently, to his **potential for success.** Guided by these findings, businessmen and industrialists, before hiring would-be young executives, often test their vocabularies as well as their special knowledge. Federal, state, and municipal agencies also commonly test vocabulary as part of their examinations for various posts. Likewise, schools and colleges have discovered that good vocabulary and good work are closely related. For all of this, we are giving the devil his due.

To just how many words do men hold fast? All answers have been debated. Estimates of the average vocabulary range from 3,000 words to 12,000. Those who read extensively may, however, have **recognition vocabularies** exceeding 50,000 words. None debate this fact: whatever the number of words in a man's vocabulary, he can easily add to it—and benefit from the addition. Before studying the steps by which vocabulary can be improved, it will be useful to understand the differences between the kinds of vocabularies.

Speaking Vocabulary—most limited of the vocabularies, it consists of the words used in conversation.

The cat is a self-centered animal, thinking only of itself, almost never of the world about it.

Writing Vocabulary—more extensive than the *speaking* vocabulary, it consists of the words used in conversation and, if the writer has a wide reading background, many thousands more.

The cat is an *egocentric* creature, *tranquil* in its *self-assurance, oblivious* of the world about it.

Reading Vocabulary—larger than either the *speaking* or *writing* vocabularies (both of which it includes), it contains words which the reader can define when he sees them, even though he neither speaks nor writes them.

"The cat understands *pure being*, which is all we need to know and which it takes us a lifetime to learn. It is both *subject* and *object*. It is its own *outlet* and its own *material*. . . . The cat has a complete *subjective unity*. Being its own centre, it *radiates* electricity in all directions. It is *magnetic* and *impervious*."

(Van Vechten, *Peter Whiffle*)

Recognition Vocabulary—largest of the vocabularies, it contains, in addition to the other three, those words which one has seen or heard previously, but cannot clearly define. He may recognize them in *context* (how they are used in the sentence), but he lacks assurance about their actual meaning.

> When you notice a cat in *profound* meditation,
> The reason, I tell you, is always the same:
> His mind is engaged in a *rapt* contemplation
> Of the thought, of the thought, of the thought of his name:
> His *ineffable effable*
> Effanineffable

113

Deep and *inscrutable singular* Name.
      (T. S. Eliot, *The Naming of Cats**)

The *erudite partisan* of cats understands that on the rare occasions when *felines* gather, they do so in a *"clowder"* and kittens in a *"kendle."* (adapted from a letter to The London *Times*) Thus, anyone who intends to improve his vocabulary must learn how to transfer into his speaking and writing vocabularies, appropriate words from his reading and recognition vocabularies. To effect the transfer involves work, but the reward is proportionate to the effort.

FOR PRACTICE: The following sentences have been selected from newspapers, speeches, magazines, books, and the like. How many of the italicized words can you define or provide a synonym for?

Next to each word, indicate to which of your four vocabularies (**speaking, writing, reading, recognition**) it belongs. Then note at the end of the exercise the sources from which the material was taken. Evaluate your own vocabulary.

* From Old Possum's Book of Practical Cats, copyright, 1939, by T. S. Eliot. Reprinted by permission of Harcourt, Brace and Company, Inc.

1. Television is here with us, *clamoring* for understanding and wise application.
2. Although Italian wines of honorable *lineage* are relatively available, wine-drinkers know little about them beyond the *ubiquitous Chianti*.
3. Those days were gone, the old brave innocent *tumultuous eupeptic tomorrowless* days.
4. Study of *scriptural* teachings, *unencumbered* by *ecclesiastical dogma*, may help to determine a *criterion* of convincing faith.
5. That *subtle* something which *effuses* behind the *whirl* of *animation*, a happy and joyous public spirit, as *distinguish'd* from a *sluggish* and *saturnine* one.

SOURCES:

1. Speaker at Town Meeting of the Air.
2. Article on wines in New York *Times Magazine*.
3. William Faulkner, *Requiem for a Nun*.
4. Letter to member of radio panel.
5. Walt Whitman, *Specimen Days*.

METHODS OF BUILDING VOCABULARY

Many roads lead to a strong vocabulary and in this section we will map several of them, first indicating some well-paved routes and some dangerous soft shoulders.

Make your study of words a passionate pursuit, not a painful prowl. When you see *denim* advertised as one of the more popular fabrics for summer wear, do you wonder why it goes by that name? If you turn eagerly to the dictionary to discover the answer, you have an affection for words that will inevitably lead to a better vocabulary.

But if, when you come upon a sentence like this:

How can the party leaders predict victory when most of the electorate are *Mugwumps?* you pass on in ignorance to the next sentence or grudgingly look up *Mugwump* in the dictionary, you are not even on a painful prowl—you are in ignoble ignorance.

Learn words that you intend to use in speaking, writing, and reading. **Don't try to learn mere lists of words.**

A Poor Method

ephemeral	short-lived
acrimonious	bitter
ubiquitous	omnipresent
clandestine	secret
obdurate	stubborn

Lists provide ineffectual study aids because:

They fail to tell whether the word is suitable for speaking, writing, or reading (since they give no reference to where or how the word was used).

They become too long and cannot easily be memorized.

They mistake **quantity** as the purpose of vocabulary building; quality (usefulness, relevance) is quite as important.

An Effective Method

1. Enter in a small notebook or on 3 × 5 index cards only those words you want to use. Discuss only one word on a page or card.

2. List the following information from the dictionary:

    a. Meanings of the word.

    b. Spelling, pronunciation, syllabication, part of speech.

    c. Origin (etymology), roots.

    d. Use as other part of speech.

    e. Synonyms, antonyms.

    Note: Reread the passage about the dictionary in Section 5: **Spelling.**

3. Copy out the sentence in which you found the word. Leave space for other sentences you may come upon.

4. Jot down examples of how you have used the word in speaking or writing.

5. Keep your notebook or pack of cards handy, and study it daily. Find occasions where you can use the word in speaking and writing. (See Below)

USING THE FAMILY OF TONGUES The word *mother* has cognates (words related in origin) in many languages:

mutter—German	*meter*—Greek
moeder—Danish	*madre*—Spanish
modhir—Icelandic	*mère*—French
mater—Latin	

After many centuries of examining interrelationships of this kind, scholars have recently discovered that men living in countries ranging from Central Asia to Western Europe speak languages derived from a parent or source language whose origin dates back about 4000 years. This parent language is commonly known as Indo-European and gave rise to the following languages:

Eastern

Sanskrit (now dead); neo-Sanskrit languages of India: Hindi, Bengali, etc.

Indo-Iranian: Persian

Armenian

Western

Celtic: Irish, Scottish, Welsh, Breton, Cornish

Italic: Latin (and other dialects like Umbrian, Etruscan); Modern Romance languages: Italian, French, Spanish, Portuguese

Hellenic: Greek

Baltic:

    EAST: Russian, Ukrainian

    WEST: Polish, Czech, Slovene

Teutonic: ENGLISH, Dutch, German, Scandinavian

Modern English passed through several stages before becoming what it is today:

Old English (Anglo-Saxon) A.D. 450–A.D. 1100.

		SYLLABICATION	PART OF SPEECH
word	**EPHEMERAL**		
pronunciation		(i fem′ar al), e-phem-er-al,	adjective
origin	Greek: *ephemeros,* of or for only one day		
meaning	Defin.—lasting but a short time, short-lived, transitory		
other uses	*ephemera*—noun; *ephemerally*—adverb		
synonym, antonym	Synonyms: *fleeting, evanescent, transient*		
	Antonyms: *permanent, lasting, eternal*		
how it is used	"All is *ephemeral*—fame and the famous as well."		
	(Marcus Aurelius, *Meditations*)		
space for other examples			
Student's use of	We waste too much time fretting about *ephemeral* things like clothes and dates. We ought to pay more heed to lasting matters. (Letter to Ed Smith)		

Typical Anglo-Saxon contributions:

ARTICLES: *the, a, an*

PRONOUNS: *that, which*

PREPOSITIONS: *in, for, to, from, without*

CONJUNCTIONS: *and, but*

VERBS: *are, have, could, sit, see, run, send*

NOUNS: *mother, father, wife, husband, house, door, bed*

Note: Many Latin words survived from the earlier period of Roman occupation, and yet more were added when Roman missionaries began to arrive in the sixth century. About these words, more will be said later.

A Danish invasion in the eighth century added yet more monosyllabic words to the English vocabulary: *leg, sky, skin,* and the pronoun, *they.*

Middle English 1100–1500

The Norman Conquest in 1066 introduced the French language to England. French has since that time deeply influenced English vocabulary, particularly words about food, clothing, law, government, and the like:

mauve	felony	debris	bagatelle
adroit	grimace	intrigue	grotesque
clique	ingénue	ennui	denouement
svelte	chauvinism	renaissance	silhouette
cliché	detour	genre	puissant

Modern English 1500–present

Early Modern English: 16th–17th centuries
Later Modern English: 18th–19th centuries
Contemporary English: Since 1900

From 1500 forward, as commerce increased, and England's contacts with the continent and the East grew, the vocabulary of the English lan-

---

SOME ENGLISH BORROWINGS FROM FOREIGN COUNTRIES (Latin and Greek will be taken separately)

ITALY	SPAIN	MEXICO	GERMANY	RUSSIA	HUNGARY	NETHERLANDS
incognito	renegade	lasso	kindergar-	vodka	goulash	skipper
salvo	corral	ranch	ten	czar	vampire	schooner
gusto	peccadillo	mesa	strafe	sable	tokay	yacht
confetti	flotilla	canyon	blitzkrieg	polka	hussar	sloop
vendetta	Negro	coyote	waltz	steppe		dock
balcony	mosquito	tomato				hull
gondola	tornado					
ditto						
bandit						
contraband						

AFRICA	PERSIA	ARABIA	SANSKRIT	HEBREW	TURKEY	EGYPT
oasis	pyjama	alcohol	indigo	amen	angora	gypsy
tangerine	chess	algebra	chintz	seraph	fez	gum
gorilla	jackal	coffee	ginger	jubilee	ottoman	paper
chimpanzee	bazaar	nadir		balsam	horde	
canary	divan	zenith		Sabbath		
		garbage		cherub		
		cipher				

INDIA	AMERICAN INDIAN	JAPAN	CHINA	MALAYA	POLYNESIA	AUSTRALIA
polo	tomahawk	kimono	tea	ketchup	tattoo	kangaroo
coolie	wigwam	geisha	chop suey	gingham	taboo	boomerang
rupee	skunk	jinrikisha	joss	caddy		
khaki	succotash	jiu-jitsu	sampan	gong		
curry	tobacco		soy	junk		

guage expanded tremendously. The preceding list merely suggests some of the borrowings which have entered our vocabulary from foreign sources.

Increasingly, Americans have realized that they live, not as a single group of people separated from the rest of the world by two oceans, but as one among a great family of nations. Not at all strange, then, is the fact that language too knows no boundaries, that English as known and spoken today is a composite of many foreign tongues. If, therefore, you build vocabulary from your knowledge of words borrowed from these foreign tongues, you can prove even better to yourself and to those about you that no man is alone.

Exercise No. 84

PART 1. Make a list of words borrowed from the Italian for the following subjects:

MUSIC	PAINTING	LITERATURE
EXAMPLE: *solo*	*chiaroscuro*	*sonnet*

PART 2. One word has been omitted from each of the following sentences. From the list of foreign borrowings below, select the appropriate word to complete each sentence. Check the meaning and pronunciation of each word in your dictionary.

a. Surely not for this, merely whistling at the passing parade, a trifle, a _____, not for this can you hang me.

b. Blindly, zealously patriotic, ignoring his own safety, Corporal Essex, a _____ to the end, gave his life for Zanzibar.

c. Wedgwood china is famed for the delicate _____ patterns which adorn it.

d. Stop wheedling! She is not the type you can _____ into making you the beneficiary of her will.

e. What might have been a happy marriage between Romeo and Juliet became instead a tragedy because of a _____ between their families.

f. No further misfortunes can befall Stella Dallas, for she is already at the _____ of her luck.

g. When Senator Flannellip really gets warmed up to his speech—about ten hours from now —we can be sure that the _____ will last for at least a week.

h. His yawl has two masts; our _____ has but one.

i. Love is the state in which man sees things most widely different from what they are. The force of illusion reaches its _____ here, sweetened and transfigured to new heights.

j. Fame pursues me, but I wish only to be obscure, to be nameless, to move _____ among the throng.

vendetta (Italian)	nadir (Arabic)
bas-relief (French)	sloop (Dutch)
incognito (Italian)	peccadillo (Spanish)
zenith (Arabic)	chauvinist (French)
cajole (French)	filibuster (Spanish)

BUILDING VOCABULARY WITH ROOTS

A root (or *stem*) is that part of a word which contains the core of meaning:

fin, meaning "boundary," is the root of such words as:

*fin*ish—to bring to an end (or, to bring to the boundary)

*fin*ite—measurable (or, having bounds)

in*fin*ity—having no bounds

de*fin*ite—precisely bounded

aster, meaning "star," is the root of such words as:

*aster*isk—the star-shaped figure used in writing as a mark of reference

*astr*onomy—the law (or, the study of the scientific laws) of the stars

dis*aster*—an unfortunate event (or, something away from the stars. *See note below*)

The greatest number of roots in English derive from the classical languages, Latin and Greek (*fin*, in the example above, is a Latin root; *aster* is a Greek root). By learning several Latin and Greek roots (there are about 160 in all, but you need not try to learn every root), you increase your mastery of words in two important ways:

You will understand more clearly the essential meaning of each part of a word by observing how roots are combined to form words:

nostos, home + *algia*, sickness = nostalgia

tele, far off + *phonos*, sound = telephone

epi, upon + *dermis*, skin = epidermis

dia, through + *therme*, heat = diathermy

peri, around + *skopein*, look = periscope

chronos, time + *meter*, measure = chronometer

You will learn words in groups by observing

how several words relate to a common root:

equ, equal, just

equal	inequality	equivocable
equate	equity	equinox
equable	adequate	equilibrium
equality	inadequate	equivalent

voc, vok, to call

vocation	avocation	revoke
vociferate	invocation	provoke
vociferous	convoke	evoke
advocate	invoke	

Note: Some words, as you have seen, follow the literal meaning of their roots, but others are only secondarily derived. *Astronomy*, for example, means literally *the law of the stars*. But *disaster, away from the stars*, does not literally signify the actual meaning of the word. Thus, you cannot force the literal meaning of the root upon all words. But, as with *disaster*, where the relationship between superstition and misfortune is implied, you can profit from understanding the correlation between the root meaning and the actual meaning.

You do not need to know Latin or Greek to profit from the tables printed below any more

A SELECTED LIST OF WORDS DERIVED FROM LATIN ROOTS (A)

ROOT	MEANING	CURRENT WORDS
AG agere	do, drive, act	agent, coagulate, actor
AM amo, amare	love	amorous, amatory, amour
ANIM animus	mind, soul life; intention	animal, animate, unanimous, magnanimous, pusillanimous; animadversion, animosity
BELL bellus	beautiful, fair	belle, belladonna+, belle-lettres
BELL bellum	war	bellicose, belligerent, rebel
CED, CESS cedere, cessus	go, yield	succeed, cede, secede, recede, process, excess, recess, abscess+
CENT centum	hundred	century, centennial
CIT citare	summon arouse	recite, excite, cite, incite
CIV civis	citizen	civic, civilization, civil, civilian
COGNIT cognoscere, cognitus	know	cognizant, incognito, cognition
COR, CORD cor, cordis	heart	core+, accord+, concord+, discord+, cordial, courage
CORP corpus	body	corpse, corps, corporal (punishment), corset, corporation+
CRED credere	believe, credit	credit, creditor, discredit, credible, credence, incredible, incredulous
CULP culpa	offense, fault	culprit, culpable
CUR, CURS cursor, currere	run	current, concourse, cursory+, precursor, discursive+

Note: Words whose meanings are secondarily derived from the root are marked +. Use your dictionary to determine the relationship between root and meaning.

than you need to know Old English, Danish, or French to speak and write effective English. Learn a few roots at a time and put them to work, first in the exercises, and then in your reading. When you come upon an unfamiliar word like *bicephalous*, don't turn immediately to the dictionary. Ask:

What does it seem to mean in context?

What is the meaning of *bi?* The answer is *two*. What is the meaning of *cephalous?* The answer is *head*.

Thus, you combine reading in context with a knowledge of roots, a significant advance towards word mastery.

Exercise No. 85

Note: Complete all of these exercises before proceeding to the next group of roots.

PART 1. For each of the LATIN ROOTS (A) above, add at least two current words not already listed.

PART 2. Complete the following sentences by selecting the appropriate choice from the list of CURRENT WORDS.

(All words are selected from the LATIN (A) roots and derivatives above.)

a. In 1981, to mark its 200th birthday, Los Angeles held a _____.

b. The speaker used harsh, fiery language in his effort to _____ the mob to fury.

c. The _____ man turns away from his enemy in craven and abject fear; the courageous man,

A SELECTED LIST OF WORDS DERIVED FROM LATIN ROOTS (B)

ROOT	MEANING	CURRENT WORDS
DEXTER dexter	right hand	dexterous, ambidextrous
DIC, DICT dicere, dictus	say, speak	dictate, predict, contradict, dedicate
DIGN dignus	worthy	dignify, condign, indignity
DUC, DUCE ducere, ductus	lead, bring	ductile, induce, deduce, product, duke, conduit
DUR durus	hard	duress, endure, obdurate+
FAC, FACT facere, factus	do, make, act	fact, factory, facsimile, effect, manufacture, factitious+, factotum
FALL fallere	deceive, err, be deceived	fallacious, fallacy, fallible, infallible
FERR ferre	bear, carry, bring	ferry, infer, transfer, refer, fertile+, suffer, defer
FERV fervere	boil	fervid, effervesce, fervor
GEN, GENER genus, generis	class, kind, race	genus, generic, general, engender, generate
GRAD, GRESS gradi, gressus	walk, go, step	gradual, digress, egress, graduate, transgress, aggression
GRAND grandis	great	aggrandize, grandiose, grandeur
IT ite, itus	go	exit, circuit, itinerant+
JECT jacere, jectus	throw, hurl	deject, inject
JUR jurare	swear	jury, abjure, perjure+
LABOR labor	work	laboratory, elaborate, collaborate, laborious

although _____ of the dangers ahead, faces the enemy and _____ taunts him.

d. To prevent the _____ agitated autograph-hunters from becoming too _____ in their attentions, the actor, although generally cordial and _____ toward his admirers, was compelled to disguise himself and mingle _____ among the wildly _____ throng.

e. A hasty, _____ study of roots will result in failure. If, however, one approaches them with diligence and enthusiasm, not _____, his vocabulary will _____ rather than _____.

CURRENT WORDS

succeed	recede	cursory
animadversion	belligerently	animated
incognito	magnanimous	incite
centennial	pusillanimous	cognizant
incredibly	amorous	

Exercise No. 86

Note: Complete all of these exercises before proceeding to the next group of roots.

PART 1. For each of the LATIN ROOTS (B) above, add at least two current words not already listed.

PART 2. Complete the following sentences by selecting the appropriate choice from the list of CURRENT WORDS:

a. The central _____ in his reasoning lies in his hard-headed, _____ assumption that _____ poets write better verse than those who can use only their left hand.

b. Although it is a _____ metal, gold would be too expensive to use in laying _____.

c. Jeeves, _____ extraordinary, was held in _____ because he _____ himself before a jury to support a clearly absurd, _____ defense.

d. Ants, _____ in their eagerness to build an empire, raid weaker foes expecting through victory to _____ their holdings in land and slaves.

e. To _____ one's solemnly dictated vow not only contradicts but also _____ the laws of human decency.

A SELECTED LIST OF WORDS DERIVED FROM LATIN ROOTS (C)

ROOT	MEANING	CURRENT WORDS
LOQU, LOC loquor, locutus	talk, speak	elocution, loquacious, grandiloquent, soliloquy, colloquial, obloquy
MEDI medius	middle, between	immediate+, medieval, mediate, medium
MIT, MISS, MISE mittere, missus	send, throw	emit, permit, commit, omission, permission, dismiss, demise+, missile, missive
MON, MONIT monere, monitus	warn, advise, remind	monument, admonition+, premonition
MOR, MORT mors, mortis	death	mortal, immortal, mortician, mortgage+, mortify
NASC, NAT nascitur	to be born	nascent, natal, nature, renascence
NOMIN nomen	name	name, nomenclature, cognomen, nominate, ignominious, nominal+
NOV novus	new	novel, innovate, novice, novitiate, renovate, novelty
OMNI omnis	all	omniscient, omnipotent, omnipresent, omnibus
PARL parlare	speak	parliament, parley, parlance, parlor
PLIC plicare	twine, twist	explicate+, complicate+, implicate+
PONDU pondus	weight	ponderous, imponderable+, preponderance+
PORT portare	carry, bring, bear	portable, transport, porter, export, importance+
RAP, RAPT rapio	seize, grasp	rape, rapine, rapture+, rapacious

CURRENT WORDS

ambidextrous	conduit	ductile
duress	obdurate	factitious
factotum	fallacy	fervid
transgress	aggrandize	abjure
perjure		

Exercise No. 87

Note: Complete all of these exercises before proceeding to the next group of roots.

PART 1. For each of the LATIN ROOTS (c) above, add at least two current words not already listed.

PART 2. Complete the following sentences by selecting the appropriate choice from the list of CURRENT WORDS opposite:

a. Whether her diction is literary or _____, the _____ Bluestocking female makes herself unpleasantly audible at all times. It is impossible to insult or _____ her, for she heeds no _____ to be silent. Conscious only of what she stupidly believes to be her supreme _____, she proceeds to analyze and to _____ the weighty, _____ problems of the universe.

b. So long as man's _____ desires for wealth and glory persist, the hopes of the world for a spiritual _____ must suffer _____ defeat, even

as they did five hundred years ago in _____ times.

CURRENT WORDS

loquacious	colloquial	medieval
admonition	mortify	renascence
ignominious	omniscience	explicate
imponderable	rapacious	

Exercise No. 88

Note: Complete all of these exercises before proceeding to the next group of roots.

PART 1. For each of the LATIN (D) roots below, add at least two current words not already listed.

PART 2. Complete the following sentences by selecting the appropriate choice from the list of CURRENT WORDS.

a. I doubt that Tom Wolfe, for all his self-concern and _____ ever gained the kind of insight and _____ that makes for a truly great novelist.

b. Paul's daughter was an evil, _____ foul-mouthed _____.

c. The _____ of our creed may seem harsh and _____, but if we hold _____ to them, the danger we face from our _____ will diminish.

d. Kaye's collection of empty Scotch bottles was

A SELECTED LIST OF WORDS DERIVED FROM LATIN ROOTS (D)

ROOT	MEANING	CURRENT WORDS
SED, SESS sedere, sessus	sit	sedentary, reside, sedate, sedan
SPEC, SPECT specere, spectus	look, see, appear	spectacle, prospectus, specie, spectator, conspicuous, introspect, perspicacious
STRING, STRICT stringere, strictus	bind, draw tight	strict, stringent, constrict, restrain, strait, distress
TANG tangere	touch	tangible, contact, tangent
TEN, TIN tenere	hold	tenable, tenure, pertinacity, tenant, tenet
TORT, TORQ torquere	twist	torque, tortuous, distort, retort, torture, contortion
TRACT trahere	draw	abstract+, attract, detract, traction, tractor, protract
VERS, VERT vertere	turn	avert, aversion, adversary, controversy+, extrovert, introvert
VIR vir	man	virago, virile, virtuous
VOC, VOK vocare	call	convoke, vocalize, advocate, vociferous+, avocation, evoke
VOL velle	wish	volition, benevolence, voluntary, volunteer, malevolent

_____ evidence that he had lied when he _____ insisted that he had an _____ to liquor.

CURRENT WORDS

introspection	perspicacity	stringent
tangible	tenaciously	tenets
vociferously	malevolent	virile
adversary	virago	aversion

Exercise No. 89

Note: Complete all of these exercises before proceeding to the next group of roots.

PART 1.   For each of the GREEK ROOTS (A), below, add at least two current words not already listed.

PART 2.   Complete the following sentences by se-lecting the appropriate choice from the list of CURRENT WORDS opposite:

a. The _____, obsessed with beauty, often leads a contemplative, _____ existence, devoid of physical activity.
b. A society that permits itself to settle into _____, forgetting that nations are an _____ of different peoples and ideas, is ripe for a _____.
c. For the _____ of perhaps his most celebrated play, Moliére chose a thoroughly unpleasant _____, the very _____ of a man-hater.

CURRENT WORDS

amalgam	sedentary	esthete
misanthrope	demagogue	protagonist
archetype	homogeneity	

A SELECTED LIST OF WORDS DERIVED FROM GREEK ROOTS (A)

ROOT	MEANING	CURRENT WORDS
AESTH aisthomai	feel, perceive	aesthetics, esthete, anesthetic+
AGOG agogos	lead, bring	demagogue, synagogue
AGON agon	contest, struggle	protagonist, antagonist, agony
ANTHROP anthropos	man	anthropology, misanthrope, philanthropist, anthropomorphic
ARCH arche	rule, govern	anarchy, archives, archetype, oligarchy, hierarchy
BIBL biblos, biblion	book	bible, bibliophile, bibliography, bibliomania
BIO bio	life	biology, biography, biotic, biophysics
CHRON chronos	time	chronicle, chronoscope, chronic, chronology, synchronize
DEM demos	people	democrat, demagogue, demotic+, epidemic, endemic
DYNAM dynamos	power	dynamic, aerodynamics, dynamometer, dynamo, dynamite
GAM gamos	marriage	monogamy, polygamy, bigamy, amalgam+
GE geo	earth	geography, geology, geodetic, geometry
GRAPH graphein	write	autograph, biography, graphic+, stenography, phonograph, or-thography, graph

Note: Almost all the sciences append the root LOGY, the science of:

anthropology	criminology	geology
archaeology	demonology	histology
bacteriology	entomology	meteorology
biology	genealogy	mythology

morphology	philology	theology
ornithology	physiology	zoology
pathology	psychology	

Not all words that end in -*logy*, however, refer to sciences: e.g., *analogy, tautology,* eulogy, trilogy. How many others can you name?

Exercise No. 90

Note: Complete all of these exercises before proceeding to the next group of roots.

PART 1. For each of the GREEK ROOTS (B), below, add at least two current words not already listed.

PART 2. Complete the following sentences by selecting the appropriate choice from the list of CURRENT WORDS opposite:

a. When a _____, fresh to the art of word study, begins to delve into _____, each prefix, suffix, and root assumes _____ importance.

b. Each man, proud of his quirks, _____, and _____, regards himself as sane, the other fellow as _____.

c. Gossip columnists, unimportant as their efforts are, nevertheless do on occasion act as _____ of sorts, adding to our vocabularies _____ like "palimony," "glitterati" and similar terms common to our _____ social life.

d. _____ toward the need for _____ in diction, many writers clutch indifferently at any word and thus submit their readers to harsh, _____ prose.

CURRENT WORDS

idiosyncrasies	cosmic	etymology
neologisms	neophyte	apathetic
euphony	cacophonic	neurotic
monomanias	cosmopolitan	philologists

Exercise No. 91

PART 1. For each of the GREEK ROOTS (C), p. 125, add at least two current words not already listed.

A SELECTED LIST OF WORDS DERIVED FROM GREEK ROOTS (B)

ROOT	MEANING	CURRENT WORDS
IDIO idios	one's own peculiar	idiom, idiosyncrasy, idiot+
ISO isos	equal	isosceles, isotope, isobar
KOSM kosmos	universe, order	cosmos, cosmic, cosmography, cosmetic, cosmopolitan
KRAT kratia	power	democracy, aristocrat, plutocrat, theocrat, bureaucrat
LOG logos	word, speech, science	logic, eulogy, etymology, philology, psychology
METER, METR	measure	diameter, metronome, symmetry
MON, MONO monos	alone	monogamy, monosyllable, monomania, monogram+, monocle+, monolith
NOM nomos	law	deuteronomy, economy
NEO neos	new	neologism, neolithic, neophyte
NEUR neuron	nerve, tendon	neuralgia, neurasthenia, neuritis, neurotic, psychoneurosis
ONYM onyma	name	pseudonym, homonym, anonymous
ORTHO ortho	correct	orthodontia, orthography+, orthodox
PATH pathos	feeling	sympathy, pathos, apathetic, antipathy
PHIL philos	loving, friendly, fond	philanthropist, Philadelphia, philosophy, philharmonic, philology
PHONE phonos	sound	phonetic, telephone, phonology, phonograph, euphony, cacophony
PHYSI physis	nature	physiology+, physicist+, physic, physiognomy

PART 2. Complete the following sentences by selecting the appropriate choice from the list of CURRENT WORDS below:

a. If many more people seek help for the future on the leather couch of the _____, advocates of the ancient art of reading the _____ will have to close shop.

b. Three-dimensional movies may represent the _____ of low taste in twentieth century entertainment, but their _____, the nineteenth century _____ must be held responsible for starting the fad.

CURRENT WORDS

prototype   stereopticon   zodiac
psychoanalyst archetype

BUILDING VOCABULARY WITH PREFIXES AND SUFFIXES

A prefix is a syllable or syllables placed (*fixed*) before (*pre-*) a word to qualify its meaning:

vocation means an occupation or trade, or, literally, *a calling.*

avocation means a hobby, a secondary occupation, or, literally, *away from a calling.*

The meaning of *avocation* has been changed, modified, or qualified by placing before it the prefix *a- (ab-)* meaning *away from.*

A suffix is a syllable or syllables placed after a word to qualify its meaning:

measure means dimension, size, or quantity.
measurable means capable of being measured.

The meaning of *measurable* has been modified by adding to *measure* the suffix *-able (-ible)* meaning *capable of being measured.*

Note that the suffix does not change the meaning of a word as drastically as does the prefix, but it does change the grammatical function. Both *avocation* and *vocation* are nouns, but the noun *measure*, because of the addition of the suffix, has become an adjective, *measurable*. Likewise, the adjective *loose* becomes an adverb when the suffix *-ly* is added (*loosely*), and the verb *commit* becomes a noun when the suffix *-sion* is added (*commission*).

Note: Certain minor changes in spelling frequently occur. These are intended to make pronunciation easier.

Most of the prefixes and suffixes in modern English derive from Old English, Latin, and Greek. They are so numerous that it is impossible to list all of them, and almost futile to try to learn every one that is listed. However, by learn-

A SELECTED LIST OF WORDS DERIVED FROM GREEK ROOTS (C)

ROOT	MEANING	CURRENT WORDS
POLI polis	city	metropolis, politician+, police+, policy+, cosmopolitan+
PSYCHE psyche	mind	psychic, psychology, psychiatry+, psychoanalysis, psychotic+, metempsychosis
PYR pyr	fire	pyre, pyromaniac, pyrotechnics
SCOP skopein	see	scope, telescope, stereoscopic, stethoscope, microscope, bishop+
SOPH sophos	wise	sophomore, philosophy, sophist+, sophisticate+, theosophy
TELE tele	far	telescope, telephone, telegraph, teleology+, telepathy
THERM therme	heat	thermal, thermometer, thermostat
TYP typos	model, impression	typical, archetype, antitype, atypical
TOP topos	a place	topography, topic+, topical+
ZO zoon	animal	zoo, zoology, zodiac+, protozoa

ing the strategic affixes, you take another long stride toward improving vocabulary:

By combining your knowledge of roots with knowledge of prefixes and suffixes, you can analyze a surprisingly large number of words:

inscription, for example, breaks down into:

ROOT: *scrip,* meaning write (Latin, *scribere*)

PREFIX: *in-,* meaning on (Latin, *in-*)

SUFFIX: *-tion,* meaning act of, state of, that which (Latin, *-tion*)

Thus (note that the definition emerges as you work *backward* from SUFFIX to ROOT to PREFIX) *inscription* means literally *the act of writing on.* The context in which the word appears usually makes the meaning more specific:

Walter found the author's *inscription* on the flyleaf.

The tombstone bore the *inscription* of the dead man's date of birth and of death.

By observing the effect suffixes have on the words you study, you add depth to your vocabulary by learning several parts of speech derived from a single word:

rational—adjective

rationalism—noun (*-ism* means state of being)

rationalize—verb (*-ize* means to make)

rationally—adverb (*-ly* means similar, or having the quality of)

Some Techniques for Changing Parts of Speech by Using Prefixes and Suffixes

To derive verbs from nouns:

Add the suffix *-ize*

terror—terrorize	drama—dramatize
economy—economize	anesthesia—anesthetize

Add the prefix *en-* or *in-*

slave—enslave	franchise—enfranchise
trench—entrench	grain—ingrain

A SELECTED LIST OF PREFIXES AND SUFFIXES FROM LATIN (A)

PREFIX	MEANING	CURRENT WORDS
AB- (a-, abs-)	from, away from	abnormal, abduct, absent, avert
AD- (a-, ac-, af-, ag-, al-, an-, ap-, ar-, as-, at-) (these varied forms are used to effect euphonious combinations with the several roots)		
AMBI-	both	ambidextrous, ambivalent, ambiguous
ANTE-	before	antedate, anteroom, antecedent
BI- (bis-)	two, twice	biped, bicycle, bimonthly, bisect
BENE-	good, well	beneficial, benevolent
CIRCUM-	around	circumstance, circumvent, circumnavigate, circumlocution
CON- (com-, co-, col-, cor-)	with	congress, colloquy, coeducation, correlate
CONTRA- (contro-, counter-)	against	contradict, controversy, countermand
DE-	from, down (negative meaning)	denounce, decry, decapitate, debase, degrade
DI- (dis-, dif-)	from, away (negative meaning)	divert, dispell, dismiss, dishonest, differ, diffuse
EQUI-	equal	equanimity, equilateral, equation
EX-	former	ex-president, ex-governor
EX- (e-, ef-, ec-)	out, from, away	exotic, exit, enervate, effulgent, ecstasy
EXTRA-	outside, beyond	extracurricular, extraordinary, extravagant, extraneous, extraterrestrial
IN- (il-, im-, ir-)	in, into, on (used with verbs and nouns)	intrude, induce, illuminate, import, imbibe, irrigate
IN- (il-, im-, ir-, ig-)	not (used with adjectives)	indecent, illiterate, improper, irreducible, ignoble, ignominious

To derive nouns from verbs:

Add the suffixes *-tion, -ion, -sion, -ation*

denounce—denunciation   compile—compilation
compel—compulsion   transpose—
                        transposition

Add the suffixes *-al, -se, -ment, -iture, -ance*

refuse—refusal   expend—expense
govern—government   buoy—buoyance

Add the suffixes *-er, -or, -ant, -ent*

audit—auditor   labor—laborer
expedite—expedient   supply—supplicant

To derive adjectives from nouns:

Add the suffixes *-ful, -less, -ious, -ous, -y*

hope—hopeful   end—endless   beauty—
sorrow—   chill—chilly   beauteous
  sorrowful   ambition—
                                  ambitious

Add the suffixes *-al, -ic, -ish, -an, -ary, -ed*

nature—natural   fever—feverish
psychosis—psychotic Sweden—Swedish
imagination—imaginary America—American

To derive nouns from adjectives:

Add the suffixes *-ness, -ity, -ce, -cy*

happy—happiness   loquacious—loquacity
romantic—romance   fragrant—fragrance

To derive verbs from adjectives:

Add the suffixes *-ize, -en, -fy*

fertile—fertilize   liquid—liquefy
thick—thicken   solid—solidify

To derive adjectives from verbs:

Add the suffixes *-able, -ible, -ive*

reverse—reversible   evade—evasive
manage—manageable   repair—reparable

To derive adverbs from adjectives:

Add the suffix *-ly*

handy—handily   excitable—excitably
angry—angrily   false—falsely

Add the suffix *-wise*

likewise, lengthwise

A SELECTED LIST OF PREFIXES AND SUFFIXES FROM LATIN (B)

PREFIX	MEANING	CURRENT WORDS
INFRA-	under, beneath	infra-red, infra-dig
INTER-	between, among	interurban, international, interchange, interfere, interpose
INTRA-	inside, within	intramural, introvert, introspect, intravenous
MAL- (male-)	bad	malefactor, malevolent, malformed, malocclusion
MULTI-	much, many	multiply, multitude, multicolor
NON-	not (*in-* and *un-* are usually more emphatic)	nonexistent, nonsense, non-Christian
OB- (o-, oc-, of-, op-)	against, out	obstruct, obdurate, obsolete, omit, occult, offend, oppose
PER-	through, throughout	persist, pertinent, perceive, perennial
POST-	after	postpone, postscript, post-graduate
PRE-	before (in *time* or *place*)	precede, predict, prevent, pre-war, prepay
PRO-	forward, in favor of	proceed, provoke, project, propose, pronoun, pro-American
RE-	again, back	repeat, return, remind, recall, refulgent, rebuild, reaffirm
RETRO-	back, backward	retroactive, retrospect, retrogress, retrograde
SINE-	without	sinecure, *sine die*
SUB- (suc-, suf-, sug-, sup-, sus-)	under, beneath	submarine, submerge, succinct, succumb, succubus, suffer, suggest, supplant, suspect
SUPER- (sur-)	above, over	superimpose, superficial, surpass, surfeit
TRANS- (tra-)	across, over	transport, transfer, transmit, traduce, traverse
TRI-	three	triangle, triumvirate
ULTRA-	beyond, outside, unusual, extreme	ultramodern, ultraconservative, ultramarine
UNI-	one	unity, uniform, unilateral, university

Note: Other suffixes related to parts of speech are listed in the tables below.

By observing the effect *prefixes* have on the words you study, you add depth to your vocabulary by learning *antonyms* (words opposed in meaning, as *good-bad, right-wrong*) for any given word:

rational—irrational (*ir-* means "not," "against")
practical—impractical (*im-* means "not")
ordinary—extraordinary (*extra-* means "in addition to")
territorial—extraterritorial

Learn a few prefixes and suffixes at a time. Put them to work first in the exercises and then in your reading.

Remember:

1. What does the word seem to mean in context?
2. What is the meaning of the root?
3. What is the meaning of the prefix? the suffix?

Combine these bits of knowledge and within a short time, the word will be yours.

Exercise No. 92

Use a selected list of prefixes and suffixes from LATIN (A).

PART 1. Separate the prefix from the stem of each of the following words. Give the meaning of the prefix, and then of the entire word.

EXAMPLE: tri/angle   tri—three
triangle: a figure whose lines intersect at three points to form three sets of angles

avert	equanimity
aggravate	equivocal
ambivalent	enervate
benefice	extraneous
colloquy	ignominious

Check your answers in the dictionary.

PART 2. Give the **negative** form of the following words. Use those prefixes which mean "not," "away from," "against." EXAMPLE: enchanted-disenchanted; literate-illiterate

congruous	plot
noble	quiet (verb)
pathetic	proper
ingenuous	inter (verb)
normal	engage

Note: Do not proceed to the next group of prefixes until you have mastered the foregoing.

Using a selected list of prefixes and suffixes from LATIN (B) separate the prefix from the stem of each of the following words. Give the meaning of the prefix, and then of the entire word.

EXAMPLE: intermediary   inter-between
intermediary: one who goes between, a mediator

introvert	obdurate
malevolent	pertinacious
refulgent	sinecure
retrogress	surfeit
traduce	unilateral

Check your answers in the dictionary.

Using prefixes from the LATIN (A) and LATIN (B) groups, give a related word for each of the following words. Give the meaning of the related word.

EXAMPLE: pertinent—impertinent
ordinary—extraordinary
grade—degrade, retrograde

Meaning

turn
urban
introvert
provoke
circumspect

Check your answers in the dictionary.

Noun Suffixes

GROUP 1: Abstract nouns. These suffixes signify state of, act of, quality of.

SUFFIX	CURRENT WORDS
-ACY	celibacy, democracy
-AGE	bondage, salvage, vassalage, marriage
-ANCE (-ancy, -ence, -ency)	severance, repentance, buoyancy, diligence, emergency
-ATION (-tion, -ion, -sion)	civilization, flirtation, union, dissension
-DOM	freedom, kingdom, serfdom
-HOOD	boyhood, manhood, falsehood
-ICE	avarice, cowardice
-ISM	communism, invalidism, Fascism, baptism
-MENT	government, agreement, statement, payment
-NESS	happiness, lewdness, deafness
-SHIP	partnership, penmanship
-TY (-ity)	security, modesty, femininity

GROUP 2: Concrete nouns. These suffixes signify one who does.

SUFFIX	CURRENT WORDS
-AN (-ant, -ent)	partisan, artisan, participant, equestrian, vagrant, student
-ARD (-art, -ary)	drunkard, braggart, notary
-EE (-eer, -ess)	legatee, auctioneer, tigress
-ER (-ar, ier, -or)	laborer, scholar, clothier, auditor
-IC (-ist, -ite, -lyte)	nomadic, sadist, Brooklynite, acolyte

Exercise No. 93

Using the noun suffixes change the following words to nouns:

EXAMPLE: endure + ance = endurance

constitute	avaricious	till (verb)
frequent	masculine	spoil
delicate	denounce	lucid
eloquent	convoke	invert
terror	supplicate	superficial
free	lag	clothe
unite	devote	

Adjective Suffixes

GROUP 1: These suffixes signify resembling, full of, or belonging to.

SUFFIX	CURRENT WORDS
-AC (-al, -an, -ar, -ary)	cardiac, seasonal, vernal, Russian, circular, imaginary
-FUL	spiteful, vengeful, hateful
-IC (-ical)	anemic, inimical, maniacal
-ISH	foolish, English, childish
-IVE	restive, furtive, secretive
-ORY	admonitory, hortatory
-OUS	mendacious, gracious, efficacious
-ULENT	succulent, fraudulent

GROUP 2: These suffixes signify capable, able to.

-ABLE	movable, curable, peaceable
-IBLE	irresistible, visible
-ILE	ductile, puerile, fertile

A SELECTED LIST OF PREFIXES AND SUFFIXES FROM GREEK

PREFIXES

PREFIX	MEANING	CURRENT WORDS
A- (an-)	not, without	apathetic, aseptic, atheism, anarchy
AMPHI-	about, around, on both sides	amphitheater, amphibious
ANA-	again, up, against	anachronism, analogy, analogue
ANTI- (ant-)	opposed, against	antonoym, anticlimax, antidote, anti-war
ARCH- (archi-)	chief, primitive (the earliest)	architect, archbishop, archangel
AUTO-	self	autocrat, automobile, autochthonous
CATA-	down, downward	catalepsy, cataclysm, catastrophe
DIA-	through, between	diathermy, dialogue, diagram, diameter, diagonal
EC-	from, out of	eccentric, ecstatic
EPI- (ep-, eph-)	upon, beside	epidemic, epilogue, ephemeral, epileptic
EU-	good, happy, well	euphony, eugenic, euthanasia, eulogy
HETERO-	different	heterogeneous, heterodox
HOMO-	the same	homogenous, homonym, homosexual
HYPER-	extreme, over, above	hypersensitive, hyperbole
HYPO-	under, below	hypocrite, hypodermic, hypochondriac, hypothesis
META-	after, beyond	metathesis, metaphysics, metabolism
NEO-	new	neologism, neophyte, neoclassical
PARA-	beside	paraphrase, paradox, parallel
PERI-	around, about	perimeter, periscope, peripatetic
POLY-	many	polygamy, polygon, polysyllable
PRO-	to, towards, before	prologue, program, proselyte
SYN- (sym-, syl-)	with, together	synagogue, synonym, synopsis, symmetry, sympathy, symphony, syllogism, syllable

SUFFIXES

SUFFIX	MEANING	CURRENT WORDS
-ISE (-ize)	to make, give	synthesize, tantalize, criticize
-OID	like	spheroid, negroid, anthropoid

Verb Suffixes

These suffixes signify **to make.**

-ATE	procreate, animate, perpetuate, facilitate
-EN	moisten, deepen, loosen, quicken
-FY	qualify, fortify, stupefy
-IZE (-ise)	magnetize, criticise, sterilize, fertilize

Exercise No. 94

PART 1. Using the **adjective suffixes** change the following words to **adjectives.**

EXAMPLE: America—Americ*an*

satire	admonish	deride
mania	work	access
virus	continue	fallacy
planet	invent	exhort
avariciousness	Briton	wonder

PART 2. Using the verb suffixes change the following words to **verbs.**

EXAMPLE: height—height*en*

liquid	class	regular
integer	hearty	item
example	symbol	personal

Separate the **Greek prefix** from the stem of each of the following words. Give the meaning of the **prefix,** and then of the **entire word.**

EXAMPLE: anti/war   anti = against   anti-war = against war.

syllogism	euphemerism	cataclysm
metaphor	euphemism	anachronism
hypercritical	euphoria	analogy
apathy	anarchic	symposium
paranoia	polyglot	synoptic
archaeology	metatarsal	neologism
epigraph	peripatetic	heterosexual
echelon	catatonic	diagnosis
		periphery

Check answers with selected list.

Review Work on Roots, Prefixes, and Suffixes

For each of the following words, add appropriate prefixes and suffixes to create as many derivative

A SELECTED LIST OF PREFIXES AND SUFFIXES FROM ANGLO-SAXON

PREFIXES

PREFIX	MEANING	CURRENT WORDS
A-	at, in, on, to	ahead, asleep, afoot, aground
BE-	throughout, over	bedaub, bedeck, besmudge, besiege
BE-	by, in	because, beside
FOR-	against, not	forbid, forbear, forlorn
FORE-	before	foretell, foreground, forehead
MIS-	error, defect, wrong	mistake, mislay, misbehavior, misconduct
OUT-	beyond, completely	outdo, outside, outbreak
UN-	not	untie, undo, uninspired
UNDER-	beneath, less than	underwrite, undertow, underrate
UP-	high	upshot, uplift, upset
WITH-	from, against	withstand, withdraw, withhold

SUFFIXES

SUFFIX	MEANING	CURRENT WORDS
-DOM	condition	freedom, wisdom
-FOLD	number, quantity	tenfold, manifold
-LESS	lacking, wanting	helpless, thoughtless
-LING	related to, belonging to	yearling, gosling, foundling
-LY	like, similar	hopefully, meagerly, evenly, closely
-MOST	(indicates superlative degree)	foremost, hindmost, inmost
-TH	state of, quality of	wealth, dearth, warmth
-WARD	in the direction of	northward, inward, outward
-WISE	way, manner	lengthwise, crosswise, otherwise
-Y	similar, pertaining to	greedy, nosy, bony, slimy

words as possible. Keep the same stem throughout. Be certain of the meaning of each derivative word.

EXAMPLE: compel (*Lat.* pellere, pulsus, to drive)

Derivative words from *compel*

NOUNS	VERBS	ADJECTIVES	ADVERBS
compulsion	compel	compulsory	compulsorily
		compulsive	
repulsion	repel	repellent	repulsively
	dispell		
pulsation	pulsate	pulsatory	
pulse			
pulsometer			

NOUNS	VERBS	ADJECTIVES	ADVERBS
propellor	propel		
propulsion			
impulse	impel	impulsive	impulsively

describe (*scribere*, write)
factor (*facere*, make, do)
pathos (*pathos*, feeling)
dependent (*pendere, -pensus*, to hang)
graphic (*graphos*, write)
spirit (*spirare*, to breathe)
sage (*sagire*, to discern)
vitalize (*vita*, life)
philology (*philos*, love)
chronicle (*chronos*, time)

BYWAYS TO BUY WORDS
LEARNING THE ORIGIN OF WORDS

Knowing the root of a word sometimes fails to produce a logical meaning. The root of *salary*, for example, is *sal*, meaning "salt," a far cry from our usage today. Yet if one thinks for a moment of a common expression such as "He is not worth his salt," he must realize that somewhere in the history of that root, a connection existed between money and salt. The connection dates back to the days of the Roman Empire when Roman soldiers were often paid for their services with enough money to buy the salt they needed for personal use. Thus what they earned was literally "salt money."

The search for the historical origins of words is called **etymology** (*etymos*, the real, or true + *logos*, the study of). The realms of etymology may be fully explored only by the professional philologist (See Walter W. Skeat's *Etymological Dictionary of the English Language*), but the amateur can have considerable and profitable fun tracing words as far back as he can.

Other examples:

CARTRIDGE—French, *cartouche*; Latin, *carta*. The Latin word, *carta*, means "paper," and the later French *cartouche* likewise meant a paper scroll on which messages were written. The first cartridges used in guns were rolled cylinders made of heavy paper; their resemblance to the letter scroll earned them the name *cartouche*, whence modern English *cartridge*.

DANDELION—French, *dent de lion* (teeth of a lion). The petals of the flower resemble teeth.

JIN-RIKISHA—Japanese. Here the roots provide the literal meaning of the word:

$$jin = \text{man}$$
$$riki = \text{power}$$
$$sha = \text{carriage}$$

EXCHEQUER—French, *eschequier*, chessboard. Edward I, King of England in the thirteenth century, handled all of his financial matters across a checkered table. The custom continued in England through the nineteenth century.

CHAPLAIN—French, *capa*; Latin, *capa*. Whenever the ancient kings of France went to war, they carried with them the cape of St. Martin of Tours. Wherever they set up camp, they kept his cape in a tent (*capella*) where it was guarded by a *chapelain*.

See what your dictionary tells about these words:

pastor	strafe	tawdry
congregation	daisy	grammar
eliminate	silly	hysteria
curfew	alphabet	taboo
assassin	hors d'oeuvre	nosegay
neighbor	phlegmatic	trivial

Words Derived from Proper Names Do you know these people?

Jean Nicot	J. A. Hansom
John Mercer	Vulcan

Amelia Bloomer James Watt
Pierre Magnol Thespis
Tantalus Hector

Each of them has given a word to the English language.

Jean Nicot—introduced tobacco to France in 1560—*nicotine*.

John Mercer—discovered a way to make cotton stronger for use as thread—*mercerize*.

Amelia Bloomer—feminist who wore a dress to fit over ankle-length pantaloons—*bloomers*.

Pierre Magnol—French botanist—*magnolia*.

Tantalus—the king in Greek mythology condemned to reach for fruit ever beyond his grasp, and for water which receded when he sought to slake his thirst—*tantalize*.

J. A. Hansom—inventor of the *hansom cab*.

Vulcan—the Roman god of fire—*vulcanize*.

James Watt—scientist who worked in electrical measurements—*watt*.

Thespis—Greek poet who invented tragedy in drama—*thespian*.

Hector—Trojan warrior, brave, but a bully—*hector* (to torment or bully).

Look up the following words:

roentgenology	quixotic	rodomontade
ampere	stentorian	simony
volt	dunce	Rosicrucian
wisteria	daguerreotype	maudlin
maverick	herculean	guillotine

Portmanteau Words, or Blended Words—like the contents of a valise (*portmanteau*) sometimes get squeezed together to form a new word:

lunch + breakfast = brunch
chuckle + snort = chortle
dance + handle = dandle

Lewis Carroll's "Jabberwocky" in *Alice Through the Looking Glass* is the finest example of the imaginative use of blended words:

slithy from *slimy* and *lithe*
mimsy from *flimsy* and *miserable*
nome from *far from* and *home*

Exercise No. 95

What are the components of the following "blend"?

flurry riffle smog squelch

SUMMARY OF METHODS OF BUILDING VOCABULARY

1. Learn only those words that you intend to use.
2. Keep a notebook or file card collection of new words.
3. Use the dictionary.
4. Try to recognize the use of the word in context.
5. Learn roots, prefixes, and suffixes.
6. Convert each new word into other parts of speech.
7. Be curious about word origins and changes in word meaning.
8. Study your words daily and *use* them in writing and speaking.

CIVIL SERVICE TESTS IN VOCABULARY (Selected Questions)

Exercise No. 96

TYPIST'S EXAMINATION

Each of the following numbered words is followed by five suggested words. Circle the word which is most nearly the same in meaning. (Choose the word most closely related to the given one, even if it is not a valid synonym.)

1. prorogue   a. blackguard b. request c. postpone d. convene e. pretend
2. desultory   a. changeable b. careful c. timely d. descriptive e. logical
3. traduce   a. transfer b. calumniate c. betray d. persecute e. subdue
4. unconscionable   a. unintelligible b. unaware c. unforgivable d. unreasonable e. unconscious
5. requite   a. reward b. delay c. regard d. acquit e. repeat
6. venal   a. poisonous b. salable c. pardonable d. sacred e. incorruptible
7. desuetude   a. unaccustomed b. despair c. disuse d. demeanor e. disinterest
8. assiduous   a. annual b. sour-tempered c. anxious d. careless e. unremitting

9. captious   a. naive b. reactionary c. captivating d. caviling e. captive

Exercise No. 97

PATROLMAN'S EXAMINATION

Same instructions as for typist's examination.

1. jocular   a. mirthful b. sympathetic c. careful d. haphazard e. morose
2. myriad   a. few b. myrrh c. content d. intent e. pertinent
3. perspicuous   a. conforming b. lucid c. perverse d. captious e. defiant
4. clandestine   a. sticking together b. faithful c. woeful d. open e. closed
5. anomaly   a. anonymous b. upper c. success d. irregularity e. prospect
6. heterogeneity   a. similarity b. question c. inference d. obvious e. ilk
7. polyglot   a. many-husbanded b. many-jewelled c. much-married d. many-languaged e. much-feared
8. jeopardy   a. demurrage b. safety c. partnership d. corpus delicti e. lis pendens
9. terse   a. poetic b. routine c. normal d. queer e. diffuse
10. collusion   a. contact b. conspiracy c. confinement d. congregation e. conjunction

Exercise No. 98

STENOGRAPHER'S EXAMINATION

Same instructions as for typist's examination.

1. plethoric   a. lean b. poor c. corpulent d. emaciated
2. ubiquitous   a. omnipresent b. obvious c. fortuitous d. ameliorate
3. pertinacious   a. pertinent b. servile c. inflexible d. rude
4. rancor   a. obesity b. chance c. resentment d. rot
5. gregarious   a. dangerous b. agricultural c. communal d. egregious
6. calumny   a. applause b. slander c. celebration d. eulogy
7. autonomous   a. self-governing b. automat c. synonymous d. apparent
8. apathy   a. emotion b. attitude c. fury d. insensibility
9. condign   a. deserved b. condemn c. belie d. conduct
10. cataclysm   a. catastrophe b. comfort c. pleasure d. prosperity
11. complaisant   a. complacent b. friendly c. unmoved d. discouraged
12. denouement   a. outcome b. end c. blessing d. help
13. credulous   a. ready to believe b. diverse c. oily d. infamous
14. derogatory   a. commendatory b. praising c. disparaging d. heinous
15. diaphanous   a. transparent b. sylph-like c. dim d. turbid

STYLE

IMPROVING THE WORD PATTERN

LEVELS OF USAGE

Diction refers to the choice of words—precise or unprecise, forceful or weak—used to express thoughts and feelings.

Usage (what people say and write) determines the correctness or incorrectness of diction. Although diction varies according to the pressures of the society in which it functions, two general levels of usage may be distinguished:

Standard English—the level of language of most educated people in English-speaking nations.

INFORMAL ENGLISH—the level most commonly used in conversation and informal writing (personal notes, diaries, dialogue in fiction and drama, and the like).

FORMAL ENGLISH—the level most commonly used in official reports, text and reference books, lectures, and the like.

Substandard English—the level of language generally considered unacceptable in polite society. It seems unlikely that any intelligent person would consider expressing himself seriously in the following way—unless facetiously:

Ed got *loaded* last night at our *shebang*, and was still *ossified* when we *carted* him home. This morning his *missus yelled at him.*

The italicized expressions are substandard, illiterate, or vulgar usages, and, when employed seriously, reflect unfavorably on the taste and education of the person who uses them.

On the other hand, pomposity characterizes the following passage, an absurdly pedantic attempt at formal usage, ill-suited both to the subject matter and to any conceivably interested audience:

Edward *underwent extraordinary inebriation* at last evening's *soiree*, and remained *comatose*

even after we *transported* him to his *domicile.* This morning his *spouse submitted him to severe verbal abuse.*

Most people, however, would accept either of the following Standard English versions:

INFORMAL: Ed got drunk at last night's party and was still unconscious when we took him home. This morning his wife berated him.

FORMAL: Edward Jones became intoxicated at a party held last night at a friend's home. The following morning his wife berated him.

In each of these passages, the language is appropriate to the subject and to the audience. The informal passage is addressed to an educated audience. Its level is standard; its mode is speech. Its diction is simpler than that in the formal passage (*drunk, intoxicated*), and its tone more personalized. The formal version, more dignified and impersonal, resembles the kind of reporting found in better newspapers.

Thus, the first step toward improving word-patterns involves discriminating between levels of usage. Substandard and pompous English have no place in the diction of an effective writer or speaker. Good diction successfully meets the demands of both the subject and the audience.

STANDARD ENGLISH

FORMAL	INFORMAL
psychotic	insane
incarcerated	jailed
policeman	cop
have dinner	dine
wed	married
May I have this dance?	Shall we dance?

SUBSTANDARD ENGLISH

VULGAR	POMPOUS
nuts	cerebral malfunctioning
slammer	immured within the confines of a cell
cop	officer of the law
grab a bite	indulge in a repast
hitched	joined in wedlock
Let's wrestle.	Shall we emulate Terpsichore?

Exercise No. 99

Give informal and formal usage for the following substandard expressions:

hog	ball and chain	square
bum	kicked the bucket	gorilla
big shot	gold digger	hot rod

INFORMAL ENGLISH Today, the informal level of usage dominates both spoken and written English. Although it carefully avoids both the vulgar and the pompous, it possesses precision and dignity. Study the diction in the passage below from "The Talk of the Town" in an old *New Yorker* magazine:

"Our cat, who for many years dozed on the hearthstone before our living-room fireplace, has changed her ways. Her favorite couch now is the top of our television set, where, basking in the warmth generated by the big tube, she naps contentedly, apparently unconscious of the racket the strange characters below are making. We've checked with a couple of other cat-and-television owners and find that her behavior isn't exceptional; sleeping on top of television sets is the mode of the day for cats. They do it even when the set is turned off, either because they're victims of habit or because they can detect some lingering emanations of heat imperceptible to their masters. Pussycat's migration from the hearth to the console embarrasses some of our staple literature, but from a cat's point of view it would seem to make sense. No more lying on the floor, exposed mercilessly to nipping dogs, roistering children, and roaring vacuum cleaners. Instead, a clean, secure, elevated haven in the one blessed spot in the room from which those flickering images are invisible."*

Words like *emanations, imperceptible, generated, migration,* and *roistering* keep the level of diction high, but the easy grace of cultivated conversation emerges in colloquialisms like *racket* and *checked with.* Note also the liveliness of phrases like *cat-and-television owners,* and *Pussycat's migration from the hearth to the console.*

No one should—or can—draw a clear-cut, final line of demarcation between the diction of formal and that of informal English. One's diction ought to be sufficiently flexible to meet the demands of formal or informal situations. Although informal English is the norm today, one may occasionally have to move to the formal level. And the transition ought to be made gracefully, not laboriously or pompously. Alert observation and unremittant practice help one to adjust to different levels. Specific instruction may accelerate the process.

Exercise No. 100

What kind of diction would you use in the following circumstances?

1. An article about community activities for your chapter of a veterans' organization.
2. A letter to the editor of your local newspaper disagreeing with his stand on school taxes.
3. An article (factual) discussing the increase in the number of emphysema victims in an area hitherto only lightly afflicted.
4. A letter to a friend serving in the army.
5. A talk about your trip around the world, to be delivered to the Ladies' Auxiliary Group.

THE DICTIONARY AND LABELED WORDS Good dictionaries label many words to indicate their appropriateness to formal and informal usage. When in doubt about using a word in a given context, check it in the dictionary.

Labels indicating that the word is acceptable for use in informal writing or speaking:

Colloq. (colloquial):

great meaning "first rate, very good": This was a *great* day for the Yankees.

* By permission, copyright, 1951, The New Yorker Magazine, Inc.

awful meaning "unpleasant, extremely bad": Marge's debut on television was simply *awful*.

Labels indicating that the word is **acceptable** for rare use in informal writing or speaking to effect novelty or particular stress:

Slang:

hook meaning "to steal": The youngsters *hooked* an apple from the fruitstand.

can meaning "to dismiss, fire": Poor Bill was *canned* when he forgot to punch his time card.

Note: Slang invigorates diction because it is often imaginative and colorful. Used too often, however, it loses its effect and degenerates into substandard prose. Neither slang nor colloquialisms are suitable for formal diction.

Labels indicating that the word is **unacceptable** for normal use in either informal or formal writing or speaking:

Illit. (illiterate, substandard):

hisn   ain't

yourn   set (for sit)

Obs. (obsolete). Obsolete words are those no longer in current use:

> *mint* meaning "a coin"
> *oblige* meaning "to please or gratify"
> *nice* meaning "foolish, silly"

Arch. (archaic). Archaic words are those no longer in current use, but still meaningful in certain contexts:

> *quoth* meaning "said"
> *methinks* meaning "I think"

But note that *ado*, although generally superseded by *to do, stir, fuss, tumult,* etc., still survives in expressions like *So much ado about so little.*

Dial. (dialect, dialectal). Dialectal words are those typical of a specific geographic region and are not in common use elsewhere. They are known also as **provincialisms, regionalisms,** or **localisms:**

corn pone (Southern for *corn bread*)

I *powdered* out of that fight. (Western for *hurried*)

poke (Western or Southern for *sack* or *bag*)

Note: Dialectal words have gradually disappeared from American English because of standardization fostered by schools and by media of mass communication. Many people, however, advocate retaining colorful local expressions, particularly in informal usage. Probably one should take a middle road. Like slang, dialect is appropriate when used discreetly, not promiscuously.

Labels indicating **British** usage as distinct from American:

Brit. (Briticism). The words an Englishman uses to describe an object often differ entirely from the words an American would use:

BRITISH	AMERICAN
underground	subway
lorry	truck
ladder (in a stocking)	run
lift	elevator
jitney	bus
pub	bar
ironmonger's	hardware store
chemist's	drug store
bobby	police officer
by-pass	highway

American English has a force and clarity of its own and Americans should use their own language.

Most words in the dictionary are not labeled, indicating that they are in current use. Note, however, that many of these words are useful only in highly technical contexts and should not be indiscriminately used merely because they are not labeled.

hurter—a buffer piece used to check the forward motion of a gun carriage.

paludal—referring to marshes or fens.

thrombus—growth of blood cells.

tierce—a liquid measure.

Exercise No. 101

Use your dictionary to determine whether the italicized words used in the following sentences are **Colloquial, Slang, Archaic, Dialectical, Illiterate,** or **British:**

1. You and your flattery—always trying *to sweet* me.

2. Butch keeps on *muscling* in where he's not wanted.
3. Their house is just down the road a *piece*.
4. Now Joe, he's a *specimen*, if ever I saw one.
5. I *suspicioned* from the beginning that he was a liar.
6. I can't *enthuse* about her new dress.
7. We went to the *cinema* last night.
8. This heat *plumb* wears me out.
9. She is an *awful* girl to take to a concert.
10. Jimmy got *mad* when I took his ball and glove.

CLARITY, EXACTNESS, CORRECTNESS, AND ECONOMY IN DICTION
Jargon, the art of saying nothing at great length.

"Caution," said Sir Arthur Quiller-Couch in his famous essay, *On Jargon*, "is its father; its mother Indolence." He was referring, of course, to the parentage of jargon, the enemy (often the mortal enemy) of clear, precise communication. Although most people want to be understood, they are frequently either afraid to say exactly what they mean, or just too lazy to say it. The results of their efforts to beat about the bush go by the name of **jargon**, or, more familiarly, **gobbledygook**, **verbomania**, **deadwood**, and **word fungus**. Jargon invades almost every realm of expression:

Government:
Such preparations shall be made as will completely obscure all Federal buildings and non-Federal buildings occupied by the Federal Government during an air-raid for any period of time from visibility by reason of internal or external illumination. Such obscuration may be obtained by blackout construction or by termination of the illumination.

TRANSLATED: During wartime, in buildings where work must continue after dark, blinds must be pulled, shades drawn, or lights turned out.

Economics:
A *soft goods recession* resulted in *negative adjustments* being brought about in many lines.

TRANSLATED: When people stopped buying "soft goods" like textiles and clothing, manufacturers suffered because they had to cut their prices.

Stocks were *easy* today.

TRANSLATED: Stock prices went down today.

Medicine:
He needed a week's vacation to recover from the effects of his *nasal coryza*.

TRANSLATED: He took a week's vacation to recover from a cold.

The fight was stopped because Jones suffered a *circumorbital haematoma*.

TRANSLATED: The fight was stopped because Jones had a black eye.

Education:
Since the good weather has made possible more free time on the campus instead of indoors, complaints have been received concerning certain exhibitionist conduct by students who apparently fail to realize that the traditional Spring time inclination to affectionately regard an attractive neighbor may not be looked upon with equally arduous approval by observers.

TRANSLATED: Stop petting in public.

Sports:
The bunt . . . is a perplexing diversion from the norm, an incisive ramification of strategic deception, though not deceit or duplicity. It is . . . a wholly unexpected subordination of the heterogeneous maximum in manual ballistics wherein we subjugate anticipated heroics to delusive legerdemain.

TRANSLATED: The bunt is a legitimate trick which sacrifices power for subtlety.

That such writing is a mockery of communication seems clear. Yet some misguided people might even defend it, insisting that many write and speak just that way. Jargon afflicts those who lack decisiveness and cannot think for themselves. Getting rid of jargon requires that a writer have the courage to *strike out* passages, however sharp the pain of parting. He must learn to eliminate irrelevancy and destroy deadwood.

Techniques for Eliminating Jargon Use precise words instead of circumlocutions (words that *talk around: circum,* "around" + *loquor,* "talk").

Circumlocution:

EXAMPLE: In the matter of deadwood, which resembles in nature jargon in that it exhibits a tendency towards circumlocution, the writer's prose suffers due to the fact that he occupies a lengthy period of time in the process of being explicit.

Substitute precise words for the circumlocutions:

In the matter of	Eliminate the phrase; it accomplishes nothing.
which resembles in nature	Use *like.*
exhibits a tendency towards circumlocution	Make the noun *circumlocution* a verb and drop the rest. Or say *beats about the bush.*
due to the fact that	Use *because.*
occupies a lengthy period of time	Use *takes too long.*
in the process of being explicit	Use *to explain.*

Clear:

Deadwood, like jargon, circumlocutes, and the writer's prose suffers because it takes too long to explain a simple matter.

Thus, **clarity, exactness, correctness,** and **economy** may be gained with a few precise words. **The fewest exact words produce the strongest prose.**

Exercise No. 102

Substitute the exact word or words for the following circumlocutions:

1. in this day and age
2. I am of the opinion that
3. as regards
4. in regard to
5. necessary funds
6. in respect to
7. relative to
8. my field of endeavor is law
9. reach a decision
10. this meets with my approval
11. during the time that
12. it is the belief of
13. come in contact with
14. in connection with
15. it is directed that
16. in view of the circumstances

Use the exact expression or word instead of a *redundant* one. Redundancy (or *tautology*) means needless repetition of the same idea.

Redundant: I asked her to *refer back* to her notes. *refer* (*re,* "back," *fer,* "carry") means send back. Thus, *back* is redundant in the sentence.

Right: I asked her to refer to her notes.

Redundant: Will you *repeat again* what you have said before I *continue on* with my typing? *repeat* means say again, and *continue* means go on.

Thus, *again* and *on* are redundant.

Right: Will you repeat what you said before I continue with my typing?

Exercise No. 103

Eliminate the redundant words from the following sentences:

1. His workmanship is absolutely unique and alone in the field of jewelry.
2. The consensus of opinion favors his retirement from office.
3. Her complexion is pink in color.
4. The modern woman of today makes up her mind without assistance from anybody else.
5. Every genius of great talent needs a wealthy millionaire to further his career onwards.
6. The audience at Simon's lecture was few in number.
7. The vase I bought was elliptical in shape.
8. These basic fundamentals, combined together, will teach any student to write well.
9. William's clothes are invariably too large in size.
10. Brett and Maria, two of Hemingway's heroines, are diametrically opposite types of women.

Use concrete words (specific words), particularly when explaining abstract ideas (general ideas).

Concrete words name or describe persons, places, or things: freedom, honesty, happiness, beauty. Both concrete and abstract words are needed in communication, but concrete words help to avoid jargon:

Excessively abstract:

In a *case* of this kind, where the diagnosis is lung cancer, the doctor must examine carefully the *condition* of the patient to determine the *degree* to which the disease has spread.

case—one of several abstract nouns too vague to be effective, may easily be omitted.

condition—the doctor ought to examine the *lung*, not the *condition*.

degree—like *case*, is vague.

Clear:

When he has diagnosed lung cancer, the doctor must examine the patient's lung carefully to determine how large an area is morbid.

Note that *lung* is repeated in this sentence. It is better to repeat a concrete word than to write around it with abstract words.

Exercise No. 104

Rewrite the following paragraph, substituting concrete and specific words for the italicized abstractions. Note that some of the italicized words, although not abstract in themselves, are inadequately specific in context.

EXAMPLE: I was so angry that I threw *something* at him.

I was so angry that I threw the cake plate at him.

Bill Wilson has the *character traits* of a man who wants *things* that lead to success and does *something* about the fact. Not only does he read in his field, but also he talks to persons who know a lot about *different subjects*. *Knowledgeability* is what he is after because he knows it will lead to improvement in his *setup* in the *legal field*. All these factors are *outstanding* in my *fundamental feeling* that Bill is going to be a *worthwhile force around here*.

Denotation and Connotation The denotation of a word is its actual meaning; its connotation, that which it suggests or implies in addition to its actual meaning. (Webster's *New International Dictionary*)

Concrete words may be connotative as, for example, *mother, soldier, skinny, fat, home*. Abstract words are more likely than concrete to have connotative meanings: *communism, fascism, liberty, love, happiness*. Words carry emotional overtones, evoke associations pleasant or unpleasant, that the dictionary does not include. To improve his diction, a writer must be sensitive to distinctions between the literal and emotional content of the words he uses.

The *young boy's* face was *whitish*, his features *small* and *round*, almost *womanly*. But his *behavior* was completely that of a boy who enjoyed rough play and who returned to his *house* after a *day of activity* with his clothes quite soiled.

Denotative words, clear but colorless, fail to evoke a vivid picture of the boy. Connotative words produce the desired effect:

The *youth's* face was *pale*, his features *delicate*, almost *feminine*. But his *mischievousness* proved him to be wholly a boy. He loved *roughhousing*, and invariably returned *home filthy* at the end of an afternoon of *rousing* play.

"Every *American boy* knows—because his *mother* has taught it to him since the *cradle*—that *family love* brings *happiness* to the individual, the community, and the nation. The *American family* has been the *cornerstone* of *freedom* in our *democracy* since the time of *Washington*, and it will remain so for as long as our nation endures. In nations under *Red domination, bureaucracy* supersedes the family. Bureaucracy becomes a cornerstone too, not of freedom, but of *tyranny*." Here is the material of the propagandist. Note how the writer has combined concrete words (*American boy, mother, cradle, American family, Washington, cornerstone*) with abstract words (*family love, freedom, democracy, Red domination, bureaucracy, tyranny*) to obscure the basic technique—pure emotional appeal, connotation. Nowhere does he rely upon the literal meaning of any of the words he uses; always he proceeds by emotional suggestion. By the time he has finished, the reader knows little, but feels much. Such writing undoubtedly has its place, but an intelligent reader must be alert to the devices involved; an intelligent writer will avoid such devices when he is trying to clarify an abstraction:

In America, young people are taught to respect the family as the principal foundation upon which democracy rests. They are urged to contrast this emphasis upon the family and its individual members with the totalitarian emphasis upon the supremacy of the state, as the basis and touchstone of individual morality.

Exercise No. 105

Read the following paragraph carefully. Underline the emotionally charged words which try to sway the reader by feeling rather than thought.

The Constitution of the United States has its foundation in the Ten Commandments and the teachings of Jesus. Therefore, all truly good men are bound by every word in the Constitution, especially today when we are troubled by dictators abroad and at home. Consider for example, the Eighth Commandment: "Thou shalt not steal." It is the basis for the Fifth Amendment: "No person shall be . . . deprived of life, liberty, or property without due process of law; nor shall private property be taken for public use, without just compensation." Now think of the robberies committed by the brazen radicals of the government who, unlike really loyal Americans, have not respected God's moral law or the Constitution. Those who have a true conscience will not tolerate a conspiracy of this kind.

Synonyms—are words which have the same or nearly the same meaning. Thus, word pairs like *gift-donation, woman-lady, intelligent-wise,* are essentially similar in denotative meaning.

Careful writers must note, however, that despite similarities, no two words are exactly alike. Usage, connotation, and idiom give to words special meanings which discriminate them from one another:

Average—mean: both words denote "a middle point between extremes." Nevertheless, whether in a specifically mathematical context or in more general usage, they differ slightly but significantly.

We swam, played tennis, and relaxed—in brief, we had an *average* vacation.
Here *average* suggests what is typical or ordinary.

The ancient Greeks set the model behavior pattern for pursuing the golden *mean.*
Here *mean* suggests a middle road, a moderate course between extremes. Neither word could be effectively substituted for the other in these contexts.

Scholar-pupil-student: each word denotes "one who studies under a teacher."

He has written several books about Eliza-bethan England, each of which has proved him a true *scholar.*
Scholar suggests a learned, erudite person.

His outstanding academic record helped him to win the coveted appointment as a Rhodes *scholar.*
Scholar means one who is enrolled in a school, either as a tuition student or as a scholarship student.

Because they had not prepared their lesson, the teacher kept her *pupils* after school.
Pupil suggests more active supervision by a teacher, whether in the classroom or in private tutoring.

A *student* of semantics, Jones has been investigating responses to connotative words.
Student (which may also mean *one who attends school*) suggests one who loves study and is capable of doing some work independent of a teacher's guidance. Thus, discriminating between synonyms is an important step towards achieving clarity and exactness in diction. Consult your dictionary whenever you are uncertain that two words are synonyms.

Exercise No. 106

In each of the following sentences choose the most suitable of the synonyms provided. Use the dictionary.

1. Nell Gwynn, the (celebrated, notorious, renowned, illustrious) courtesan and mistress of King Charles II, was illiterate but intelligent.
2. The head cashier (embezzled, purloined, stole, looted) the bank's funds and (decamped, fled, absconded, skipped).
3. She eliminates jargon from her prose and writes (concisely, tersely, compendiously, pithily).
4. Hemingway's descriptions of bullfights are so (graphic, colorful, vivid, pictorial) that one almost feels and smells the struggle between matador and bull.
5. Her lively puns merely attest to her (intelligence, wit, brilliance, alertness) but in no way prove her (intelligence, wit, brilliance, alertness).
6. If he violates the law, he is (exposed, liable, susceptible, prone) to punishment.
7. I admire a man who, despite the honors heaped upon him, remains (humble, meek, modest).
8. The heavyweight wrestlers faced one another,

two (colossal, big, monstrous, prodigious) specimens of living but unthinking animal matter.

9. Andersen's fairy tales abound in (sound, robust, wholesome, hale) charm.

10. The man who ridicules sincerity is a (misogynist, cynic, misanthrope, pessimist), and must be carefully distinguished from the (misogynist, cynic, misanthrope, pessimist) who thinks he is a woman-hater.

FRESHNESS AND VIVIDNESS IN DICTION

Scientists frequently write prose that is clear, exact, and economical, but rarely **vivid**. To be vivid, diction must be concrete but imaginative, capable of awakening the reader's sense impressions and arousing his feelings.

Note how Mark Twain uses verbs, adjectives, and adverbs in the following passage to describe how it feels to be shaved by a Parisian barber:

I sat *bolt upright, silent, sad,* and *solemn.* One of the *wig-making* villains lathered my face for ten *terrible* minutes and finished by *plastering* a mass of suds in my mouth. . . . Then this outlaw *strapped* his razor on his foot, *hovered* over me *ominously* for six *fearful* seconds, and then *swooped* down on me *like the genius of destruction.* The first rake of his razor *loosened* the very hide from my face and *lifted* me out of the chair. I *stormed* and *raved* and the other boys enjoyed it.

Test the effectiveness of Twain's diction by substituting:

putting for *plastering*

stood for *hovered*

began to shave me for *swooped down on me like the genius of destruction*

cut my face for *loosened the very hide*

protested and argued for *stormed and raved*

The substitute words, although clear, lack the vividness of Twain's diction.

Making Verbs Vivid Simple Anglo-Saxon verbs like *go, come, say, walk, run, think, know, get, fix,* and the like are indispensable. In some sentences, however, they fail to do the job as effectively as a more colorful (connotative) verb:

Weak: Toby *walked* into the room and *said,* "I'm going to commit suicide."

Improved: Toby *walked furiously* into the room and *said hysterically,* "I'm going to commit suicide."

The adverbs help slightly, but *walked furiously* is not a really sensible description.

Vivid: Toby *burst* into the room and *shrieked,* "I'm going to commit suicide."

The single verb, clear, accurate, and vivid, is more dynamic than the verb-adverb combination.

Linking verbs sometimes serve to make useful distinctions:

Angela *appears* innocent, but actually she *is* a dangerous paranoiac.

The difference in meaning between *appear* and *is* underscores the effect of the sentence.

Generally, however, linking verbs do not communicate as directly or vividly as verbs of action. Furthermore, linking verbs require additional clauses or phrases to clarify their meaning, and thus weaken the economy of the sentence.

Weak: Language is what we call the sounds by which man *is* able to communicate his ideas and observations to his fellow man. Animals *are* also able to communicate by means of sound, as *is* evident if we *are* willing to watch puppies, kittens, mice, and young lions. Man, however, *was* to take an extra and important step forward when he *was* able to invent a method which *was* to preserve his speech forever.

The passage suffers from an excess of linking verbs which deaden the impact of meaning.

Better: "Man communicates his ideas and observations to his fellow man by means of sounds we call *language.* But animals too communicate through sound; witness puppies, kittens, mice, and young lions. Man, however, advanced significantly beyond animals by inventing printing, a method designed to preserve his speech forever."   (Van Loon)

The linking verbs have been eliminated, and live, vigorous verbs substituted to shorten the passage, and vivify its content.

Exercise No. 107

Substitute for the verb in parentheses one that more appropriately suits the context of each of the following sentences:

EXAMPLE: He placed the mint julep on the cocktail table, and listlessly (*sat*) on the divan. (use *settled* instead of *sat*)

1. The young slattern in the bright red suit (walked) across the street.
2. Matthews (thought) that repairs on his barn would amount to two thousand dollars.
3. The cabin cruiser, its engine (making noise), (went laboriously) through the rough sea.
4. Rickie (sat) atop the radiator, his eyes (moving) lightly from his aunt to his fiancée.
5. As Rose Ann (rested) on the windowsill, the odor of summer, borne by a southerly wind, (came) by her and into the house.

Exercise No. 108

Eliminate the linking verb by recasting the following sentences:

1. The subject of the governor's address was the elimination of housing shortages.
2. Words which are taken out of context are not always likely to mean the same as they do when they are in context.
3. His answer was an evasion of the question which had been put to him.
4. Shortages of raw materials are the cause of increase in price.
5. It appeared to me that he was a philosopher who was in search of a universal truth that was applicable only to him.

Making Adjectives and Adverbs More Vivid

Adjectives and abverbs cannot take the place of well-chosen verbs, but when they are fresh and lively, they contribute to vigorous diction.

Sara was an *extraordinarily lovely* girl and everyone watched her as she walked *casually* by.

Extraordinarily and *casually*, the adverbs, and *lovely*, the adjective, fail to convey the desired picture because the verbs, *was, watched*, and *walked* are dull.

Sara's *piquant* loveliness *turned* heads whenever she *minced* by.

Two verbs, *turned* and *minced*, supplemented by an appropriate adjective, *piquant*, achieve the picture.

Avoid "dead" adjectives like: *nice, pretty,* *awful, terrific, fierce, rotten, horrible, dumb, mean, big, little*, etc. Avoid overusing adverbs like: *rather, quite, very, somewhat,* etc.

Colloquially acceptable, but dull and inaccurate: Jim has a *nice* wife, and we had a *swell* time at their party.

Improved: Jim's wife is a *warm, genial* person, and she helped make our evening *delightful.*

Colloquially acceptable, but dull and inaccurate: The evening was *rather hot*, and so we walked along the shore beneath the *very tall* and *big* poplars.

Improved: The evening was so *sultry* that we sought fresh air near the shore beneath the *towering* poplars.

Avoid excessive use of adjectives and adverbs. Used indiscriminately, they lead to "overfine writing," or "purple prose."

"Purple prose": Jeff wandered disconsolately, alone amidst the moon and star-brightened darkness. Vast western hills loomed purple and gray against the black sky, as if to reflect the melancholia seeping perniciously through Jeff's spirit. Through the impenetrable stillness that bore down upon his seething consciousness came the irritable chirp of a cricket and a mismated echo from a bullfrog. Jeff plodded wearily onwards, his nostrils filling with the barely perceptible sweetness of moist young grass. The blood began to pound wildly in his ears and every fiber of his tortured being shrieked ceaselessly for escape.

Symptoms of ability show through the thick, ornate diction. But the passage needs to be completely rewritten and simplified.

Exercise No. 109

Substitute for the adjective or adverb in parentheses one that more appropriately suits the context of the sentence.

1. Harry has a (big) heart, but he is (very slow) at following a (smart) conversation.
2. Stale butter has a (sour) taste and a (sour) smell.
3. I felt the (awful) heat of the blast furnace sear my face.
4. Winter makes the city (old) like the fur of win-

ter bears; Spring makes the city (new) like
kissing on the stairs.

5. Before us stretched the (big) expanse of the
Gobi Desert.

6. He has an (awful) nerve daring to invite me
out with his (dumb) sister.

7. The actors gave a (terrific) performance, but
the play was (rotten).

8. (Cute) children are (quite sweet), but the
noise they make in a (little) apartment is
(something) (fierce).

9. Elene heard the (loud noise) of the (big) air
raid siren.

10. Enter the (big) Mrs. Fezziwig, one (big) smile
decorating her (big) face.

Figures of Speech—vary expressions by using
words to evoke images or to suggest relationships different from their usual meanings. The
figures most common in current use are:

Metaphor: an implied comparison between
two unlike objects or ideas sharing a single
likeness.

The chambered nautilus is *a ship of pearl*.

Sweet day, so cool, so calm, so bright, the
bridal of the earth and sky.

Simile: a stated comparison (using *like* or
as) between two unlike objects or ideas sharing a single likeness.

The grandeur of God flames out *like shining
from shook foil*.

*Like as the waves make towards the pebbled
shore,*

So do our minutes hasten to their end.

Figures of speech enliven both prose and
poetry. They must, however, impress the reader
with their originality if they are to evoke memo-
rable pictures. Originality comes hard and writers face two dangerous hazards—the cliché and
the overwrought figure.

The cliché (*trite, hackneyed,* or *stereotyped*
expression) is a word or phrase that has become
stale from overuse. It occurs in several forms:

1. *Quotations* like "He who hesitates is lost,"
"Footprints on the sands of time," "The calm
before the storm," "Home, Sweet Home."

2. *Figures of speech* like "cold as ice," "meek as
a lamb," "he is a rat (skunk, louse, mouse,
tiger, lion)," "Mother Nature," "Father Time,"

"Old Man River," "busy as a bee."

3. *Catch phrases* like "hit the nail on the head,"
"burn the midnight oil," "it stands to reason,"
"crack of dawn," "shadow of a doubt," "little
by little."

Although it is difficult to avoid clichés entirely,
a careful writer will try to keep them at a minimum. He will, moreover, try to create the appropriate figure of speech—the one that suits
his need—and he will search for the fresh and
natural phrase—the one that energizes his
writing.

The overwrought figure bungles the effect it
strives for because it strives too hard. If an
original figure of speech eludes a writer's grasp,
he is wiser to depend upon clear, exact words
than to destroy clarity and precision with a far-
fetched, confused, or unconvincing analogy.

Overwrought: The age of the atom has transfigured man, but the transfiguration has been
from spirituality to materialism, exactly the reverse of the counsel of the ancient prophets.
Today, man surges forward in his march of
mind, but his soul is mired in an abyss of false
yearnings. In splitting the atom, man has split
his own being and lost the unity of his molecular whole.

The writer begins with an interesting image—
transfiguration—but shortly afterwards loses it
in an unrelated figure about a *march of mind*.
Furthermore, he gets his metaphors tangled
when he gets a soul *mired* in an *abyss*. Finally,
he returns to the atom, but the original image
of transfiguration has now entirely disappeared,
and the reader wallows in the murky depths of
a *molecular whole*. A simple, unadorned statement of facts would be better:

The atomic age has halted man's spiritual development. Intellectually, he has surged forward, but his ideals and his values have stood
still. If man's moral being regresses, atom splitting may prove an illusory advance.

Exercise No. 110

Revise the following sentences. Provide fresh
images for the clichés and simplify the overwrought
figures.

1. To borrow a leaf from olden days, I promise to don the shining armor of a crusading knight and struggle onwards for enduring peace and freedom.
2. Sadder but wiser, the shivering mongrel crawled out of the icy pond.
3. Luke favored his company with a rendition of songs redolent of the good old days.
4. Hayfever spreads like wildfire during the summer months, but scientists keep searching for new methods to iron out the problem.
5. Jones is the one man in a hundred who can lead us out of the morass of corrupt politics without beating about the bush.
6. It stands to reason that Mother Nature must protect the denizens of the deep lest the devotees of the hook and rod uproot them from their watery homes.
7. We watched with bated breath as the blushing bride, her eyes starry, her dress white as snow, approached the altar of matrimonial bliss.
8. Hector's jokes are too funny for words. They make the other comedians green with envy.
9. He's a dead duck now that these disclosures of his graft and corruption have been put on the record.
10. Little by little, a fool and his filthy lucre come to the parting of the ways.

SUMMARY OF WAYS TO IMPROVE WORD PATTERNS

Clarity, Exactness, Correctness, and Economy

Choose the **level** of usage appropriate to the subject and the audience.

Choose **concrete** words wherever possible, and especially when explaining abstractions.

Choose **denotative** and **connotative** words discriminatingly.

Choose the **precise**, not the approximate synonym.

Freshness and Vividness

Choose "live" parts of speech, paying especial attention to verbs.

Choose **vigorous** and **original** figures of speech.

The Pitfalls

Avoid the vulgar and the **pompous**.

Avoid the **trite** and the overwrought.

IMPROVING THE SENTENCE PATTERN

THE PURPOSE OF A SENTENCE

Words, phrases, and clauses—the structural elements of communication—derive their import from sentence context. The sentence is the basic unit of communication. Its function, then, is to communicate: with force and grace if possible, but with clarity and precision at least. Whatever blocks or distorts the meaning of the sentence, whatever obscures its point or impedes its readability, whatever, in short, detracts from its effectiveness as a vehicle of communication, must be corrected—no matter what temporary surgical pain it may cause the author.

Clarity and precision, of course, do not necessarily equal simplicity. Some ideas will not yield to simple expression: to explain the theory of relativity or the philosophy of existentialism, the writer needs sentences different from those he would need to describe the right way of baking a cake, different and more complex. Nevertheless, any idea may be rendered excessively difficult by a writer who rejects the first principle of style, to get his idea across to his reader.

But isolating lucidity from the other prose virtues is ultimately an artificial procedure. To get his idea across as he experienced it, with all its force and all its immediacy, the writer must emphasize what is important, subordinate what is minor, and eliminate what is inconsequential. He must call on all the resources of style to tell the truth as he felt the truth. For the writer, therefore, morality has its center in the integrity of his sentences.

CLARITY AND COHERENCE

ECONOMY You should write sentences that the reader can understand with a minimum expenditure of energy. The great law of style, a philosopher observes, is to economize your reader's attention. In order to practice this kind of economy, marshal your words so that they proceed in firm, close array to the objective you have set for them. Make your sentences hang together: make them coherent and unified. Compare:

Incoherent: I like herring, and it is a fish which to the poor man is what sturgeon is to the rich man.

Coherent: I like herring, the poor man's sturgeon.

Coherent: When I realized that I would remain poor, I determined to develop a taste for herring, the poor man's sturgeon.

Note the variety of other faults in the first sentence, faults which issue from its incoherence and disunity (the two are inseparable): the three copulas which impair force; the wordiness which blurs lucidity; the clumsy rhythm which undermines euphony. The reader has to work too hard for too little, and justly blames the writer. His pen or typewriter initiated his thought. Had he performed his duty—planned before writing—he could have conformed to the "law of economy."

Exercise No. 111

The following sentences are uneconomically phrased. Improve them.

1. I am fond of ice-cream, and it is a high-caloric food.
2. Emma Lazarus was born in 1848. It was a year of revolutions.
3. I rarely eat oysters, but they are shellfish.
4. By repeatedly performing an action, one acquires a habit; it denotes a fixed response to a given stimulus.
5. A bunt is a smut that destroys wheat kernels, and is a baseball term too: "a lightly batted ball."

CONSISTENCY You should never leave the reader in doubt as to who is speaking to whom and about what.

Inconsistent: We have utterly forgotten the slang of the generation before ours. We never, for example, hear of a *cake-eater* nowadays. He is with the *flapper.* Yet we can remember when it was on everybody's tongue.

Who is *we?* In the first and second sentences *we* seems to mean "people in general." In the last sentence, however, *we* seems to refer to the author; for if people in general have "utterly" forgotten the slang of a past generation, they can hardly recall the particular slang term referred to, though perhaps the author can. But what slang term does he refer to—*cake-eater* or *flapper? Cake-eater* seems the likelier antecedent of the pronoun *it* in the last sentence (in spite of the fact that *flapper* is nearer and ought logically to be the antecedent). But in the third sentence the author has referred to the *cake-eater* as *he.* And if *cake-eater,* like the other slang of its generation, has been utterly forgotten (a dubious contention, by the way), should not the author define it? Finally, which is "the generation before ours"? One could perhaps answer—if he knew, as he does not, whom *we* represented.

Consistent: People forget the slang of the generation before the one in which they came of age. Nowadays, for example, no one ever hears of the *cake-eater.* That effeminate trifler has joined the *flapper.* And yet I [or *we,* if it is consistently used to mean "the author" or "the authors"] can remember when he [or *cake-eater*] was on everybody's tongue.

Exercise No. 112

Rewrite each of the sentences below, removing the inconsistencies they contain.

1. We often get into difficulty by not defining technical terms precisely; in order to avert the difficulty, we shall begin by defining as precisely as we can all the technical terms employed in the ensuing pages.
2. We seldom care about the history contained in a historical novel. Nevertheless, we have been careful to include in ours no incidents which have not a sound basis in fact. If any of them appear dubious to you, I suggest that you refer to the notes at the end of each chapter.
3. The reader will think the present writer conceited, perhaps; but I ask you to consider my great and enduring achievements.
4. People climb mountains because they are there.
5. People who live in our industrial society are different in some ways.

LOGIC Your sentences must be structured logically, internally consistent. Avoiding the loose and illogical thinking which breeds muddled writing is a more difficult matter than a few paragraphs can successfully demonstrate. Be wary of these pitfalls:

Equivocation or Double Meaning Maintaining a nuisance is a crime; barking dogs are generally nuisances; therefore maintaining a dog is generally a crime. (Here *nuisance* has been given its legal meaning in the first premise, its common meaning in the second.)

Begging the Question (circular reasoning) God exists because the Bible says He does. (Here the premise assumes as true the proposition to be proved, since the word of the Bible is valid only if God exists.)

Facile Assumption Everybody loves a lover. Since I love you, I am a lover. Consequently, you love me. (The proverb uncritically accepted often leads to error.)

Non sequitur (a conclusion that does not follow from the premises) All blackbirds are black. Some hawks are black. Therefore, some hawks are blackbirds. (Here the writer affirms solely that blackbirds are black. He does not maintain that they are the only black birds.)

Junior will one day be a great singer: he has absolute pitch. (Here the easy generalization operates: Junior may possess a frog-like voice or he may hate music.)

Ignoring the question (arguing off the point)
(1) Arguing against the man.

No wonder you believe in evolution—you look like an ape. (Here the argument attacks the man, not the idea he advocates.)

(2) Referring to authorities.

Students of government from Jefferson to Taft have agreed that the best government is the one which governs least. (Here the force of authority substitutes for the force of ideas and facts. But an equally impressive group of counter-authorities ["from Hamilton to Roosevelt"] may be cited for a different theory of government.)

(3) Appealing to prejudice.

He must be a good senator because the ignoramuses hate him. (Here the argument ignores the non-ignoramuses who may hate him—and also the possibility that the ignoramuses, though generally without understanding of political matters, might be right about this one.)

Misuse of Statistics He earned fifty dollars a week in 1929, one hundred dollars a week in 1949. Thus, his purchasing power doubled in twenty years. (Here the fallacy consists of ignoring the possible decrease in the purchasing power of the dollar in twenty years.)

False Cause Brandy is good for colds: I drank a half bottle of Metaxas and my cold disappeared. (Here the supposition that the earlier act is the causative act—as if day were the cause of night because it inevitably precedes night.)

Exercise No. 113

Point out the logical fallacy in each of the first seven sentences; correct the errors in linkage in the others.

1. Albert Smith, a great thinker, has backed Jojo for governer; consequently Jojo must be a better candidate than his opponent.
2. Five out of six smokers queried say that cigarette A tastes better than any other cigarette. Most people, therefore, will prefer the taste of cigarette A to that of any other cigarette.
3. All dogs are animals; a man is an animal; therefore, men are dogs.
4. Some women have read Toynbee; my wife has read Toynbee; hence my wife is *some* woman.
5. A. Our leader is a holy man: he speaks with God every day.
   B. How do you know he does?
   A. He says so.
   B. He may be lying.
   A. Ridiculous! Would anyone who speaks with God every day lie?
6. Oysters ought to be eaten only in months spelled with an *r*. It follows that oysters ought not to be eaten in May, June, July, and August.
7. I coughed each morning after I smoked a cigarette. From that fact I deduced that not smoking cigarettes was an anti-cough measure.
8. Jack Spratt could eat no fat, while his wife could eat no lean.

9. Although he married, he came of a long line of bachelors.
10. Look when you leap.

LEVEL OF LANGUAGE Unless you calculate a special effect, you should employ the same level of language throughout. Inconsistency in tone—formal phrases alternating with colloquial and slang phrases—distracts the reader and generally snarls the writer.

Faulty: She was graduated from the Cacophonic School of Music, which turns out lots of hep cats each year.

The formal *was graduated from* jangles with the informal *turns out*, the colloquial *lots of*, and the slang *hep cats*.

Informal: She graduated from the Cacophonic School of Music, which graduates many jazz musicians each year.

Here the words and phrases are appropriate to their informal context.

Exercise No. 114

Rewrite informally or formally:

1. One cannot always be on the lookout for chiselers, however aggravating such characters may be.
2. A scrumptious "looker," she unfortunately possessed several grave intellectual deficiencies.
3. When the auditor asked for the phone number of the D.A., Mr. Cagliostro seemed to be in a pretty fix.
4. I opine that the gent who drew the five aces has been playing dishonestly.
5. As you suggest, I am going to give you the straight stuff.

LENGTH You should keep long winding sentences to a minimum. The reader tends to lose his way in them. At least the modern reader does. The sentences he reads in popular magazines and newspapers average from ten to twenty words, in "quality" magazines and serious books from twenty to thirty words. (One authority declares that twenty-one words is the average length of sentences written by professional authors.) The nineteenth-century reader faced longer sentences as a rule—probably between five and ten words longer, and the eighteenth-century reader had to cope with sentences averaging between thirty-five and forty words.

Consider how difficult the following sentence is to comprehend, how the author gets caught in its coils toward its end; yet it was written by a great Victorian stylist, John Ruskin.

Excessively long: If there be—we do not say there is—but if there be in painting anything which operates as words do, not by resembling anything, but by being taken as a symbol and substitute for it, and thus inducing the effect of it, then this channel of communication can convey uncorrupted truth, though it does not in any degree resemble the facts whose conception it induces.

Most modern writers would break this tortuous sentence into three or four smaller ones:

Simpler: Words induce the effect of things by being taken as symbol and substitute for them. If there be anything in painting—we do not say there is—which operates as words do, then this channel of communication can convey the uncorrupted truth. For then paintings can induce in us a conception of facts, though not in any degree resembling them.

Note that *painting* has been changed to *paintings*: "painting" corresponds to "writing"; "paintings" seems better because it corresponds to "words." But perhaps the original sentence needs more extensive repairs—perhaps a total reconstruction.

Exercise No. 115

Break up the long and cumbersome sentences below, making whatever revisions you consider necessary.

If we endeavor to form our conceptions upon history and life, we remark three classes of men, the first consisting of those for whom the chief thing is the qualities of feelings and who create art; the second of the practical men, who respect nothing but power and respect power only so far as it is exercised; and a third class consisting of men to whom nothing seems great but reason and who, if force interests them, it is not in its exertion, but in that it has a reason and a law. For men of the first class, nature is a picture; for men of the second class, it is an opportunity; for men of the third class it is a cosmos so admirable that to penetrate to its ways seems to them the only thing that makes life worth living, and these are the men whom we see possessed by a passion to learn, just as other men have a passion to teach and to disseminate their influence; who, if they do not give themselves over completely to their passion to learn, do not because they exercise self-control; who are the natural scientific men, and who are the only men that have any real success in scientific research.

COORDINATION AND SUBORDINATION

You should avoid the "primer sentence." It is as bad, in a different way, as the overlong sentence.

Primer sentence: Modern English is full of bad habits. This is especially true of written English. The bad habits spread by imitation. They can be avoided. But one must take the necessary trouble.

Improved: Modern English, especially written English, is full of bad habits which spread by imitation and which can be avoided if one is willing to take the necessary trouble.

(Orwell)

Not only does the primer style become dreadfully monotonous after a few paragraphs, but also it inhibits any sustained and thoughtful treatment of a subject. To fathom, to explore, to distinguish—**to write accurately and subtly**—you must coordinate thoughts of equal importance, subordinate those of lesser importance.

From improperly attributing equality to ideas that are not equal stem most errors of coordination.

Excessive Coordination I was a private in the army once and then I discovered that sergeants were often impolite and they were generally most impolite when they had least cause to be.

The structural likeness of the clauses joined by *and* leads the reader to suppose that they are all of equal importance.

Improved: As a private in the army, I discovered that sergeants were often impolite, generally most impolite when they had least cause to be.

Excessive coordination: I want to go to Europe next summer, and so I am hoarding my money.

Improved: I am hoarding my money because I want to go to Europe next summer.

Unnatural Coordination—(joining clauses apparently unrelated).

Unnatural coordination: Robert Frost was born in California and he writes about the New England landscape and New Englanders.

There seems to be no connection between the two clauses.

Improved: Although Robert Frost was born in California, he writes chiefly about the New England landscape and New Englanders.

Improved: Robert Frost was born in California, but having lived for many years in New England he writes chiefly about its landscapes and its people.

Unnatural coordination: He lived in an attic and he could see only a blank wall.

Improved: He lived in an attic, his only vista a blank wall.

From improper analysis of the relation between ideas stem most errors of subordination.

Upside-down Subordination—(illogical subordination).

Upside-down subordination: When I gave her custody of our Asiatic ibexes, she asked for it.

Right-side-up subordination: When she asked for custody of our Asiatic ibexes, I gave it to her.

Upside-down subordination: He besought her hand daily for twenty years, finally seeking elsewhere.

Right-side-up subordination: After beseeching her hand daily for twenty years, he finally sought elsewhere.

Thwarted Subordination Andrew Jackson courted a wealthy lady named Rachel Donelson, and whose family helped him in getting on.

The *and* before the subordinate clause thwarts subordination.

Proper subordination: Andrew Jackson courted a wealthy lady named Rachel Donelson, whose family helped him in getting on.

Proper subordination: Andrew Jackson courted Rachel Donelson, who was a wealthy lady and whose family helped him in getting on.

Exercise No. 116

By subordination and coordination, convert the primer sentences below into mature prose.

In 1823 the Whitmans moved from West Hills to Brooklyn. Brooklyn was then a country town of seven thousand people. There Walt attended public school for a few years. It was the only formal education he ever had. By 1831–32 he was working in printing offices. He was learning the trade. He was employed for four or five years in printing offices in Brooklyn and New York. He then taught school for a few years in several small schools on Long Island. He "boarded round" at the homes of his students. Meanwhile he began to contribute to New York journals and magazines. He wrote sentimental stories and poems for them. His writing was in the tradition of the time.

FORCE AND VIGOR

PERIODIC AND LOOSE SENTENCES You can achieve a more emphatic utterance by the strategic employment of suspense. Normally, the English sentence has **loose** structure: it discloses its meaning near its inception; that is, it declares its subject and verb early. **Periodic** structure may constitute an effective variation from the normal pattern. The periodic sentence suspends its meaning until it nears its end; that is, it withholds its subject and verb to the last.

Loose: "It [snow] was falling on every part of the dark central plain, on the treeless hills, falling softly on the bog of Allen and, farther westward, softly falling into the dark mutinous Shannon waves."   (James Joyce)

Periodic: "Yet if the only form of tradition, of handing down, consisted in following the ways of the generation before us in a blind or timid adherence to its successes, 'tradition' should positively be discouraged."

                                    (T. S. Eliot)

The first three words in the loose sentence quoted disclose the subject and the verb. Though the sense unfolds progressively, each phrase reveals a segment of meaning. The loose sentence approximates speech rhythm; its movement seems natural, spontaneous. For that reason, it is the sentence norm: more than ninety percent of English sentences are loose in structure.

The periodic sentence quoted above attains suspense by withholding its verb to the end of the sentence. It builds to a climax; satisfying the curiosity it arouses by the *if-clause* after a purposeful delay. Since climax connotes delayed effect, periodic sentences are generally longer than loose sentences. Somewhat unnatural, the periodic sentence should be sparingly employed: orators (who often overuse it) find it valuable for emphatic statement and writers of fiction for dramatic revelation.

Exercise No. 117

Convert the loose into periodic sentences and the periodic into loose sentences.

1. The boxer acknowledged defeat after ten rounds, during which he lost precisely four teeth and about two quarts of blood.
2. Having penetrated the enemy's flank and reassembled our forces, we struck hard.
3. Not by force only but by fraud also are people enslaved.
4. He despised children although he liked dogs and tolerated cats.
5. He faltered when he saw, a bit foggily, the vague luminous form approach with slow deliberate steps.

PARALLELISM You should employ parallelism when it is appropriate to your thought. Parallelism achieves its effects by balancing like grammatical units against each other—similar parts of speech (noun against noun, verb against verb, and so on), phrases, clauses, sentences. Sometimes one element echoes the other.

How shall I curse, whom God hath not cursed?

And how shall I defy, whom the Lord hath not defied?

Here the second line repeats the idea of the first. But parallelism may embrace contrasting statements as well:

For the Lord knoweth the way of the righteous;

But the way of the wicked shall perish.

Here the second line opposes the first.

Balanced sentence structure gives discourse neatness and precision; it allows no part of a thought to get lost. However, when the elements of a sentence have no mutual correspondences, when they neither echo nor contrast with each other, forcing them into a sham parallelism of structure distorts meaning. The writer who balances his sentences relentlessly often finds himself unable to tell the truth. An important technique for securing structural form and precision when used temperately, parallelism can become a pernicious device when used promiscuously. Here is parallelism employed with consummate skill:

But in a larger sense, we cannot dedicate, we cannot consecrate, we cannot hallow this ground. The brave men, living and dead, who struggled here, have consecrated it far above our poor power to add or detract. The world will little note nor long remember what we say here, but it can never forget what they did here.

(A. Lincoln)

Exercise No. 118

Restore the parallelism to these famous sentences:

1. Out of his (Nicholas Machiavelli's) surname people have coined an epithet for a knave; they use "Nick" as a synonym for the Devil.
2. [Boswell was] regarded in his own age as a classic; today it is as a companion that we think of him.
3. I come to bury Caesar; praising him forms no part of my intention.
4. The evil that men do lives after them, and, with their bones, whatever good they have done is oft interred.
5. The Puritan hated bear-baiting, not because it gave pain to the bear, but for the reason that the spectators received pleasure from it.

EMPHASIS You should give emphatic expression to the ideas you regard as important. Perhaps the most obvious way of gaining emphasis is italicization (underlining).

We *never* liked puns or pundits.
That way, however, is mechanical, artificial—easily abused.

There are more telling ways of securing emphasis, ways less liable to misapplication. To the writer who wants to be emphatic without being mannered, psychology offers an important clue. One psychological law says that, other things being equal, the stimulus which comes first, last, or oftenest, is the stimulus that impresses us most forcefully, the one most easily recalled.

To gain emphasis, then, place the important words at the beginning of the sentence or at the end of the sentence or repeat them during the course of the sentence.

Weak: Of late, Romanticism has appealed to many poets who seemed to have taken up residence in the Wasteland.

Stronger: "Romanticism has of late appealed to many poets who seemed to have taken up residence in the Wasteland." (John Henry)

Weak: . . . closed fists beat against breasts which were contrite all of a sudden.

Stronger: ". . . closed fists beat against suddenly contrite breasts." (James T. Farrell)

Weak: . . . that government of, by, and for the people shall not perish from the earth.

Stronger: ". . . that government of the people, by the people, for the people, shall not perish from the earth." (A. Lincoln)

Repetition carried to excess may, however, become an irritating device. Used rarely and discreetly, it can compel attention. Matthew Arnold, many people may be inclined to think, rather overdoes the repetition of (especially) *truth and seriousness* and *diction and movement,* pairs that act in the following passage almost as refrains.

". . . the superiority of poetry over history consists in its possessing a higher truth and a higher seriousness. Let us add . . . that the substance and matter of the best poetry acquire their special character from possessing, in an eminent degree, truth and seriousness. We may add yet further what is in itself evident, that to the style and manner of the best poetry their special character, their accent, is given by their diction, and, even yet more, by their movement. And though we distinguish between the two characters, the two accents, of superiority, yet they are nevertheless vitally connected one with the other. The superior character of truth and seriousness, in the matter of the best poetry, is inseparable from the superiority of diction and movement marking its style and manner. . . ."

There are several other repetitions in the course of the paragraph; it is easier to be emphatically repetitious than to be emphatic through repetition.

Exercise No. 119

Rephrase the following sentences more emphatically.

1. Science answers many questions, but never "Why?" the ultimate one.

2. The ultimate question, "Why?" science never pretends to answer.

3. As every intelligent observer knows, dictatorship means the triumph of the inferior man, not of the superior one.

4. To be sure, the Psalms are a passionate criticism of life.

5. Though I speak with the tongues of men and of angels and have not charity, I am become as sounding brass or a tinkling cymbal. Grant, furthermore that I possess the gift of prophecy and understand all mysteries and all knowledge; assume additionally that I enjoy comprehensive faith, enough to move mountains; yet devoid of charity I am nothing. Even should I bestow my goods to feed the poor and give my body to be burned, if I am without charity it profits me nothing.

VARIETY AND EUPHONY

You should vary the length and structure of your sentences, always striving, moreover, to form sentences pleasing to the ear.

VARIETY Vary the length of your sentences. Too many long sentences strain the reader's attention. Sameness, in sentence length as in other matters, produces monotony. Changing pace by introducing an occasional terse sentence, particularly at the end of a paragraph, helps prevent monotony. Thoreau here speaks of John Brown:

"Literary gentlemen, editors, and critics think that they know how to write, because they have studied grammar and rhetoric; but they are egregiously mistaken. The *art* of composition is as simple as the discharge of a bullet from a rifle, and its masterpieces imply an infinitely greater force behind them. This unlettered man's speaking and writing are standard English. . . . It suggests that the one great rule of composition—and if I were a professor of rhetoric I should insist on this—is, *to speak the truth*. This first, this second, this third; pebbles in your mouth or not. This demands earnestness and manhood chiefly."

Vary the openings of your sentences. Sentences all cut to the same pattern, all wearing the same uniform, move woodenly—or the reader after a while thinks they do, which amounts to the same thing. Inevitably, monotype sentences become monotonous sentences.

Since the beginning often determines the form of the sentence, become aware of the different kinds of beginnings. Delay introducing the subject by beginning with a phrase, clause, participle, absolute, or other subordinate construction.

TYPICAL: He followed truth too closely at the heels and had his teeth kicked out.

CLAUSE: Because he followed truth too closely at the heels, he had his teeth kicked out.

PHRASE: By following too closely at truth's heels, he had his teeth kicked out.

PARTICIPLE: Having followed [or, Following] truth too closely at the heels, he had his teeth kicked out.

Vary the pattern of your sentences. The subject, the verb, and the object or complement (if any)—that constitutes the pattern of the English sentence. But for both variety and emphasis, sometimes reverse the sequence: sometimes, not too many times; else your sentences will appear artificial and unidiomatic.

Normal pattern: Emerson said, "Speak with the vulgar, think with the wise."

Reversed pattern: "Speak with the vulgar, think with the wise," said Emerson.

(Object-verb-subject)

Normal pattern: The theory of divine right and the head of Charles I fall together.

Reversed pattern: Together fell the theory of divine right and the head of Charles I.
(Verb-subject)

Normal pattern: I hate croaker and cold mutton equally.

Reversed pattern: Croaker and cold mutton, I hate equally. (Object-subject-verb)

Normal pattern: The days of our glory are vanished.

Reversed pattern: Vanished are the days of our glory. (Complement-verb-subject)

Vary the kinds of sentences. An occasional question or exclamation or command may relieve the monotony of the declarative. Be wary, though: overuse (of the question particularly) may become an obnoxious mannerism. In the paragraph quoted below, Emerson resorts naturally and skillfully to the exhortation and question, enforcing his point and varying his mode.

"A foolish consistency is the hobgoblin of little minds, adored by little statesmen and philosophers and divines. With consistency a great soul has simply nothing to do. He may as well concern himself with his shadow on the wall. Speak what you think now in hard words and tomorrow speak what tomorrow thinks in hard words again, though it contradict everything you said today.—'Ah, no you shall be sure to be misunderstood.'—Is it so bad then to be misunderstood? Pythagoras was misunderstood, and Socrates, and Jesus, and Copernicus, and Galileo, and Newton, and every wise and pure spirit that ever took flesh. To be great is to be misunderstood."

The paragraph might stand as a mode of supple, varied expression.

Vary the complete-sentence norm. Though using nonsentences—"sentence fragments," elements containing neither subject nor predicate—demands sober control, abstention may deprive the writer of an excellent (occasional) resource, one modern writers avail themselves of increasingly. The danger, of course, is that intemperate use of nonsentences will fragment communication, make it sporadic, discontinuous, wearisome. Nevertheless, from the non-sentence artfully disposed accrue advantages worth the risk.

"The tractors came over the roads and into the fields, great crawlers moving like insects, having the incredible strength of insects. They crawled over the ground, laying the track and rolling on it and picking it up. Diesel tractors, puttering while they stood idle; they thundered when they moved, and then settled down to a droning roar. Snub-nosed monsters, raising the dust and sticking their snouts into it, straight down the country, across the country, through fences, through dooryards, in and out of gullies in straight lines. They did not run on the ground, but on their own roadbeds." (John Steinbeck)

Here the prose gives the direct impress of a man's thinking, of the movement of his mind. The nonsentences seem to require neither subject nor verb: the reader feels their absence not at all.

Exercise No. 120

Rewrite the passages below, varying the length and structure of the individual sentences.

1. The vice president of the Chesapeake and Ohio Railway asked his traffic department whether it could deliver rain. It was an unusual question to direct to traffic. There was, however, a reason for the question. The reservoir of one of the manufacturing plants belonging to the company was dry. Therefore, the plant was about to shut down.

2. California is the fabulous state. It is bounded by mountains and forests on the north and the Mexican desert and the Colorado River on the south. It has the Sierra Nevada to its east, and the Pacific to the west. It has many mountain peaks. The highest of them is Mount Whitney. Mount Whitney is only sixty miles from Death Valley. Death Valley is the lowest point in the nation.

3. The age we live in is a most dangerous one. It is an age of supersonic airspeeds, of biological warfare, of atomic and hydrogen bombs. Nobody knows what is next. We all exist on borrowed time today; that is no exaggeration. We of this generation may deserve no better fate. We are sure our children do, however.

LANGUAGE You should, as a rule, phrase your sentences directly, employing the passive and other indirect constructions only for specific reasons. If the agent is unknown, or (for some reason) better left unidentified, or less important than his act, the passive is a legitimate construction.

> Black masses are conducted nightly.
> He was called Oedipus.
> French is spoken here.

However, the passive breeds circumlocution. It has not the pulse of normal speech. It shortly waxes boring. Compare:

Indirect: A style consistently laconic, excessively terse, is defeated by itself.

Direct: A style consistently laconic, excessively terse, defeats itself.

Indirect: False words ought to be hated and true ones sought by you.

Direct: Hate false words and seek true ones.

You should use fresh, vivid, imaginative language. It vivifies writing, adds reality to it. Compare:

Dull: In Trollope's novels, right and wrong are very plain.

Better: In Trollope's novels right and wrong are as palpable as a clergyman's gown or a barrister's wig.

Note that the language ought to be appropriate to the context: "as a tractor," for example, would not fit the context in the sentence quoted.

Imaginative: "Often, if the emergency brake [of the Model T Ford] hadn't been pulled all the way back, the car advanced on you the instant the first explosion occurred and you would hold back by leaning your weight against it. I can still feel my old Ford nuzzling me at the curb, as though looking for an apple in my pocket."   (Lee Strout White)

"Welcher was a rich lawyer, with a face like a bad orange. Yellow and blue. A little grasshopper of a man. Five feet of shiny broadcloth and three inches of collar. Always on the jump. Inside or out. In his fifties. The hopping fifties. And fierce as a mad mouse."   (Joyce Cary)

Exercise No. 121

Rephrase the following sentences, substituting active for awkward passive constructions and vivid for dull language.

1. Lots were drawn by the three conspirators to determine the one by whom the assassination would be undertaken.
2. The sleeves of the shirt were stretched out on the drying line.
3. Pope made an odd impression on people: his back was humped and so weak that he could not stand erect.
4. Julia's dainty leg is white and has no hair.
5. What awaits him when a door is opened by him is known by no man. Surprises may be harbored in even the most familiar room.

EUPHONY You should construct sentences that are pleasing to the ear.

Avoid the jingling recurrence of the same sound:

> I bathed, made my bed, and ate a breakfast of bread and butter.

Here the alliteration of *b*'s, the assonance of long *a*'s, and the rime of *bed* and *bread* distract the reader from the sense, focus his attention on the sound. The example given is extreme, of course; but more moderate recurrences of sound, because they are more moderate, often escape the notice of the writer. Yet they may be irritating to the reader. Read your sentences aloud; your ear will usually inform you of jingles that your eye misses.

Avoid the needless repetition of the same word. "Elegant variation"—the piling up of synonyms—does not constitute the alternative: if only one word meets your need precisely, repeat it. But a sentence like this demands rewriting:

Repetitive: The woman whom I marry must be a woman who does not regard me as someone whose chief function is to convert her into a woman who has children.

Improved: The woman whom I marry must not regard me chiefly as the father of her potential children.

Avoid heaping phrase on phrase in your sentences. A succession of phrases (especially prepositional phrases) imparts a jerky rhythm to your sentences.

Jojo refused to come out of the pool onto the tiles.

Avoid a too marked rhythm in your sentences. Prose has a harmony other than verse, a great critic noted. Some great writers offend—but not in their great passages. This passage is from Dickens: it has been set as verse, though originally written as prose.

I think in every quiet season now,
Still do those waters roll, and leap, and roar,
And tumble all day long;
Still are the rainbows spanning them
A hundred feet below.
Still when the sun is on them, do they shine
And glow like molten gold.
Still when the day is gloomy do they fall
Like snow, or seem to crumble away,
Like the front of a great chalk cliff,
Or roll adown the rock like dense white
    smoke.

Either as prose or poetry the writing fails. This, from Disraeli, is even worse:

"Why am I here? are you not here? and need I urge a stronger plea? Oh, brother dear, I pray you come and mingle in our festival. Our walls are hung with flowers you love; I culled them by the fountain's side; the holy lamps are trimmed and set, and you must raise their earliest flame. Without the gate my maidens wait to offer you a robe of state. Then, brother dear, I pray you come and mingle in our festival."

To read this paragraph without intoning it seems only less difficult than to read it without ridiculing it.

All good prose has rhythm, a rhythm which bears the imprint of the man who writes it, which rises and falls in response to the demands of his theme. Here is a passage that might easily have fallen into a te-dum-te-dum-te-dum rhythm, had not the author skillfully varied his stresses:

"Fair today and warmer. A hot sun ballooned on high, held to the sweltering earth by the thin line of a well-ordered universe. The hovering clouds, like cream turned sour by the heat, curdled into spoondrift."   (Ellis St. Joseph)

Exercise No. 122

The sentences below contain harsh or unpleasing combinations of sound. Eliminate them.

1. Why did you bring these two books to me to read out of?
2. The man who tries to live and die in peace is often grieved.
3. The boy's toys are noisy.
4. Since she is not of a suspicious nature, she seldom searches her spouse's trousers.
5. His mother thought that his adolescent ambition to fly was flighty.

A GLOSSARY OF FAULTY DICTION

Accept, except

Though frequently confused, these words are nearly antonyms.

Accept means "to take what is offered."

Except (as a verb) means "to exclude."

Right: Jojo was willing to accept all invitations, but all excepted Jojo from their invitations.

Adapt, adopt

Adapt means "to adjust or fit."

Adopt means "to take, receive, or assume as one's own."

Dr. Hyde adopted a child who shortly adapted himself to his new environment.

Affect, effect

As a verb, *affect* means "to act upon or influence." As a verb, *effect* means "to produce or accomplish."

Intemperate living will affect his health.

Temperate living will effect his cure.

As a noun, *affect* has a psychological connotation: "feeling, emotion, desire." As a noun, *effect* means "result or consequence."

Right: The effect of an affect is to influence behavior or consciousness.

Aggravate

In the sense of "irritate or annoy," *aggravate* is colloquial. In standard English it means "to make worse or less endurable."

Right: He aggravated injury by insult.

Agree to, agree with

English idiom demands that one *agrees to* a scheme, plan or project and *agrees with* a person. Additionally, a thing may *agree with* a person, and two things may *agree with* each other.

I agree to a quarrel.

I am happy to disagree with you.

Brandy agrees with me.

The verb agrees with the noun in person and number.

Ain't

Originally a contraction of *am not*, by extension *ain't* became a contraction of *is not* and *are not*, even of *has not* and *have not*. Dictionaries agree in labeling *ain't* "dialectal or illiterate."

No contraction of *am not* has proved generally acceptable, and so the rejection of *ain't* by educated speakers and writers may legitimately be cause for regret.

Some liberal grammarians call *ain't* "colloquial" as a contraction of "am not," substandard as a contraction of *is not, are not, has not, have not*. But educated colloquial usage seems to be increasingly against them.

Alibi

Alibi means "a plea of having been, at the time of an act, at a place other than the place of the act."

Sutton's alibi, that he was in jail when Arnold Shuster was murdered, seemed flawless.

Colloquially, alibi has come to mean "excuse or protest." (Ring Lardner's *Alibi Ike* probably established the colloquial sense of the word firmly.)

Allude, refer

Allude means "to touch on lightly and indirectly." *Refer* means "to mention distinctly and directly."

Wrong: He alluded at great length to General MacArthur.

Right: In passing, he alluded to a certain general who had commanded the American armies in the Pacific.

Right: I refer to General MacArthur, commander of the American armies in the Pacific.

Alright

Alright, a simplified spelling of *all right*, has not yet won its way to dictionary approval. But it is a popular spelling, probably because of its likeness to *always* and *altogether*, and eventually will gain dictionary acceptance. (Don't be a pioneer, however.)

Alternative

Alternative derives from Latin *alter*, "the second of two," a fact that people who esteem origins regard as decisive. To them, alternative means only "a choice between two courses":

This is your alternative: believe either his report or your own eyes.

But educated usage and most dictionaries define *alternative* as signifying not only "choice between two courses," but also "choice"—though commonly they label the latter meaning "loose" or "less strict."

Acceptable: It was his only possible alternative.

Acceptable: We had three alternatives.

Among, between

Between is used when speaking of two things or persons; *among*, when speaking of more than two.

He had a pumpkin between his ears.

He had a nose carelessly located among his features.

However, when used to denote contrast, or to express interrelation, *between* sometimes refers to more than two.

Right: Though *Sanctuary, This Side of Paradise,* and *The Masters* all deal with college life, there is a great difference between them.

Right: The treaty between the three governments lacked three signatures.

Amount, number

Amount applies to mass or bulk, *number* to separate units.

They had a large number of children and a small amount of money.

Apt, liable, likely

Apt means "suited, pertinent"; or "inclined, disposed"; or "ready, prompt to learn."

An apt student of the classics, Mr. Coolidge was apt to disregard "the illusion of reality"; but now and then he would emerge from his studies with apt comments on men and affairs.

Likely means "probable" and *liable* means "responsible for consequences," or "in danger of incurring something disagreeable."

He is not likely to write love letters to Miss Becky Sharp, but all men are liable to make mistakes—and liable for them.

Careful writers keep the meanings of *apt*, *likely*, and *liable* distinct. But most writers are not careful and use the three words interchangeably; consequently, they are *informal* synonyms.

As, like

As introduces a clause, *like* a phrase.

Like Jane, Mary was tall as a giraffe.

Colloquially, the distinction between the two words is generally disregarded.

Like may function, in colloquial usage, as a conjunction:

He stood there without moving, like he was thinking of putting down roots.

As regards, in regard to

The idiomatic usage is *in regard to* or *as regards; in regards to* is a nonstandard confusion of the two idioms.

Wrong: Jojo would say nothing in regards to his English lessons.

Right: Jojo would say nothing in regard to (*or* as regards, *or* with regard to, *or* regarding) his English lessons.

In the sentence quoted—and generally—*about* serves the purpose more clearly and less clumsily:

Jojo would say nothing about his English lessons.

Awful

Awful, as a loose substitute for "very, excessively" or for "ugly, extremely bad, shocking, ludicrous," is a colloquial usage—perhaps a low colloquial usage. In standard English it means "awe-inspiring, appalling."

> The awful shadow of some unseen Power
> Floats though unseen among us.
> (Shelley)

Because of, due to

Because of introduces an adverbial phrase, *due to* an adjective phrase.

Right: Because of Adam and Eve, we have

been excluded from Eden. (The phrase modifies *have been excluded*.)

Right: Our exclusion from Eden is due to Adam and Eve. (Phrase modifies *exclusion*.)

However, the use of *due to* as a preposition introducing an adverbial clause has gained wide acceptance—certainly among writers, and even among liberal grammarians.

Beside, besides

Beside means "at the side of," *besides* "additionally."

Right: No one sat beside me. (That is, the adjacent chairs were vacant.)

Right: No one sat besides me. (That is, everyone else stood.)

Between, among   *See* Among, between

Bust

Dictionaries label the verb *bust* as slang in the sense of "to become bankrupt," "to burst," "to reduce in rank," or "to strike."

However, one may on the standard level, refer to Teddy Roosevelt's busting of trusts or broncos.

Cannot help but

There are three acceptable idioms, each having a meaning slightly different from the others:

I can but hope means "I can only hope."

I cannot but hope means "I cannot do anything except hope."

I cannot help hoping means "I cannot keep away from hope."

The differences, though, have been obscured, the variant meanings being generally confounded.

Cannot help but, deriving from the popular confusion of *cannot but* and *cannot help*, has gained reluctant acceptance as a colloquial usage.

Contact

Contact in the sense of "get in touch with" is a colloquial usage—one that many people abominate because it is greatly overused. It functions as a loose substitute for *communicate with, write to, talk to, meet, telephone, call upon, inform*, and *ask about*.

Continual, continuous

Continual implies a regular but interrupted succession; *continuous* a constant and uninterrupted succession.

The continual rains of California (Florida) are beneficial to the orange crop.

The continuous roar of Niagara depressed the honeymooners.

Could of

Avoid writing *could of*, a corruption of *could've* (*could have*).

Cute

Cute is colloquial for *shrewd, petite, dainty, charming, pretty*, and the like (almost what one likes). An overworked word, it deserves a rest—perhaps interment.

Data

Data is the plural form of *datum*. Theoretically, one ought to say "This datum is enough," and "These data are enough." However, *data* often connotes a singular idea and properly functions as a singular noun.

Right: The data of science differs from the data of ethics.

Different from, different than, different to

The standard idiom is *different from*. Some grammarians rank *different to* as "standard" likewise, whereas others insist that it is "colloquial." *Different to* is chiefly a British usage.

Right: Man, said a French savant, is different from woman.

Acceptable: She was different than he had supposed. (Note that *different than* is a convenient formula when a clause follows. If *different from* were employed, the preceding sentence would have to be altered: She was different from what he had supposed.)

Disinterested, uninterested

Disinterested means "impartial," *uninterested* "not interested." An uninterested judge, it has been pointed out, might fall asleep on the bench; a disinterested one might be passionately interested in the progress of a trial, but he presides over it without bias, nevertheless.

Though the distinction between *uninterested*

and *disinterested* seems a useful one, still observed by careful writers, it has been popularly disregarded. Most dictionaries now give "uninterested" as the usual meaning of *disinterested*.

Disregardless, irregardless

Disregardless and *irregardless* are both nonstandard. Employing them humorously has become trite.

Doubt that, doubt whether

Doubt that implies little uncertainty, *doubt whether* much.

I'm no weather prophet, but I doubt that it will rain cats and dogs.

He doubted whether he could become a weather prophet—a foolish doubt.

Doubt if, a less formal idiom than *doubt whether,* has the same meaning.

Due to, because of *See* Because of, due to

Each other, one another

Each other and *one another* may be used interchangeably in standard English. But some formalists still distinguish between them, holding that *each other* implies two only and that *one another* implies more than two:

Let us love, be true to each other.

Poets often write for one another.

Effect, affect *See* Affect, effect

Emigrant, immigrant

An *emigrant* leaves one country to enter another. An *immigrant* enters one country from another.

The French emigrants sailed from LeHavre.

The French immigrants arrived in New York. Note that an emigrant must subsequently be an immigrant.

Enthuse

Many writers detest *enthuse,* a colloquialism meaning "enthusiastic" or "make enthusiastic."

Equally as good

Equally as good mixes two good idioms, *as good as* and *equally good,* to produce a bad blend.

Wrong: A picture is equally as good as a thousand words.

Right: A picture is as good as a thousand words.

Right: A picture and a thousand words are equally good.

Etc.

Etc. is the abbreviation of *et cetera,* Latin for "and so forth" (*et* "and" plus *cetera* "other things").

Use *etc.* sparingly.

Do not use *and etc.* at all: it equals "and and so forth."

Except, accept *See* Accept, except

Farther, further

Farther and *further* may be used interchangeably in standard English, though many careful writers prefer *further* when they intend "more" or "more extended."

Right: Heaven is no further (or farther) on sea than on land.

Acceptable: I have nothing farther to say.

Preferable: I have nothing further to say.

Fewer, less

Fewer applies to number—to things countable. *Less* applies to quantity—to things that are measured.

The Mormons made an interesting discovery: the fewer wives, the less trouble.

Colloquially, *less* functions as a synonym for *fewer.*

Good, well

Good functions only as an adjective, *well* as both an adverb and an adjective.

Wrong: She dances good.

Right: She dances well.

Got, gotten

The verb *get* has two perfect forms: *got* and *gotten.*

In the sense of "obtain," both *got* and *gotten* are standard American usages.

Right: He has got (or gotten) the plans from the enemy.

In the sense of "must" or "possess" *got* ranks as a cultivated informal usage. (*Gotten* is almost never used in this sense.)

I have (I've) got to go.

I have (I've) got plenty of nothing.

Graduate

The formal idiom is "to be graduated from"; more general, however, is to "graduate from."

Formal: He will be graduated from high school in June.

Standard: He will ultimately graduate from Miss Hotchkiss' School for Boys. It is incorrect to use *graduate* as a transitive verb meaning "to receive a diploma."

Wrong: He graduated the City College.

Right: The City College graduated him.

Had ought, hadn't ought, didn't ought

Had ought, hadn't ought, and *didn't ought* are nonstandard. Use *ought* (or *ought not*) alone: it says all that *had ought* says—without redundancy.

Half a

Half a is the standard idiom, *a half* the more formal idiom.

Standard: Half a league onward rode the six hundred.

Formal: A half league onward rode the six hundred.

Avoid the redundant *a half a.*

Human, humans

Human is an adjective. It is colloquial as a noun.

Colloquial: A multitude of humans gathered at Coney Island.

Standard: A multitude of human beings gathered at Coney Island.

Hang, hung

If a man is suspended by the neck until he is dead, he is preferably *hanged.* However, pictures, draperies, trophies, and the like are *hung.*

Hardly, scarcely, barely

Hardly, scarcely, and *barely* are negatives implying "not quite." Avoid using any of them with another negative.

Wrong: He admitted that he scarcely didn't escape death by drowning.

Right: He admitted that he scarcely did escape death by drowning.

If, whether

Standard usage prefers *if* to introduce a condition, *whether* to introduce an indirect question, an expression of doubt or uncertainty, or an alternative.

Condition: If we strike, the enemy will scatter.

Indirect question: He asked whether lightning had struck once.

Doubt: She wondered whether he was guilt stricken.

Alternative: They often strike their sails, whether the fish are striking or not.

Immigrant, emigrant   *See* Emigrant, Immigrant

Imply, infer

Imply means "to suggest or hint." (A writer or speaker *implies* to his audience.)

Infer means "to conclude or derive from." (An audience *infers* from a writer or speaker.)

The chairman of the Selective Service Board implied that a truce might result in fewer draft calls. College students inferred from his statement that they might continue their studies with less fear of interruption.

In, into

In implies "location, situation, or position."

Into implies "direction, or motion towards a location."

I sat in the darkened room watching moths fly into the candleflame.

In back of

In back of, used to mean "behind," is colloquial. Standard usage prefers *behind.*

Colloquial: At the theater, we sat in back of our friends.

Standard: At the theater, we sat behind our friends.

Wrong: We sat in back of the room.

Right: We sat at the back (rear) of the room.

In regard to, as regards   *See* As regards, in regard to

Incredible, incredulous

Incredible means "unbelievable or too far-fetched to believe."

Incredulous means "skeptical or disinclined to believe."

The children recounted an incredible tale about killing a talking snake. Their parents listened; then smiled incredulously.

Individual, party, person

Person means "a single human being." Standard usage prefers this reference to *humans*.

Individual means "a single person or group of persons of distinct characteristics."

Party means "a group of people." It may be used to refer to *one person* only in the legal sense of "one involved in a transaction." Used to denote "a person" it is substandard.

Right: He is the person to whom I gave the book.

Right: Poets and bankers differ in attitude as strongly as individuals can.

Right: If the party to the deed signed the affidavit he will be released from further responsibilities.

Irregardless, disregardless   *See* Disregardless, irregardless

Is because   *See* Reason is because

Is when, is where

Do not use *is when* and *is where* in definitions. However, *when* and *where* may properly be used after *to be* to introduce a noun clause of time or place.

Right: This house is where Edgar Allan Poe lived.

Right: The time to attack is when the enemy retreats.

Wrong: Fascism is when one person may impose his will on all minority groups.

Right: In Fascism, one person may impose his will on all minority groups.

Right: Fascism is a system in which one person may impose his will on all minority groups.

Wrong: Heredity is where parents transmit their traits to their children.

Right: Heredity is the transmission of traits from parents to children.

Kind of, sort of

These are colloquial adverbs used to mean *rather* or *somewhat*.

Colloquial: I was kind (sort) of disappointed by his writing style.

Standard: I was rather disappointed by his writing style.

Note: Avoid using *a* or *an* after colloquialisms *sort of* and *kind of*.

Wrong: What kind of a vacation did you have?

Colloquial: What kind of vacation did you have?

Note: *Kind of* and *sort of* are acceptable in sentences like:

What kind of man is he?

Later, latter

Later, the comparative form of *late*, means "more late."

Latter means "the second mentioned of two things."

Hurry! It's later than you think.

He ate mussels and snails. The latter gave him ptomaine poisoning.

Note: To designate more than two, use *last*, *last-named*, or *last-mentioned*.

Learn, teach

Often confused, *learn* and *teach* are nearly antonyms. *Learn* means "to gain knowledge or acquire skills." *Teach* means "to impart knowledge or to show how."

Students learn most when they have been taught how to study.

Leave, let

Avoid expressions like "Leave me go," or "Leave me alone." *Leave* means "to go away from or to depart." *Let* means "to allow or permit."

Right: If you won't let me alone, at least let me pack my clothes and leave this house.

Note: *Leave* used as substantive, meaning *allow*, is substandard.

Wrong: Leave me do it.

Less, fewer   *See* Fewer, less

Liable, likely, apt   *See* Apt, liable, likely

Lie, lay

The irregular verbs *lie* and *lay* cause much confusion because certain of their forms are identical.

Lie, an intransitive verb, means:

1. To recline.
2. To utter a falsehood.

Lay, a transitive verb, means "to put or place."

Note the trouble spots:

Lie (to recline) PRESENT
Lie (to deceive) PRESENT
Lay (to recline) PAST
Lay (to put) PRESENT

Right:

Lie (to recline):	I lie down when I'm tired. (*Present*)
	I lay down last evening. (*Past*)
	Often, when exhausted, I *have* (or had) *lain* down. (*Past Part.*)
Lie (to deceive):	Why do you lie when you know I'll learn the truth? (*Present*)
	He died to the police to protect his aunt. (*Past*)
	He has (or had) lied too often to be trusted. (*Past Part.*)
Lay (to put):	Lay that revolver on the table. (*Present*)
	We laid our money on the counter. (*Past*)
	We have (or had) laid our plowshares besides our scythes. (*Past Part.*)

Like, as *See* As, like

Loan, lend

Although both *loan* and *lend* are established as standard English, *lend* is preferred in formal contexts.

Standard: Will you loan me your pen?
Formal: Will you lend me your pen?

Avoid confusing *lend* (or *loan*) with *borrow* (to accept a loan).

Wrong: I loaned ten dollars from Buzz.
Right: I borrowed ten dollars from Buzz.

Mutual

Strictly, *mutual* implies a reciprocal relationship—John is to Jojo as Jojo is to John.

Right: John and Jojo are mutually dependent. (That is, John depends on Jojo and Jojo depends on John.)

Common, in the sense of "that which is shared equally by two or more people," should be preferred to *mutual* in such phrases as "our mutual friend," "their mutual fondness for oysters," "your mutual astonishment." So, at any rate, say precisionists; but *mutual* and *common* are generally used interchangeably.

Phrases like "mutual cooperation" are redundant and ought to be avoided.

Nice

Nice, accepted as colloquial, should be avoided; overuse has made it trite. Use words that precisely meet your meaning.

Colloquial: Your furniture has a nice finish and should wear nicely.

Better: Your furniture has a rich, glossy luster, one that will last.

Note: *Nice* used to mean "precise, discriminating," makes an effective adjective.

Right: Good diction aims at nice distinction between words.

Not so, not as

Both *not so* and *not as* are accepted as standard English in negative expressions like *not so . . . as* or *not as . . . as*.

Few writers today distinguish between *so . . . as* to indicate negation, and *as . . . as* to indicate affirmation. *Not so . . . as* is formal.

Right: He's not so much a bore as we had expected.

Right: He's not as much a bore as we had expected.

Nowhere, nowheres

Avoid *nowheres*, a dialectal substitution for *nowhere*.

He was nowhere in sight.

Number, amount *See* Amount, number

Off of

Although frequently used as a colloquialism, *off of* is generally considered to be an uncultivated usage. *Of* is unnecessary.

Poor: Keep off of my property.

Right: Keep off my property.

One another, each other   *See* Each other, one another

Over with

(See *Off of.*) *With* is unnecessary.

Poor: I'm glad my vacation is over with.

Right: I'm glad my vacation is over. (ended)

Party, person, individual *See* Individual, party, person

Practical, practicable

Easily and often confused, *practical* and *practicable* are not synonyms.

Practical means "useful or workable, as opposed to theoretical." It may apply to persons or things.

Practicable means "possible or feasible, particularly in reference to projects, schemes, or plans." It applies only to things, never to persons.

Right: Twenty years ago practical businessmen showed no desire to invest in practicable schemes for jet-propulsion. Today jet-engines are as practical as gasoline engines.

Prefer to, prefer than

Standard usage favors *prefer to.*

I prefer modern literature to medieval.

Note: Also acceptable in combination with *prefer* are *rather than, above,* or *before.*

Proved, proven

Linguists differ about the acceptability of *proven,* their judgments varying from "archaic" to "acceptable." *Proved,* however, is preferred.

Hitler had proved that tyranny cannot prevail.

Raise, rear

Raise, in the sense of "bringing up children" is colloquial. *Rear* is the preferred standard usage.

Colloquial: The twins were raised by their uncle.

Standard: The twins were reared by their uncle.

Raise, rise

Do not confuse *raise,* a transitive verb, requiring an object, with *rise,* an intransitive verb that does not require an object.

Right: I rise early because I raise roosters.

Right: When the conductor raised his baton to begin the national anthem, the audience rose.

Rarely ever

Substandard for *rarely,* or *hardly ever.*

Vulgar: I rarely ever get to the theater.

Right: I rarely (hardly ever) get to the theater.

Rear, raise   *See* Raise, rear

Reason is because

Reason is because is colloquial; *reason is that* is standard. Many linguists object to the redundancy of *reason is because,* since *because* means "for this reason."

Colloquial: The reason I am late is because the drawbridge jammed.

Standard: The reason I am late is that the drawbridge jammed.

Reason why

Reason why is accepted by most linguists as standard. A few purists continue to regard *reason why* as colloquial.

The reason why he collects books is that he enjoys reading them.

Refer, allude   *See* Allude, refer

Rise, raise   *See* Raise, rise

Said

As an adjective, *said* means "previously mentioned" and should be used only in legal documents. In standard English substitute a noun or pronoun.

Legal: The said parties are under subpoena to appear in court on June 15, 1979.

Standard: These persons are to appear in court on June 15, 1979.

Set, sit

Set, a weak transitive verb, means "to place or put." Its intransitive uses, when it means "to decline or wane," are limited: *The sun sets.*

Sit, a strong intransitive verb, means "to be seated."

Right: I set the dog in his box and he sits there.—PRESENT

I set the dog in his box and he sat there.—PAST

I have set the dog in his box and he has set there.—PERFECT

Someplace, anyplace, noplace, everyplace

These expressions are widely used as colloquialisms for the standard English words *somewhere, anywhere, nowhere, everywhere*. Because many linguists label them substandard, they ought to be avoided in formal contexts.

Colloquial: I've looked everyplace, but my watch is noplace in this room.

Standard: I've looked everywhere, but my watch is nowhere in this room.

Teach, learn *See* Learn, teach

Their, there, they're

Do not confuse these homonyms.

Their is the possessive form of they.—Pronoun

There means "at that place or at that point." —Adverb

They're is the contraction for *they are*.—Pronoun and Verb

If they're willing, we'll drive their car. Otherwise we'll take our car and leave theirs there.

This here, that there

These (and related expressions like *these here* and *those there*) are redundant. *This* and *that* are wholly adequate as demonstratives.

Right: Give this check to that man.

Thusly

Substandard for thus.

Thus he decided to avoid vulgarity.

Transpire

From Latin, *trans*, across or through, and *spirare*, to breathe, *transpire* literally means "to leak or emit through the pores." By extension it has come to mean "to become known or to come to light."

Right: The secret of the atom bomb transpired to foreign agents despite careful security measures.

Transpire should not be used in the sense of "to occur or happen."

Even in its acceptable usage, *transpire* is pompous and should be avoided.

Uninterested, disinterested *See* Disinterested, uninterested

Unique

Unique means "the only one of its kind." Thus, it should not be confused with *unusual, rare,* or *outstanding*, which can be compared, as *unique* cannot.

The unique manuscript of *Beowulf* is in the British museum.

Very

In formal writing, avoid using *very* to modify a past participle which is not clearly an adjective. Insert between *very* and the past participle one of the following adverbs: *much, deeply, greatly*.

Doubtful: I am very interested in Jeffer's prosody.

Right: I am very much interested in Jeffer's prosody.

Doubtful: He is very disgusted with his domestic life.

Right: He is very much disgusted with his domestic life.

Ways

Colloquial for "distance." Prefer *distance*.

We must travel a long distance before we reach Xanadu.

Well, good

Good, an adjective meaning "satisfactory or excellent," is often confused with *well*, an adverb meaning "in a satisfactory or excellent manner." *Good* cannot be used as an adverb.

Wrong: If her voice is well, she'll sing good.

Right: If her voice is good, she'll sing well.

Note: Well used as an adjective means "good health."

He looked well after his ulcer healed.

Whether, if *See* If, whether

You all

You all is dialectal (Southern) for the plural of you.

LETTER WRITING

THE LETTER IN MODERN SOCIETY

Though few people depend upon writing as their chief source of income, most have often found it necessary to compose a personal or business letter. Almost every man and woman who belongs to a club or organization or community needs to know the principles of effective letter writing.

More than two hundred years ago, the Earl of Chesterfield, one of the most famous of letter writers, gave his son excellent advice about both the personal and business letter. For **personal letters** he urged the **charm and wit of extemporaneous conversation;** for **business letters clarity and directness:** "Every paragraph should be so clear and unambiguous that the dullest fellow in the world may not be able to mistake it, nor obliged to read it twice in order to understand it."

One wonders what the Earl would say about a business letter of the 1980's which read like this:

Dear Sir:

Yours of the 5th inst. at hand. We beg to state in re your inquiry concerning your purchase order X-2930-C, that the above order was shipped from our warehouse in Las Vegas via Smith collect.

We regret most sincerely any delay you have been caused, but feel assured that the order is en route to you now. If any further delay is encountered, an immediate reply from you will be appreciated. We trust that we may continue to be of service and remain

Very truly yours,

Or how the Earl might react to the "charm" and "wit" of this personal note:

Dear Jim,

Well, you sent me a letter, and now I guess I owe you one. Gosh, but I hate to write letters, especially because there's never really anything around here to write about. We did go to the movies last night, one of those horror films, but you know what they're like.

Ma and Sis are ok, and we saw your Aunt Joan last week. She's ok too and sends her regards.

Well, I guess that's all that's new in this neck of the woods. Let me hear from you again soon, and tell me about life in the armed forces. I'd be kind of interested to know.

Regards from everybody.

Your friend,

In the modern world, crammed as it is with excitement and movement, only laziness or ignorance explains letters like the preceding two. The sections below attempt to direct the modern letter writer to effective communication that is correct, precise, and vigorous.

ESTABLISHED CONVENTIONS IN LETTER WRITING

In communication, as in clothing, good taste is dictated by custom and convention. Therefore, some rules must arbitrarily be followed in both personal and business correspondence.

STATIONERY AND GENERAL APPEARANCE

Business Letters *Choose stationery (letter paper and envelopes) of appropriate quality, color, and size.*

Use good quality, plain *white* bond paper in a standard size (for business stationery 8½ by 11 inches and 5½ by 7 inches).

Use white envelopes proper for standard letter paper: 4⅛ by 9½ inches and 3⅝ by 6½ inches.

Use a typewriter.

Almost all business letters written today

Figure 1   THE LETTER PICTURE

AVOID THIS

1 Oakly Avenue
Elmont, New York 11003

June 24, 1981

Box C123
Times
New York, N.Y. 10018

Dear Sir:

For the last six years I have been fortunate
enough to work at an occupation I really enjoy -- sales
promotion. At college I prepared for the work I knew I
would devote my life to. Since then, I have helped, both
as a salesman and as a sales executive, to develop successful techniques of marketing plastics in the United States
and in South America. I believe that I am now ready
to assume the responsibilities of complete sales promotional
management.

I have enclosed a personal data sheet outlining my qualifications for the position you offer. If my qualifications interest you, I should be grateful if you would
allow me to come in and talk with you.

Very truly yours,

Warren Finzer

Warren Finzer

1 Oakly Avenue
Elmont, New York 11003
June 24, 1981

Box C123
Times
New York, N.Y. 10018

Dear Sirs:

For the past six years I have been fortunate enough
to work at an occupation I really enjoy -- sales promotion.
At college I prepared for the work I knew I would devote
my life to. Since then, I have helped, both as a salesman
and as a sales executive, to develop successful techniques
of marketing plastics in the United States and in South
America. I believe that I am now ready to assume the
responsibilities of complete sales promotional management.

I have enclosed a personal data sheet outlining my
qualifications for the position you offer. If my qualifications interest you, I should be grateful if you would
allow me to come in and talk with you.

Very truly yours,

Warren Finzer

Warren Finzer

DO THIS

are typed. Only when specifically requested to do so ought one to write by hand, and then only in blue or black ink. Never use pencil.

In the better business organizations, no corrections or erasures are permitted in correspondence. The typescript must be mechanically perfect.

Use one side of the paper only, whether the letter is typewritten or handwritten.

Arrange the letter on the page so that the writing becomes a picture, the white space a frame. (see Figure 1)

Keep margins of at least one inch on all sides of the paper.

Be particularly careful not to crowd the right hand margin or the bottom of the page.

Estimate the length of the letter and frame it to make the most attractive arrangement. *Fold letters properly.* (see Figure 2)

To prepare an 8½ by 11 inch letter for a standard, **small commercial envelope** (3⅝ by 6½ inches):

Step 1. Starting from the bottom, fold the sheet upward to within one eighth inch of the top. The slight margin makes it easier to separate the ends when opening the letter.

Step 2. Now, starting from the left of the creased sheet, fold once from the left and once from the right to divide the width of the sheet into three equal sections.

Step 3. Place the letter in the envelope so that the left fold is down, the right fold up, and so that the right flap of the letter faces the back of the envelope.

To prepare an 8½ by 11 inch letter for a standard, **long commercial envelope** (4⅛ by 9½ inches):

Step 1. Starting from the bottom, fold the sheet upward to slightly more than one third the length of the sheet.

Step 2. Now, starting from the top, make the second fold at the edge of the bottom of the page as it lies folded.

Step 3. Place the letter in the envelope so that the two flaps face the back of the en-

velope, and the top edge of the letter rests on the bottom of the envelope.

Make certain that the folded letter fits the envelope perfectly. If the fit is wrong, the fold has been made incorrectly.

Figure 2 FOLDING THE LETTER

a. 8½"x11" LETTER IN SMALL COMMERCIAL ENVELOPE

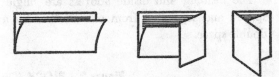

b. 8½"x11" LETTER IN LONG COMMERCIAL ENVELOPE

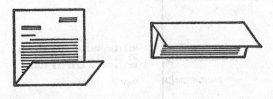

c. THE FOUR PAGE LEAFLET

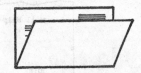

Personal Letters The writer has more leeway in selecting stationery for personal correspondence. Although a wide variety of colors and sizes is available, the standard size is a four page leaflet 5½ by 7 inches, the standard colors are white, buff, light blue, and gray. Envelopes match the page in size and color.

Most personal correspondence is handwritten, especially when the content is intimate. Nevertheless, typewritten personal notes have gained wide sanction and are generally acceptable.

Make the letter legible and neat. Avoid crowding margins at the right and bottom. Avoid garish contrasts between ink and paper.

The four-page leaflet should be folded once, in half, and placed in the envelope with the crease at the bottom.

HEADING AND INSIDE ADDRESS FOR TYPED BUSINESS LETTERS

The heading and inside address must be consistent in form (*block* or *indented*) and punctuation (*open* or *closed*). (see Figure 3 and Figure 4)

Open punctuation (no punctuation) and *block form* are generally preferred in both heading and inside address.

The heading and inside address are single-spaced and separated from one another by a double space.

The heading provides the address of the writer and the date. It is placed in the **upper right** side of the first page.

Note: Many firms use printed headings and type only the date.

Use no abbreviations such as Ave., St., Blvd., Rd.

Avoid 4th, 2nd, 1st. Use the numbers alone or, if there is a possibility of confusing a street number with a house number, spell it out: 36 East Thirty-third Street.

Abbreviations are generally approved for

Figure 3   BLOCK FORM, OPEN PUNCTUATION

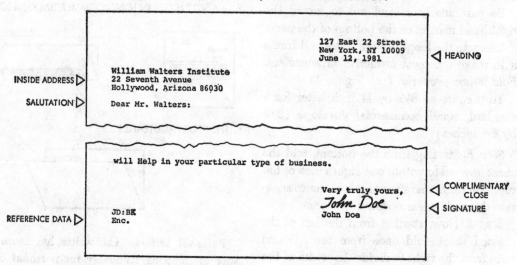

Figure 4   INDENTED FORM, OPEN PUNCTUATION

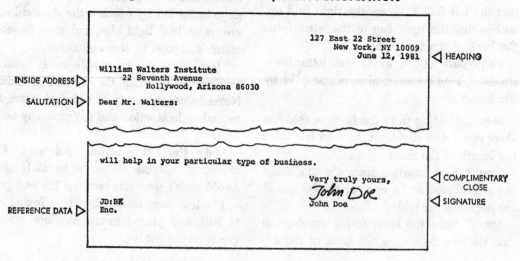

city-state relationships, such as: New York, NY and Washington, DC.

Do not abbreviate the names of the months. Do not write Dec. 7; write December 7. Do not use figures for months: 7/28/81. Do not write June 15, '81.

The **inside address** gives the exact name of the person, firm, or organization written to. It is placed flush with the left hand margin, and separated from the last line of the heading by a double space.

Observe the same rules for abbreviations as discussed under heading.

Provide full and accurate information so that the letter may reach the proper individual or department quickly:

> TO A DEPARTMENT
> Dombel's Department Store
> Adjustment Department
> 250 West 34 Street
> Avondale, IL 60435

> TO AN INDIVIDUAL
> Edward Jones and Sons
> Attention: William Cole
> 26 Lincoln Road
> Kansas City, MO 64125

THE SALUTATION—is placed flush with the left hand margin. It is separated from the last line of the inside address by a double space. (see Figure 3 and Figure 4)

In business letters, the salutation is followed by a colon:

Dear Mr. Smith:

In personal letters, the salutation is usually followed by a comma:

Dear Bill,

Note: The salutation is never, under any circumstances, followed by a semi-colon.

When the letter is addressed to a firm or organization rather than to an individual, use any of the following salutations:

Gentlemen: Dear Sir:
Ladies: (or Mesdames:)   Dear Sirs:

Note: A more formal usage is:

My dear Sir:
Sir: Madam:

When the letter is addressed to an individual, use any copy of the following salutations:

Dear Mr. Lump: Dear Miss Jones:
Dear Mrs. Eichen: Dear Dr. Pangloss:
Dear Professor Middlebrook:
Dear Lieutenant Dreyfus:

Note that abbreviations are permissible only with Mr., Mrs., and Dr.

Below is a list of salutations to be used when addressing dignitaries:

GOVERNMENT OFFICIALS
The President
> My dear Mr. President:
> My dear President McKinley:
> Sir:

Cabinet officers
> My dear Mr. Secretary:
> My dear Secretary Adams:
> My dear Mr. Lowell:
> Sir:

Judges
> My dear Judge Garth:
> My dear Sir:

Military officials
> My dear General Atwater:
> My dear General:
> My dear Sir:

MEMBERS OF THE CLERGY
The Pope
> Your Holiness:
> Most Holy Father:

Cardinal
> Your Eminence:

Archbishop
> Most Reverend Archbishop:
> Most Reverend Sir:

Bishop (Roman Catholic)
> Your Excellency:

Bishop (Episcopalian)
    Right Reverend and Dear Sir:
    Dear Bishop Mather:

Bishop (Methodist)
    Dear Sir:
    Dear Bishop Bradford:

Priest (Roman Catholic)
    Reverend Father:
    Dear Father Malachy:

Clergyman
    Dear Sir:
    Dear Mr. Link:

Rabbi
    Reverend Sir:
    Dear Sir:
    Dear Rabbi Lewisohn:
    Dear Mr. Pool:

Mother Superior
    Reverend Mother:
    My dear Reverend Mother Noonan:

Nun
    Reverend Sister:
    Dear Sister Anne:

EDUCATORS
    President of a College
        Dear Sir:
        Dear President Gallagher:

    President of a Catholic College
        Very Reverend and dear Father:
        Dear Father Malachy:

    President of a Theological Seminary
        Dear President Weston:
        Dear Dr. Weston:

    Dean of a College
        Dear Dean Walters:
        Dear Sir:
        Dear Dr. Walters:

FOREIGN DIGNITARIES
    Prime Minister
        My dear Mr. Prime Minister:
        My dear Mr. Teetering:

Duke or Duchess
    Dear Lord Asquith:
    Sir:
    Dear Duchess Asquith:

Baron or Baroness
    My dear Lord Essex:
    Sir:
    My dear Lady Essex:

Ambassador
    Excellency:
    My dear Mr. Ambassador:

THE COMPLIMENTARY CLOSE—(*see Figure 3 and Figure 4*)—should be placed on a separate line and to the right of the middle of the page. It should be separated from the last line of the body of the letter by double spacing.

Capitalize only the first letter of the complimentary close. A comma should be used after it.

Keep the complimentary close in harmony with the salutation. If the salutation is formal, the close ought to be formal.

Formal close
    Very truly yours,
    Yours very truly,
    Yours truly,   Note: Use *yours* in
Personal close   all complimentary
    Sincerely yours,   closings.
    Yours sincerely,
    Cordially yours,
    Faithfully yours,
Official close
    Respectfully yours,
    Yours respectfully,
    Very respectfully yours,

Note: Avoid outdated phrases like "Your obedient servant"; "I am, dear sir, expectantly yours"; "Your humble servant."

THE SIGNATURE—(*see Figure 3 and Figure 4*) The writer's name should be in his own handwriting and should be placed two spaces below the complimentary close. In a business letter, a typewritten name should be added and should be placed two spaces below the handwritten signature.

Note: Letters from business organizations are usually signed with the name of the firm, typewritten, and the signature of the letter-writer, handwritten:

Mills Bottling Company

L. M. Smith

If a woman gives no specific marital identification, she is assumed to be single. If she wishes to be addressed as one who is married, she should sign her own name (*not* her husband's) and precede it with *Mrs.* in parentheses; write her husband's name preceded by Mrs., enclose it in parentheses, and write it on the line below her signature.

Single woman: Mabel Seckert or (Miss) Mabel Seckert

Married woman: (Mrs.) Annabelle Lee

Married woman: Annabelle Lee (Mrs. Edgar Allan Lee)

Reference data are placed flush with the left margin, below the signature. (see Figure 3 and Figure 4)

The writer who dictates a letter usually places his initials first, followed by a colon and his secretary's initials. When errors or problems occur, identifying the writer is thus simplified.

When *enclosures* are added, the fact should be noted directly below the initials.

ADDRESSING THE ENVELOPE—(*see Figure 5 and Figure 6*)

The Address

Write the address legibly. Use pen or typewriter.

Place the address in the right middle part of the envelope or post card.

At the request of the United States Postal Service, indent each succeeding line after the

Figure 5   THE ENVELOPE

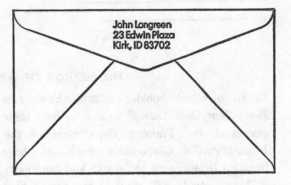

first line of the address, and leave a space between lines.

Do not abbreviate names of cities, streets or avenues.

Include the zone number of addresses in cities.

Indicate clearly requests for special handling: air mail, registry, special delivery, and the like.

Affix the stamp in the upper right corner.

The Return Address

The return address of the sender of a business letter should always appear in the extreme upper left corner of the face of the envelope.

The return address of the sender of a personal letter may appear either in the extreme upper left corner of the face of the envelope, or in the top center portion of the back flap of the envelope. (see Figure 6)

Use block form and open punctuation for the return address.

Write the full name of the sender but do not use "Mr."

Exercise No. 123

Make any necessary corrections in the mechanical details of the following letter:

122 E. 44th St.
Chic., IL 65059
Sept., 5, '81

Attention Mr. Smith
Catnip Corp. of America

Dear Mr. Smith;

_____
_____
_____
_____
_____

Very truly yours,

Exercise No. 124

Make any necessary corrections in the form of the address and return address on the following envelope:

Mr. Wm. Denton
120 W. 4th St.
New York, NY 10003

Mr. Edwards
Compton Tea Co.
Manager
Paterson, NJ 20309
USA

THE METHOD OF WRITING BUSINESS LETTERS

In an excellent booklet *Letters—Have You Read Your Own Lately?* written to help their personnel, the Training Department of the Johns-Manville Corporation explained how business letters came to be stiff and pompous:

"Many people still cling to the notion that business letters must be very formal. . . . There has been a sort of traditional business language used in business letters and nowhere else. That is the poor background we start with.

"Do you remember dictating your first letter? You were probably a little in awe of the importance of business correspondence. You certainly didn't want your letter to sound simple or childish or different from the rest.

"So you listened to the others in the office, read their letters, and copied their style and phraseology. You hunted up impressive phrases like 'We hereby acknowledge your letter of the 16th and in reply wish to advise,' or 'We trust the above action meets with your entire approval.' Then you were in the groove!—or, should we say,—the rut?

"Or you might have bucked the current for a while and then, because it's easier to drift than to swim, you, too, started saying 'In the above instance' and 'Beg to advise that shipment has gone forward.' Thus the old-fashioned style perpetuates itself. It is passed along from generation to generation."

Progressive business organizations are trying to change the letter-writing habits of this generation by writing fresh, vigorous letters.

Good business letters (as well as office memoranda, reports, and bulletins) should be *planned* before they are written and *revised* after they are written. During both stages of composition the writer ought to ask:

What are the facts involved?
What message do I want to convey?

Good business letters must be *clear* and *correct.*

Vague: Have you anything about good salesmanship or how to start a course of that kind? Any books, pamphlets, or references?

The reader probably will be able to figure out what this letter means, but he must first untangle the bad prose, and then try to determine what the writer wants.

Clear: We are planning to begin courses in effective salesmanship. Because we know that you have conducted excellent training programs, we should like your assistance. Can you recommend any course syllabi, reading references, film-strips, or other audio-visual aids?

Good business letters must be direct and natural.

Artificial:

This will acknowledge receipt of your letter in regard to the error you claimed we made in billing the shipment of toothpicks, your order 18L14, invoice 1287A.

This is to advise you that we have located the error in the billing, which was due to a transfer of our files. With reference to this error, a new invoice, 1398A, will be sent you in due course, which same should reach you soon.

We regret any inconvenience caused you and trust that our action as stated above will prove satisfactory.

Only Colonel Blimp, or one of his pompous American counterparts in business would speak this way. Furthermore, what the letter really has to communicate appears—and then only vaguely—in the second paragraph. The first paragraph merely repeats what the reader already knows; the third paragraph doesn't convince because it is too wordy and too trite.

Direct and Natural:

Your claim is wholly justified. Our billing is wrong and we are sorry about our error.

We are mailing at once a corrected billing on our invoice 1398A.

This letter gets directly to the point, clearly explains the facts, and stops.

Most of the troubles with business letters derive from roundabout language, "deadwood," or jargon. If weasel-words were cut out, letters would communicate the sprightliness their writers display in talking, but not in writing. In the pamphlet already mentioned, the Johns-Manville Corporation lists some of the more offensive examples of jargon and indicates effective alternatives:

Use Familiar Words—You're not explaining the Einstein Theory.

WHY BE SO FORMAL?	MAKE IT FRIENDLY
communication	letter, wire
the writer	I or me
maintain an inventory	keep a stock
discrepancy	difference
assistance	help
unable to effect cancellation	cannot cancel
We regret most sincerely	I'm very sorry

Use Active Voice

PASSIVE	ACTIVE
No billing has been received	We didn't get a bill
It is desired that we receive	We want, We'd appreciate
An immediate reply will be appreciated	Please answer promptly, We'll appreciate a prompt reply.
The question was raised by you	You raised the question (or You asked)
Your letter of July 15th has been received and the contents of same carefully noted	(Just don't say it at all)

Stay out of the Squirrel Cage—Use Straightforward Language

SQUIRREL CAGE	STRAIGHTFORWARD
We are in receipt of	We received
Please arrange to return	Please return
We are not in a position to	We cannot
May we suggest that you	Please
We will take steps to	We will
Please see that an investigation is made to determine	Please find out

Why use a Phrase ... When a Word is Enough

inasmuch as	because
in order to	to
along the lines of	like
in the event that	if
at the present time	now
in regard to	about
with reference to	about
pertaining to	about
in the nature of	like
for the reason that	because
in the amount of	for

Avoid Letter Fungus

MOLDY MORSELS	TASTY TIDBITS
attached please find	here is *or* I am attaching
enclosed please find	here is *or* I enclose

MOLDY MORSELS	TASTY TIDBITS
this will acknowledge receipt of—	
replying to your letter of—	
with reference to your letter of—	(These are all time and space fillers. Let's omit them and get on with the message)
we wish to advise that—	
please be advised that—	
contents noted—	
we take this opportunity to—	
for your information—	
under separate cover	(Say how sent—by parcel post, etc.)
according to our records	(But naturally, Why say it?)
above (as, "the above")	
subject (as, "subject order")	(Name what you are talking about or just say "your order," or "it")
same (as "thank you for same")	
at this writing	now
even date	(Name the date)
our Mr. Jones	Mr. Jones, our representative (our engineer, etc.)
forward	send
the shipment will go forward	we will ship
favor us with	send us *or* give us
your favor	your letter, order, request

MOLDY MORSELS	TASTY TIDBITS
we trust	we hope, believe, think
by return mail	
at an early date	(Omit unless special attention is necessary. Then say, "Please answer promptly" or "Please send us your reply by April 15")
at your earliest convenience	
in due course	soon, promptly, at once

Good business letters must be **courteous** and **personalized**.

Offensive: We will send you the copy of Whitman's *Leaves of Grass* when you tell us which edition you want. Until such time as you send us this information, we will hold your order in abeyance.

This letter makes the customer feel that he has been stupid, or committed an unpardonable sin. A wiser procedure involves considering the point of view of the customer and putting him at his ease.

Courteous: We have in stock the third, fifth, and seventh editions of Whitman's *Leaves of Grass*. The price is the same for each of these editions, and all are in excellent condition. Please let us know which edition you prefer, and we shall fill your order at once.

TYPES OF BUSINESS LETTERS

THE LETTER OF APPLICATION

WANTED: Sales promotion manager, extensive experience with manufactured products, college graduate, some knowledge of Spanish preferred. Write, stating full details. Box C123, *Times*.

245 North Avenue
Bronx, NY 10454
June 24, 1981

Dear Sir:

In response to your ad in Sunday's *Times*, I believe that I am the man for the job.

I am 31 and graduated from College in 1972. Since then, I have held several jobs dealing with sales promotion and succeeded at all of them. I am sure I could do the same for your organization.

You can reach me for an interview by calling between seven and nine at 673/7770.

Very truly yours,
Edward Rack

Would you hire this man?

You ought not, for his letter indicates (perhaps erroneously) that he is tactless, inaccurate, and vague:

1. He has omitted the *inside address*.

2. Paragraph 1:

He fails to state what job he is applying for. The firm may have inserted several advertisements. (Incidentally, in letters of application, use *advertisement*, not *ad.*)

His tone is obnoxiously immodest.

3. Paragraph 2:

He fails to state the college from which he was graduated.

He fails to give his marital status if applicable.

He fails to make *specific* references either to the firms he worked for or to the duties he performed.

He ignores the reference to knowledge of Spanish.

His tone is again unjustifiably self-confident.

4. Paragraph 3:

His tone challenges the employer: "Here I am; come get me."

Thus, the letter of application must, like all business letters, be:

Clear and Correct.
Direct and Natural.
Courteous and Personalized.

Specifically, the letter of application must:

1. Establish a point of contact with the employer

How I know about the vacancy (advertisement, agency, third person, or an unsolicited letter of application)

What job I am applying for

2. Arouse the interest of the employer

My general qualifications: include age, although it is not a legal requirement.

My education, training, and experience

3. Convince the employer

Why I think I can do the job

Others who will vouch for my ability

4. Gain an interview with the employer

Request for an interview

Arrangements necessary for an interview

Each of the letters below illustrates the principles of effective applications for jobs.

A.

1 Oakley Avenue
Elmont, NY 10438
June 24, 1981

Box C 123
Times
New York, NY 10036

Dear Sir:

I am writing in answer to your advertisement in Sunday's *Times* for a sales promotion manager.

I am twenty-nine years old, married, and a graduate of the Wharton School of Business with a B.B.A. degree. At college I majored in sales management and marketing, and minored in Spanish.

Since my graduation in 1947, I have worked for Glo-Set Extruders, 11 Easter Avenue, Westchester, New York. During my first three years with this firm, I was a salesman. Since then, I have been assistant sales promotion manager. My special duties include training new sales personnel; writing all correspondence in Spanish to our clients in South America; and organizing marketing and promotional programs. I believe that my experience has prepared me to assume the responsibilities of complete sales promotional management.

I have permission to refer you to my employer, Mr. Leland Logan, and to Mr. Edward Taylor, chairman, Department of Business Administration, The Wharton School of Business, University of Pennsylvania, Philadelphia, Pennsylvania.

I should be pleased to give you any further information you request. May I have an interview at your convenience?

Very truly yours,

Warren Finger

Home phone: 254-5698
Office phone: 952-6574

B.

Note: Another way to answer an advertisement and get results is to write a brief letter and to enclose, on a separate page, a personal data sheet:

>1 Oakley Avenue
>Elmont, NY 10438
>June 24, 1981

Box C 123
Times
New York, NY

Dear Sir:

For the past six years I have been fortunate enough to work at an occupation I really enjoy—sales promotion. At college I prepared for the work I knew I would devote my life to. Since then, I have helped, both as a salesman and as a sales executive, to develop successful techniques of marketing plastics in the United States and in South America. I believe that I am now ready to assume the responsibilities of complete sales promotional management.

I have enclosed a personal data sheet outlining my qualifications for the position you offer. If my qualifications interest you, I should be grateful if you would allow me to come in and talk with you.

>Very truly yours,

>*Warren Finzer*

Personal Data Sheet

Name: Warren Finzer   Age: 29 years
Address: 1 Oakley Avenue   Height: 5' 10"
   Elmont, NY 10438   Weight: 175
Telephone: Home—254-5698
   Office—952-6574
Education: B.B.A., 1947, The Wharton School of Business, University of Pennsylvania.
Major subject: Sales management and marketing.
Minor subject: Spanish (I read, write, and speak the language fluently.)
Experience: Glo-Set Extruders, 11 Easter Avenue, Westchester, NY 10281

1947–1950: salesman
1950–present: Assistant sales promotion manager in charge of: Training new sales personnel; Writing all correspondence to clients in South America; Organizing marketing and promotional programs.

References:
   Mr. Leland Logan, president
   Glo-Set Extruders
   11 Easter Avenue
   Westchester, NY 10481

   Mr. Edward Taylor, chairman
   Department of Business Administration
   The Wharton School of Business
   University of Pennsylvania
   Philadelphia, PA 19106

INQUIRIES AND REPLIES—vary considerably. Correspondents may either inquire about the adaptability of a product to their specific needs or request information having little or nothing to do with a purchase. Likewise, a reply may give details about a product or simply offer a special service unrelated to sales. Certain conventions, however, distinguish both the inquiry and the reply:

The Inquiry   State specifically the kind of information you need, and why you are asking the person to provide it.

Explain clearly how and when you intend to use this information.

Express your appreciation. Avoid "Thank you in advance" and like expressions which seem to prevent the other fellow from refusing or to indicate your unwillingness to write again.

The Reply   Answer the questions asked.
When necessary, give detailed explanations.
Offer additional service.

Example of an Exchange of Inquiry and Reply[*]
Dear Sir:

Recently I heard a brief but complimentary reference made to Clingtite Letters. I intend to buy a movie titling kit, but most of those I have seen are too cumbersome for my needs. Since

[*] By permission of Clingtite Letters, Chicago, Illinois.

my local photographic dealer does not stock your product, I should like the following information:

1. Can this equipment be used conveniently both indoors and outdoors?
2. To what substances will the letters adhere.
3. May I see samples of the letters?
4. Where can I purchase the kit?

I shall appreciate your answering these questions.

Very truly yours,

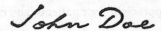

John Doe

Dear Friend:

Thank you for your inquiry on CLINGTITE LETTERS. We are pleased to send you samples of our letters with our handy booklet "Titling Can Be Easy."

CLINGTITE LETTERS stick on contact with glass, steel, plastic, metal and all other non-porous surfaces. Imagine the speed and ease in titling right on location while shooting your movies. You eliminate all need for splicing in titles at a later date. Our booklet is packed full of ideas and suggestions.

CLINGTITE LETTERS are carried by leading dealers and cost $2.95. A set consists of two 8″ × 10″ titling boards and over 150 letters, numerals, symbols and animated characters. If your local dealer is out of stock and you wish to purchase a kit immediately, follow our "buy by mail" instructions below.

Well-made titles add interest and continuity to your slides and movies and CLINGTITE LETTERS make your job easier.

Sincerely yours,

Lawrence A. Roberts

Sales Promotion Manager

IF YOU ARE BUYING BY MAIL—

Send $2.95 in cash, check, money order or stamps with your name and address (you can use the back of this letter). Please print or write legibly.

We pay postage for fourth class delivery of parcels. Please consult your postmaster for zone rates.

C.O.D. orders are sent at $2.95 plus postage and C.O.D. charges, or a total of $3.42. No first class C.O.D.'s.

Note: ALL KITS PURCHASED BY MAIL MAY BE RETURNED FOR COMPLETE REFUND IF YOU ARE NOT FULLY SATISFIED!

ORDER AND REMITTANCE Most business organizations provide printed forms to make the task of ordering simple and efficient. When no form is available, the correspondent should observe the following conventions:

Tabulate the items to be ordered.

Specify the quantity, quality, shape, style, color, price. If the material is listed in a catalog, give the catalog number.

List substitutes, or state that no substitutes will be accepted.

Specify the method of shipment.

Where will the order be shipped?

How will the order be shipped: overnight courier, express, first class, parcel post, United Parcel, and the like?

When will the order be shipped? If a time limit is important, state the deadline.

Specify the method of payment: personal check, certified check, charge card, C.O.D., and the like.

Example:

Dear Sir:

I have enclosed a check for $29.50 for the following items:

1 Croton stainless steel aquarium, 5 gallon size, No. X27	$13.00
1 Croton fluorescent light fixture for use with five gallon aquarium	2.00
1 Three pound bag of washed sand	.50
1 Argus thermostat, No. M4	2.00
1 X-Cel Tank thermometer, No. 2	1.00
1 Superba Air Pump, No. 522	10.00
	$29.50

Please ship these items, without substitution, by parcel post. If there are any shortages or changes in price, please let me know before shipping the order.

ACKNOWLEDGMENT Most acknowledgments are sent out on the day an order is received and take the form of printed postal cards or brief form letters. On occasion, a letter acknowledging an order from a new customer or an old one warrants a special letter. In all letters of acknowledgment, the following conventions prevail:

Statement of appreciation for the order.

Reference to the date of receipt of the order.

Statement of when the order will be filled and when it will be shipped.

Statement of desire to be of further service to the customer.

Example:

Dear Sir:

Thank you for your order of June 12.

Shipments have been slightly delayed, but your order will be sent to you as soon as possible. If you have not received it within two weeks, please notify us.

We appreciate your patience and cooperation.

Very truly yours,

TYPES OF PERSONAL LETTERS

THE CONVERSATIONAL LETTER Naturalness, sincerity, originality, and ease characterize the conversational letter. Keep in mind the personality of the one to whom you write. Reread his last letter to you and discuss the things he has shown interest in. Tell him about people and events you are both familiar with and curious about. Avoid a patronizing tone or an artificially literary or crudely vulgar style.

Dear A—— and H——,

Here's news of more than average proportions—the C——s are seriously considering—no, they are intently planning on a move to California. Yes, lock, stock, and deep-freeze, they plan to amble off to the sun-baked surface of the California desert where M's brother has been baking these past several years.

Maybe the migration causes no surprise. You might remark, "Oh, well, a couple of screwballs—they might do anything." That would probably be true, but seriously we have thought the situation over carefully, and I do want to tell you why we arrived at this unusual decision. Fundamentally, I've grown to dislike the city. My sentiments are outlined in Abraham Cowley's poem, "The Wish"—"This busy world and I shall ne'er agree." And I simply don't want to work any longer in D.C. So, all in all, we've decided to take a gamble—as we've done before—

sell the house, take the money, and move to what may be a desert mirage, but what we hope will really be greener fields. We've tried to eliminate the wishful thinking, but maybe you never really can do that.

Well, there it is. We'll visit you before we leave, of course. When, however, I can't at this moment even guess. But wish us luck, will you? Keep well and enjoy life.

THE "BREAD AND BUTTER" LETTER When you have been a guest for dinner or a weekend, write a brief note of appreciation within a day after your visit. Write even though you have already thanked your host in person.

Dear B——,

The ingredients of your recipe I haven't yet discovered. But somewhere in it you have used magic, for the enchantment of the weekend remains. I look forward to more of your delightful witchcraft.

Sincerely yours,

THE "THANK YOU" LETTER When you receive a gift or a favor, acknowledge it as soon as possible. The letter should not become too sentimental, but ought to reveal your sincere appreciation.

Dear J——,

I had thought myself too old for surprises, but when the postman left a huge package from

Vienna, I blinked and scratched. The portfolio of Bosch's prints (the best edition I have ever seen) is astonishingly beautiful. I wish I might knock at your distant door and sit with you to admire them. Is someone knocking?

THE CONGRATULATORY LETTER When a friend wins an award or gains a post of honor, send him a note of congratulation.

Dear L——,

We rejoice in your winning a travelling fellowship to Ireland. Certainly you have long deserved it, and we hope your travels and research will be exciting and productive.

THE LETTER OF CONDOLENCE Letters expressing condolence should contain a brief but sincere statement of sympathy.

Dear Miss Lee,

We want to express our sincerest sympathy and to tell you how deeply sorry we were to learn of your loss.

THE FORMAL SOCIAL NOTE Invitations and replies are either printed or handwritten on small white cards or notepaper. They are never typed.

Invitations should be mailed at least two weeks before the date of the scheduled event.

Replies should be prompt and definite in their expression of acceptance or regret.

Formal notes are written in the third person. Every word is spelled out, except street numbers, Mr., Mrs., Dr.

Invitation

The Boonesville Buddy Boys
request the pleasure of
Mr. Louis Wigan's
company at a reunion party
on Saturday evening, July the third
at eight o'clock
Miller's Tavern
Eastern Avenue.

Reply

Mr. Louis Wigan
regrets that he is unable to accept
(accepts with pleasure)
The Boonesville Buddy Boys'
kind invitation to a reunion party
on Saturday evening, July the third
at eight o'clock.

Note: Neither invitation nor reply uses:
Inside address
Complimentary close
Signature

TEST NO. 2

Final Test

GRAMMAR

Identify the part of speech of each of the italicized words.

1. With *how* sad steps, O Moon, thou climbest the skies.
2. I bring fresh showers for the *thirsting* flowers.
3. You shall *not* crucify man upon a cross of gold.
4. My children do *whatever* they wish to do.
5. I will not go; *however*, you are free to go if you wish.

USAGE

Part I: Choose the correct form for each of the following:

1. Neither of his friends (*is, are*) more literate than he.
2. Randolph is the man (*who, whom*) I believe is best suited for the promotion.
3. There is so much talking (*in back of, behind*) me that I cannot hear the speaker.
4. I am so tired that I (*can scarcely, can't scarcely*) stand.

5. My tastes in women are different (*from, than*) his.

6. Had you been there, you (*heard, have heard, would have heard*) him.

7. I don't know (*if, whether*) I should tell you about my decision.

8. The mink coat (*lay, laid*) where the politician's wife left it.

9. I (*shall, will*) arrive tomorrow, and thereafter I am determined that all (*shall, will*) obey my commands.

10. She disliked liquor that tasted (*bitter, bitterly*).

11. Everyone expects (*his, their*) candidate to win.

12. June is one of those people who (*collect, collects*) grievances.

13. In the hot weather I feel (*bad, badly*).

14. I am willing to (*accept, except*) any excuse (*accept, except*) those which are manifest lies.

15. Florence has (*swam, swum*) in many oceans.

Part II: Rewrite the following sentences to assure clarity and correctness.

1. When driving through the tunnel, the air pressure affected his ears.

2. A love like ours only comes once in a decade.

3. Pat's charm was not only her physical beauty but she was also gracious and intelligent.

4. Being that he is that kind of a person, he cannot be expected to in any circumstance be popular.

5. Ought we watch television or to have an evening of discussing politics.

SPELLING

Correct any misspelled word. If the word is correct, let it remain as it is.

allies	irrefuteable	procede
consumate	benefited	lieutenant
aclimate	foundrys	innoculate
freind	supercede	rarify
decieve	preceed	innuendo

PUNCTUATION

Insert punctuation wherever it is necessary.

1. He gave the order however only a few obeyed it.

2. If it is essential that we work then work we must.

3. My friend who loves the name Jojo despises the name Archibald.

4. Onwards and upwards said his father but Tommy answered what if I want to go backwards and downwards.

5. With men of a speculative turn writes Teufelsdrockh there come seasons when in fear you ask that unanswerable question Who am I.

VOCABULARY

Part I: Add suffixes needed to change the following words to adjectives.

EXAMPLE: America—American

1. deride
2. maniac
3. admonish
4. secret (*noun*)
5. exhort

Part II: Give at least one word derived from each of the following roots.

1. nostos (*home*)
2. therme (*heat*)
3. dermis (*skin*)
4. cognosco (*know*)
5. genus (*kind, class*)
6. tangere (*touch*)
7. gamos (*marriage*)
8. pathos (*feeling*)
9. skopein (*see*)
10. ferre (*carry, bring*)

ANSWERS

TEST NO. 1

SENTENCE ERRORS

PART I:

1. are (see Agreement)
2. go (see Agreement)
3. has (see Agreement)
4. was (see Agreement)
5. who (see Case)
6. me (see Case)
7. her, me (see Case)
8. him (see Case)
9. he (see Reference)
10. its (see Reference)
11. sweet (see Adjectives)
12. surely (see Adverbs)
13. sought (see Verbs)
14. saw (see Verbs)
15. would have seen (see Verbs)

PART II:

1. If we all strive towards peace, *we* may hope. . . . (see Shifts)
2. Wash your hair with *Squeaky Lotion* and then massage it with *Silky Conditioner.* (see Parallelism)
3. I expect Bill to arrive early and to bring his cousin Ann. (see Parallelism)
4. Put the warm sodas in the refrigerator. (see Modifiers)
5. His ankle broken, the racing colt had to be destroyed by his owner. (see Modifiers)

SPELLING

Listed below are correct spellings for the misspelled words.

embarrassed	marriage	receipt
forcible	height	picnicking
boundaries	dynamos	benefited

PUNCTUATION

1. Jane, answer the telephone. (see Direct Address)
2. correct (see Restrictive Clauses)
3. If I draw . . . bank, I shall be . . . (see Subordinate Clauses)
4. Millie, who has several suitors, loves none of them. (see Non-Restrictive Clauses)
5. "Gretchen," he begged, "won't you, for goodness' sake, share a doughnut with me?" (see Quotation Marks)

VOCABULARY

PART I:

1. asymmetrical
2. benevolent
3. monogamy
4. malignant
5. taciturn

PART II:

1. epicure
2. accidental
3. abundance
4. reward, recompense, pay
5. acting; affected, artificial

TEST NO. 2

GRAMMAR

1. adverb (modifying *sad*)
2. adjective (modifying *flowers*)
3. not (adverb of negation) modifies verb *shall crucify.*
4. whatever (indefinite pronoun)
5. however (conjunctive adverb)

USAGE

PART I:

1. is
2. who (subject of *is*)
3. behind
4. can scarcely
5. different from
6. would have heard
7. whether
8. lay
9. shall, shall
10. bitter
11. his
12. collect
13. bad
14. accept, except
15. swum

PART II:

1. When driving through the tunnel, he felt the air pressure.
2. A love like ours comes only once in a decade.
3. Pat's charm was not only her physical beauty but also her grace and intelligence.
4. Since he is that kind of person, he cannot be expected in any circumstances to be popular.
5. Ought we watch wrestling or discuss politics.

SPELLING

Listed below are the correct spellings for the misspelled words.

consummate	irrefutable	proceed
acclimate	foundries	inoculate
friend	supersede	rarefy
deceive	precede	

PUNCTUATION

1. He gave the order; however, only a few obeyed it.
2. If it is essential that we work, then work we must.
3. My friend, who loves the name Jojo, despises the name Archibald.
4. "Onwards and upwards," said his father, but Tommy answered, "What if I want to go backwards and downwards?"
5. "With men of a speculative turn," writes Teufelsdrockh, "there come seasons when in fear you ask that unanswerable question: 'Who am I?'"

VOCABULARY

PART I:

1. derisive
2. maniacal
3. admonitory
4. secretive
5. exhortatory

PART II:
1. nostalgia, nostalgic
2. thermostat, thermal, thermometer
3. epidermis, dermatologist
4. cognition, recognize, reconnaissance
5. generic, general
6. intangible, tangent
7. monogamy, polygamy, amalgam
8. sympathy, pathetic
9. periscope, scope, telescope
10. transfer, ferry, refer

Exercise No. 1

1. Death spares none.
2. Nonsentence.
3. Nonsentence.
4. [You] let no man be called fortunate until he is dead. (Subject understood.)
5. Nonsentence.
6. Nonsentence.
7. Life is made up of marble and mud.
8. It is life near the bone where it is sweetest.
9. Variety [i]'s the very spice of life.
10. Life is just one darned thing after another.

Exercise No. 2

1. *Mary*—noun
   had—verb
   little—adjective
   lamb—noun
   Its—pronoun
   fleece—noun
   was—verb
   white—adjective
   snow—noun
   And—conjunction
   everywhere—adverb
   went—verb
   He—pronoun
   followed—verb
   her—pronoun
   to—preposition
   school—noun
   one—adjective
   day—noun
   was—verb
   against—preposition
   rule—noun
   It—pronoun
   made—verb
   children—noun
   in—preposition
2. adjective; adverb
3. verb; adjective
4. adjective; noun

5. verb; noun
6. verb; noun
7. *quick*—adjective
   brown—adjective
   fox—noun
   jumps—verb
   over—preposition
   lazy—adjective
   dog—noun
8. *He*—pronoun
   stood—verb
   hesitantly—adverb
   on—preposition
   board—noun
   gazed—verb
   longingly—adverb
   at—preposition
   water—noun
   but—conjunction
   never—adverb
   dived—verb
   into—preposition
   it—pronoun
9. interjection
10. *But*—verb
   me—pronoun
   no—adjective
   buts—noun

Exercise No. 3

1. The Hudson, a river 306 miles long, flows south to New York Bay. It was discovered by a Dutch explorer named Henry Hudson.
2. The students—who came from China and Japan—preferred science to history, Esperanto to English, mechanics to music. All, however, were required to take a course entitled ["] Introduction to American Government. ["]

3. Both Mammon and Mercury were gods once. Today, *mammon* means "riches" and *mercury* signifies "a heavy silver-white metallic element."

Exercise No. 4

1. Abstract: proportion, manners, customs, amusements, nation, regulations, penal code.
2. Concrete: men, battles, bull-fights, combats, gladiators, hanging, burning, rack.

Exercise No. 5

Collective nouns: board (when employed to signify "group": e.g., *board of directors*), class, ministry, nation, people, group, assembly.

Exercise No. 6

duties	swine	appendix
fly	spoonfuls	series
monkeys	louse	p's and q's
brother	court-martial	stratum
geese	passers-by	oases
mongooses	hangers-on	mesdames
sheep	die	beau
Negroes	step-ins	seraph
dominoes	geniuses, genii	mathematics
halves	apparatus, apparatuses	dilettante

Exercise No. 7

1. spinster
2. bitch
3. filly
4. baroness
5. signore
6. tomcat
7. landlord
8. poetess
9. Mistress (*or* Miss), Mrs., Mme.
10. widower

Exercise No. 8

1. *Cleo*, nominative case, subject of verb *refused*. *Tony*, objective case, object of verb *refused*.
2. *David*, nominative case, predicate nominative after linking verb *was*. *king, priest, prophet*, nominative case, appositives of *David*. *people*, objective case, object of preposition *of*.
3. *Man*, nominative case, subject of linking verb *is*. *architect*, nominative case, predicate nominative after linking verb *is*. *character*, objective case, object of preposition *of*.
4. *Judgment*, nominative case, word in direct address. *beasts*, objective case, object of preposition *to*.
5. *Brutus*, objective case, object of verb *have played*. *Brutus*, nominative case, subject of verb *has lost*.
6. *King of England's*, possessive case, indicates possession (or habitual residence). *palace*, nominative case, subject of linking verb *is*. *hour's*, possessive case, idiomatically indicates duration. *ride*, nominative case, predicate nominative after linking verb *is*. *center*, objective case, object of preposition *from*. *London*, objective case, object of preposition *of*.
7. *plural*, nominative case, subject of verb *baffled*. *forms*, objective case, object of preposition *of*. *ingenuity*, objective case, object of verb *baffled*.

grammarians, objective case, object of preposition *of*.

time, objective case, object of preposition *for*.

8. *Guiness'*, possessive case, indicates manufacturer.

Stout, objective case, object of verb *try*.

goodness', possessive case, idiomatically indicates attribute.

sake, objective case, object of preposition *for*.

9. *Shelley*, objective case, object of verb *did see*.

10. *man's*, nominative case, subject of verb [*i*]*'s*.

shirt, objective case, object of preposition *without*.

Exercise No. 9

1. *He*, personal pronoun.
   whoever, compound relative pronoun, nominative case, subject of verb *trusted*.
   him, personal pronoun.
2. *whomever*, objective case, object of preposition *by*.
3. *myself*, reflexive pronoun, objective case, object of verb *bit*.
4. *we*, personal pronoun, nominative case, subject of verb *despise*.
   ourselves, reflexive pronoun, objective case, object of verb *despise*.
5. *all*, indefinite pronoun, nominative case, appositive of nominative *we*.
   I, nominative case, appositive (with *Einstein* and *Fermi*) of *we*.
6. *each other*, reciprocal pronoun (denoting interaction involving two people).
7. *who*, relative pronoun, nominative case, subject of verb *knew*.
   whom, relative pronoun, object of preposition *to*.
8. *whose*, relative pronoun, possessive case, indicates possession. (Preferred because *hill* seems personified, and *whose* refers to people.)
   everything, indefinite pronoun, objective case, object of preposition *at*.
9. *the use of which*. (Preferred because *of which* refers to things; but *whose* is also acceptable.)
   nobody, indefinite pronoun, nominative case, subject of verb *knows*.
10. [*u*]*'s*, personal pronoun, objective case, object of verb *let*.
    me, personal pronoun, objective case, appositive of [*u*]*'s*.

Exercise No. 10

1. Everybody has a right to *his* own opinion, right or wrong. (*Everybody*, antecedent of *his* is singular.)
2. Either the marines or their gallant commander, Captain Jinks, may be relied upon for *his* customary rescue, to occur just before the final curtain. (When *either . . .* or connects nouns of differing number, the pronoun agrees with the noun closer to it.)
3. "In America," he said, "we know that we are free; but sometimes we become a little afraid, for we are not yet acclimated to freedom."
4. What a sweet child it [he] is; it [he] seems the image of your friend Jack. (A baby may be referred to as *it*; but then *it* must be consistently employed.)
5. If the pig or the fool is of a different opinion, it is because he knows only his side of the question.

Exercise No. 11

1. *me*, object of the preposition *between*.
   he, subject of the verb *knows*.
   she, subject of the verb *knows*.

2. *them*, object of the preposition *like*.
3. *we*, predicate nominative after linking verb *was*.
4. *them*, subject of the infinitive *to be*.
5. *me*, appositive of *person* (in objective case).
6. *he*, subject of (understood) verb *is*. (You are, very obviously, as ugly as he [is].)
7. *whom*, object of verb *love*.
   who, subject of verb *are*.
8. *who*, subject of verb *envies*.
9. *him*, object of preposition *but* (here signifying "except").
10. *who*, subject of (understood) verb *is*. (He is more audible than who [is audible], would you say?)

Exercise No. 12

1.	2.	3.
sit: I	*may:* A	*let:* T
pity: T	*have:* T	*make:* T [that
had: T	*be:* L	or which (un-
landed: I	*can:* A	derstood) is ob-
was: L	*are:* C	ject of *make*]
should be: A	*had:* T	*does:* A
had: T		*mean:* T

Exercise No. 13

1. Because he burst my balloon, I struck (punched) him on the nose.
2. He dived fifty feet into a wet handkerchief.
3. He has got gold, but the process has frozen the gentle current of his soul.
4. I have lain awake on rainy mornings, wondering why I had laid away money for them.
5. When the warden rang the bell, the prisoner was hanged.
6. I bore the burden that I was born to bear.
7. Because he had drunk so much, his wife wrung his neck.
8. The sun shone over Ruth as she bound the sheaves.
9. The Romans lent Antony their ears.
10. When the bee stung him, he sprang to his feet.

Exercise No. 14

1. Neither John nor I is utterly senseless.
2. The herd of cattle which is [are] grazing on the field has [have] been sold down the river. (Singular verbs are to be preferred because the herd was apparently sold as a unit; however, plural verbs are also defensible—if consistently employed.)
3. He is one of the men who need lobotomy like a hole in the head.
4. There are a table, a chair, and a tape recorder: now talk!
5. Tactics wins battles.
6. He is one of those pedagogues who have given *pedantry* its signification.
7. It is I, not he, who am at fault.
8. There are ['re] gold pieces in plenty here.
9. Seven days without water makes one week.
10. The general, together with five thousand picked troops, storms the tavern.

Exercise No. 15

1. *had reached:* past perfect
2. *will have collected:* future perfect
3. *have had:* present perfect

4. *insists:* present
 shall be: future
5. *had risen:* past perfect
 had been: past perfect
 had decreased: past perfect
 lost: past
 had lingered: past perfect
6. *believes:* present
 was: past
 tied: past
 believe: present
 had [*n't*] *been:* past perfect
 would have been: past perfect [verb-phrase made with modal auxiliary]
7. *made:* past
 had distinguished: past perfect
8. *can be found:* present [verb-phrase made with modal auxiliary; passive voice]
 will deny: future
 can exist: present
 has reached: present perfect
 is turning: present [progressive form]
9. *is:* present
 has set: present perfect
 will soften: future
10. *will have been decimated:* future perfect [passive voice]

Exercise No. 16

1. were		6. is not
2. is		7. consider
3. were		8. suspect
4. are		9. were
5. be		10. be

Exercise No. 17

1. Everybody had a most enjoyable time.
2. Most teachers believe that people write passive sentences when they have not thought out the communication they intend before they set pen to paper.
3. Correct, since *head*, not *quack*, should be emphasized.
4. He saw that she wanted to be kissed, and he kissed her.
5. After Jonathan J. Logorrhea had spoken for an hour, nobody listened to what he was saying.
6. I admit that the bank notes which her father flashed before my eyes impressed me.
7. Correct.
8. Correct if Caesar is the center of the communication. If Cleopatra is, rewrite: Cleopatra first conquered, then cuckolded Caesar.
9. Soldiers read books—comic books, chiefly.
10. Correct, since who read the books does not matter.

Exercise No. 18

Progressive	Emphatic
1. I am playing	I do play
2. you were fiddling	you did fiddle
3. it will be fizzing	
4. she has been constituting	
5. they had been asseverating	
6. he will have been explicating	
7. (if) he be laughing	
8. he is being slugged	

Exercise No. 19

1. [*the:* limiting (definite article)]
 full: descriptive
 African: descriptive (proper)
 wide: descriptive
 lovely: descriptive
2. *invisible:* descriptive
 those: limiting
 immortal: descriptive
 their: limiting (pronominal, possessive)
3. *which:* limiting (pronominal, relative)
4. *which:* limiting (pronominal, interrogative)
5. *pixilated:* descriptive
 any: limiting (pronominal, indefinite)
6. *black:* descriptive
 hot: descriptive
 sweet: descriptive
7. *subtle:* descriptive
 specious: descriptive
8. *other:* limiting (pronominal, indefinite)
 Holmesean: descriptive (proper)
 worst: descriptive
 best: descriptive
9. *brilliant:* descriptive
 corrupt: descriptive
10. none

Exercise No. 20

1. a, a	7. a;
2. a, a, the	a;
3. the, the	the;
4. a, a, a; the, the, the	the, the, the, the
5. the	8. The, —, the, the, —
6. An, a, a	9. The
	10. the

Exercise No. 21

1. lesser
2. eldest
3. most kind
4. first, most, fundamental
5. cleaner, more intelligent
6. best known, most bloodthirsty
7. better (idiomatically, *best*)
8. more absurd, more (less) happy
9. bigger, redder, hotter
10. inner (inmost)

Exercise No. 22

1. *almost:* degree, *professionally:* manner
2. *therefore:* conjunctive
3. *formerly:* time
4. *west:* place
 consequently: conjunctive
5. *There:* place
6. *badly:* manner
7. *badly:* manner
 hence: conjunctive
8. *Yes:* conjunctive
9. *seldom:* degree
 sensibly: manner
 never: degree
10. *Well:* conjunctive
 now: time

Exercise No. 23

1. wisest, best
2. farther (further), worse
3. tougher, more tender (or, to establish antithesis, *tenderer*)
4. most (least) distinctly
5. highest, most highly

Exercise No. 24

1. *neither . . . nor:* coordinating (correlatives)
2. *...when:* subordinating
3. *as:* subordinating
4. *when:* subordinating
5. *yet:* coordinating
6. *because:* subordinating
7. *so that:* subordinating
8. *lest:* subordinating
9. *But:* coordinating
   for: coordinating
10. *not only . . . but also:* coordinating (correlatives)

Exercise No. 25

Preposition	Words related
1. in	heraldic—heat
on	scorpion—stone
2. into	nose—porridge
of	bread and butter—mine
for	man—himself
for	God—us
3. in	what is bred—bone
out of	will . . . come—flesh
4. from	came—Switzerland
through	came—France
over to	came—England
among	stayed—us
5. to	speak—whom

Exercise No. 26

1. *biting:* takes *dogs* for its object, is itself object of the preposition *to*.
2. *reading:* subject of verb *has served*, modified by the phrase *in abnormal psychology* and by the adjective *avid*, takes *Jojo's* for its subject.
   making: takes *him* for its object, is itself object of the preposition *of*.
3. *spurning:* subject of the verb *demonstrates*, it takes *her* for its object and *his* for its subject (not *he spurning*, since the subject of a gerund is in the possessive case).
4. *gilding:* subject of verb *was*, takes *his* (not *him gilding*) for its subject.
5. *having read:* subject of verb *has . . . raised*, it takes *their* for its subject, *all the selections* for its object.

Exercise No. 27

1. *Desperate:* modifies *reporter*, is modified by the phrase *for news*.
2. *Having read:* modifies *normality* (dangling), and should modify *Jojo*. Revised: *Having avidly read books on abnormal psychology, Jojo was oppressed by his normality*. In the revised sentence, *books* is object of the participle *having read*, which is modified by *avidly*.
3. *Having been spurned:* modifies *lady*, is modified by the phrase *by Jojo*.

4. *Having gilded:* modifies *he*, takes *lilies* for its object, is modified by *with loving devotion*.
5. *Having read:* modifies *intelligence quotients* (dangling) and should modify *they*. Revised: *Though they read all the selections of the book clubs, their intelligence quotients remained static*. The revised sentence has a clause doing the work of the participle.

Exercise No. 28

1. He wanted to see the headless horseman.
2. I think the criminal to be him.
3. To write with precision it is necessary to have thought logically first. (Split infinitive in original sentence.)
4. I know him to be a sheep in wolf's clothing. (Subject of the infinitive *to be* should be in the objective case.)
5. Invariably to be kind to children, one requires angelic qualities. (Split infinitive and dangling modification in original sentence.)

Exercise No. 29

1. *in the hand:* prepositional phrase, used as an adjective to modify *bird*.
   in the bush: prepositional phrase, used as an adjective to modify *two* [*birds*].
2. *Having seen three birds:* participial phrase, modifying *he*.
   in the bush: prepositional phrase, used as an adjective to modify *birds*.
   in his hand: prepositional phrase, used as an adjective to modify *one* [*bird*].
3. *in the bush:* prepositional phrase, used as an adjective to modify *birds*.
   having been captured: participial phrase, modifying *birds*.
4. *to snare:* infinitive phrase, used as an adverb to modify *lived*.
   [*to*] *burn:* infinitive phrase, used as an adverb to modify *lived*.
5. *To part from friends:* infinitive phrase, used as a noun (subject of verb *is*).
   to die a little: infinitive phrase used as a predicate nominative (after linking verb *is*).

Exercise No. 30

1. *where she was going:* noun clause, object of verb *knew*.
   how she would get there: noun clause, object of verb *knew*.
2. *when I was hungry:* adverbial clause, modifies *ate*.
   whenever he could: adverbial clause, modifies *drank*.
3. *which he concealed:* adjective clause, modifies *purpose*.
4. *who have status:* adjective clause, modifies *criminals*.
5. *While making hay:* adverbial clause, modifies *ought*.
   whether the sun is shining: noun clause, object of *to see*.

Exercise No. 31

1. *Compound:* Jack loves Jill, but Jill loves herself.
   Complex: Jack loves Jill, whereas Jill loves herself.
2. *Compound:* The nickel has a diminished value; for example, it no longer buys a telephone call.

Complex: The nickel, which has a diminished value, no longer buys a telephone call.

3. *Compound:* Ideas have consequences; moreover, the consequences are sometimes far-reaching.
   Complex: Ideas have consequences which are sometimes far-reaching.
4. *Compound:* He reached for the moon and he stubbed his toe.
   Complex: While reaching for the moon, he stubbed his toe.
5. *Compound:* The American way of speaking and writing differs from the English way, but it is not therefore inferior.
   Complex: Although the American way of speaking and writing differs from the English way, it is not therefore inferior.

Exercise No. 32

1. scratches ("One . . . scratches")
2. is ("Cause . . . is")
3. were ("months . . . were")
4. are
5. is

Exercise No. 33

1. confront ("ordeals that confront." Verb here agrees with the antecedent of the pronoun.)
2. fail
3. have
4. confuse
5. need

Exercise No. 34

1. irritate (Compound subject "Laughing and giggling" requires a plural verb.)
2. go (Reverse the word order: "There I go, but for the grace of God.")
3. were
4. were
5. add

Exercise No. 35

1. has (Either one or the other *has* played the trick.)
2. dominates
3. understand (When compound subjects joined by correlatives do not agree in number, the verb agrees in number with the nearer subject, in this case, the plural *teachers.*)
4. were
5. is

Exercise No. 36

1. enters (*along with* does not affect the number of the verb whose subject remains the singular *soldier.*)
2. dislikes
3. was
4. searches
5. leads

Exercise No. 37

Correct Form	Antecedent
1. their	all
2. his	each
3. their	lass and lad
4. their	authors
5. him	anyone

Correct Form	Antecedent
6. it	none
7. his	whoever
8. its *or* their	team (the antecedent may be taken collectively as a singular noun, or separately, as "members of the team," to make the pronoun plural.)
9. they	some
10. they	groups

Exercise No. 38

Hesitantly, feeling the gloom enclose me, I approached the darkened stairwell. Although I was trembling, I began to mount the worn old steps I had trod so often in the happier times of my youth. I sensed that at the summit of those steps my whole life would change, but I had to go on.

Exercise No. 39

1. I (*I* is part of the compound subject *Ed and I.*)
2. who (*who* is subject of the verb *may make.*)
3. his (Before a gerund, the pronoun is usually in the possessive case. If you intend to stress the person, *accepting* must be considered as a participle and the objective case, *him,* should be used.)
4. her (part of compound object of preposition *about*)
5. him
6. us (object of preposition *against. Boys* is the objective complement of *us* and is also in the objective case.)
7. they (predicate nominative after linking verb *is*)
8. his (see 3 above)
9. Whom (Reverse the word order: You wish to send this letter to whom? *Whom* is object of the preposition *to.*)
10. him, me
11. him (*But* acts here as a preposition.)
12. they (Complete the ellipsis: "as intelligent as they are.")
13. himself (Reflexive pronoun is justified when the action reflects upon the subject.)
14. him, me (Apposition with *people,* object of preposition *of*)
15. Whoever (Subject of verb *assumes*)
16. who (Subject of verb *asked. I believe* is merely an interrupter.)
17. me (Complete the ellipsis: "better than it *fitted* me.")
18. us (see 6 above)
19. we (Predicate nominative after linking verb)
20. him (Objective case after infinitive *to be*)

Exercise No. 40

1. The Happy-Thought-of-the-Day Club sent to its readers a magazine which had many wholesome suggestions.
2. If it does not fit your head, have your hat made smaller.
3. Ed's father is happy to be returning from abroad.
4. The financial experts say that everything will get better next year.
5. In order to cut down the annual deficit, transit officials will increase the fare, a procedure that will be a hardship on commuters.
6. In *The Canterbury Tales* Chaucer writes entertainingly about the Middle Ages, those years in which

feudalism and religion exercised profound influence on noble and serf alike.

7. Although I found the party dull, many, amazingly enough, enjoyed it.
8. If you borrow from another writer's work, acknowledge your source.
9. Franklin's *Autobiography* gives precepts on thrift.
10. Beethoven's later works are remarkable, more so when one considers that he was deaf when he wrote them.

Exercise No. 41

1. had labored over
2. had once seen
3. wore
4. visited
5. had neglected
6. having been born
7. to be
8. to have read
9. Having been taught
10. Reaching

Exercise No. 42

1. shall	5. will	8. will
2. shall	6. shall	9. shall
3. shall, shall	7. will	10. shall
4. will		

Exercise No. 43

1. can	3. could	7. can, should
2. may (might. Both are defensible.)	4. would	8. would
	5. should	9. can
	6. ought	10. would

Exercise No. 44

1. well (Modifies the verb *hear*)
2. easily (Modifies the verb *won*)
3. almost
4. fresh (Modifies *marlin*)
5. really (Modifies adjective *good*)
6. well
7. sweet (Modifies *gladioli*)
8. surely, good (*surely* modifies *feels; good* modifies *air*)
9. bad
10. tightly
11. well
12. firm
13. helplessly
14. loudly
15. softly, clearly
16. cacophonous
17. gently
18. angry (Modifies *prisoner*)
19. heartily
20. quickly, surely, really, noisy

Exercise No. 45

1. Most students believe that their writing is better than *that of* their fellow students. (Or "than their fellow students' writing")
2. Correct.
3. We think that our cat is unique.
4. Keeping tropical fish is almost as time-consuming as raising cactus, if not more so.
5. Lydia has more trouble taking care of Philip than other parents encounter with their children.
6. Correct.
7. Correct.
8. Correct.
9. Many soldiers have found that being in politics is not so simple as being in the military.
10. I have heard both his speeches, and I think yesterday's clearly the better.

Exercise No. 46

Following are suggested answers. Others (using subordinate clauses) are possible.

1. Hanging from the bell tower, the fanatic prepared to leap as crowds watched.
2. Having entered his car, he immediately rolled down the windows.
3. Gingerly walking barefooted on the cobblestones, he saw a silver coin.
4. Listening to the concert with rapt attention, he felt more than ever that Beethoven was a magnificent composer.
5. Working too hard and earning too little, I feel my ulcer starting to bother me again.
6. Tired and indisposed, I shall not work tonight.
7. Leaving his apartment in a violent temper, she became increasingly furious as she thought of his insolence.
8. He saw her diamond necklace hanging round her neck.
9. Because he had spilled gravy on her gown, Dante had ruined his evening with Beatrice.
10. Entering the drug store, he let his cigarette dangle limply between his lips.

Exercise No. 47

Following are suggested answers. Others are possible.

1. To travel in comfort, one must have money.
2. To smoke safely, use filters.
3. Wearing gloves permits one to row all afternoon without getting blisters.
4. Maintaining moderate speed is essential to get ten miles to the gallon.
5. To work as a pianist, one must practice constantly.

Exercise No. 48

Following are suggested answers. Others are possible.

1. One must make reservations before leaving for Europe.
2. After he had attacked me for lateness, my employer fired me.
3. On his first attempt at flycasting, the fisherman snared a trout.
4. When entering the theater, I was surprised at the clothes worn by the audience.
5. While turning the page, he spilled the ashtray onto his book.

Exercise No. 49

Following are suggested answers. Others are possible.

1. When he was three years old, John's mother taught him archery.
2. While I was visiting in Concord, the weather was excellent.
3. Once she had allowed it to relax, Hilda's back felt better.
4. Stephen kept watching the light until it turned green.
5. Although famished, he refused to eat caviar.

Exercise No. 50

Following are suggested answers. Others are possible.

1. Even the most intellectual of his listeners will be confused by Dr. Sermione's lectures.
2. Vivien reads only the best in Irish literature.
3. The baby walked nearly across his playpen.

4. Teeth may be ruined if candy is eaten frequently.
5. Scarcely had I opened the door when the dog leaped at me.

Exercise No. 51

Following are suggested answers. Others are possible.
1. The girl woke with a cry as a scream tore through the house.
2. Indians inhabit a village in eastern Mexico called Patzcuaro.
3. Columbus vowed that he would claim the New World for Ferdinand and Isabella as soon as he landed.
4. In all my travels I have never seen a cathedral like that one.
5. In the laboratory I located the trouble with my television set.

Exercise No. 52

Following are suggested answers. Others are possible.
1. We set out towards the end of the rainbow for the city in which we lived.
2. When we visited foreign lands, we spoke with inhabitants and tried to learn their folkways.
3. He examined in the microscope the specimen that was in a glass slide.
4. As we were leaving he promised to visit us.
5. Letters that show personality and spirit can win friends.

Exercise No. 53

Following are suggested answers. Others are possible.
1. Dr. Johnson despised the Scots, although he befriended Boswell and spent many pleasant hours with his Scottish biographer.
2. I warned him that I would take no more of his nonsense, even though we had spent many years together and had shared experiences neither of us would ever forget.
3. Correct.
4. He tried suddenly and violently to swerve his car away from the oncoming truck.
5. The view from the waterfront in New Orleans is as dismal as that from the New Jersey docks, if not more so.

Exercise No. 54

Following are suggested answers. Others are possible.
1. One should listen carefully to his employer if *he* wants promotions.
2. Lorelei was a cold-hearted girl whose best friends were diamonds.
3. Beethoven's *Fifth Symphony is* a famous musical achievement. (Although created in the past, works of art remain permanently great, and thus take the present tense.)
4. If he were to take an old friend's advice, he *would* leave his job.
5. I know that I wouldn't go out with that gang unless *I* wanted to get into trouble.
6. A true democrat accepts the opinion of the majority even if *he* disagrees with it.
7. When Job heard the Voice from the Whirlwind, he *knew* that his moment of reckoning *had* come.
8. Everyone has some favorite recipe that *he concocts* for *his* friends.

9. Tom and Huck shared the universal fright that afflicts those who enter cemeteries at night.
10. Smart wrestlers know how to feign agony, and *one can* always tell that they *are* not really hurt.
11. Directing strangers is not always easy, but one must try to give simple, specific instructions to prevent them from getting lost. In any event it is only courteous to try to guide them as well as possible.
12. The Indians defeated Custer and exterminated his troops.
13. If I allow him enough rope, *he'll* hang *himself*.
14. Correct.
15. One must practice if *he* wishes to succeed.

Exercise No. 55

Following are suggested answers. Others are possible.
1. Some public officials, better called "publicity hounds," always investigate dead scandals.
2. He believes that courage is better than *fear* and that faith is truer than doubt. (All nouns; *fearing* is a gerund.)
3. I want stouthearted men who will fight when necessary.
4. The Indian Summer of life should be sunny and sad, like the season, and possess infinite wealth and depth of tone.
5. The school commission voted to improve building facilities and to enlarge the teaching staff. (All infinitives instead of mixed phrase and infinitive.)
6. Find time to learn goodness and *to give* up laziness.
7. The child eagerly awaited the hour of his birthday, knowing that soon he would have all his new presents.
8. Saying is one thing; *doing* is another.
9. What Charles needs is a doctor and *a* rest.
10. We studied the life of the ant and its method of operating a social community.

Exercise No. 56

Following are suggested answers. Others are possible.
1. They couldn't decide whether *to leave* the theater or *to hiss* the performance.
2. Either Bill stops mimicking me or I will bang his head. (Each correlative must be followed by corresponding part of speech: here noun or pronoun; in the original *Either* is followed by the verb *stops, or* by the pronoun *I*.)
3. Franklin was not only a skillful politician but also an *inventive genius*.
4. Neither can he do as he is told, nor can his parents hope to change him.
5. Billy wants to be either a business tycoon or an actor when he grows up.

Exercise No. 57

Following are suggested answers. Others are possible.
1. Henry Adams wrote history, fiction and an essay on architecture inspired by the cathedrals at Chartres and Mt. St. Michel.
2. Dumas has always excited readers young and old and will continue to do so.
3. The yokels were attentive *to* and then swindled by the huckster.
4. The artist decided to exhibit his paintings, which hardly deserved public attention, and *to give* lectures.

5. The doctors warned Jones that to work would prove fatal, *that* to travel might prove helpful, but *that* to rest would effect complete recovery.

Exercise No. 58

Following are suggested answers. Others are possible.
1. Conscious of the Martian invasion of Oregon, the president warned against relaxing vigilance.
2. Extremely hungry, he opened the refrigerator and grabbed the chicken leg.
3. He promised them that the two large specimens of walrus in the city zoo would be delightful to watch.
4. If he takes the time to study French—and he must work hard—he will surely succeed. (The original is parallel in form, but not in thought.)
5. Infuriated by his attacks on her intelligence, the timid girl fled from the room. (*Timid* is a general state; *infuriated by attacks* ... is a specific. Thus, the original sentence is not parallel and must be recast.)

Exercise No. 59

Following are suggested answers. Others are possible.
1. The house was burned, but the children *were* saved.
2. I remember Al Capone better than *I remember* Vincent Coll.
3. I have six calculators, but he *has only* two.
4. The teacher *whom I offered as a reference* would not write a letter for me.
5. My dog and *my* girl friend are going with me on my vacation.
6. He has bought as many books as any man has *bought* or can buy.
7. Our only chance was *that* Johnson might send out an alarm.
8. The patient moaned, perspired, and *displayed* other symptoms of delirium.
9. The major problem is *that* she is not at all interested.
10. We were more familiar with the Smiths than *with* the Joneses.
11. His highly effective recitation was admired by all.
12. Possibly because rainmakers are "seeding" too many clouds, tornadoes and typhoons are becoming more frequent.
13. So far as his writing is concerned, *it is* sometimes pointless in its thinking.
14. His vision at night was almost as good as *that of* a cat.
15. Harold read about and collected relics from New England.

Exercise No. 60

1. c, f (topic sentence), e, b, a, d
2. b (topic sentence), a, d, c
3. b (topic sentence), d, c, e, a
4. b (topic sentence), c, a, d
5. c (topic sentence), a, b, d, g, e, f

Exercise No. 61

1. Never! I would rather die!
2. Die you shall!
3. Jason asked why Luster had turned left.
4. He exclaimed angrily that he welcomed opposition.
5. "Never!" did you say?
6. Well played!

7. May I suggest that you reply with a certified check not later than June 1, 1955.
8. O Scotia! my dear, my native soil!
9. "Heigh-ho!" he exclaimed.
10. Bah! He's [he's] never met his deadline.

Exercise No. 62

Note: The brackets indicate options.

1. Just as the procedure of a collection department must be clear-cut and definite, the steps being taken with the sureness of a skilled chess player, so the various paragraphs of a collection letter must show clear organization, giving evidence of a mind that [,] from the beginning [,] has had a specific end in view. (Civil Service Exam.)
2. In some jobs [,] it is necessary to understand, interpret [,] and apply rules and principles. In others, it is necessary also to discover principles from available data or information. These types of reasoning ability can be tested by different kinds of tests—for example, questions on the relationship of words, understanding of paragraphs [,] or solving of numerical problems. (Civil Service Exam.)
3. A plane figure consists of a square, ten inches on a side, and an isosceles triangle whose base is the left edge of the square and whose altitude, dropped from the vertex opposite the ten-inch base of the triangle common to the square, is six inches. (Civil Service Exam.)
4. Few people take the trouble of finding out what democracy really is. Yet this would be a great help, for it is our lawless and uncertain thoughts, it is the indefiniteness of our impressions, that fill darkness, whether mental or physical, with spectres and hobgoblins. Democracy is nothing more than an experiment in government, more likely to succeed in a new soil, but likely to be tried in all soils, which must stand or fall on its own merits as others have done before it. For there is no trick of perpetual motion in politics, any more than in mechanics. President Lincoln defined democracy to be "the government of the people by the people for the people."
5. I went to the woods because I wished to live deliberately, to front only the essential facts of life, and to see if I could not learn what it had to teach [,] and not, when I came to die, discover that I had not lived.
6. In all my lectures [,] I have taught one doctrine, namely, the infinitude of the private man. This the people accept readily enough, and even with loud acclamation, as long as I call the lecture Art [,] or Politics [,] or Literature [,] or the Household; but the moment I call it Religion [,] they are shocked, though it be only the application of the same truth which they receive everywhere else to a new class of facts. (R. W. Emerson)
7. When Melville died on September 28, 1891, he left in manuscript a novelette, *Billy Budd,* which was not published until 1924, though written about 1888–1891.
8. Man was not made for any useful purpose, for the reason that he hasn't served any; he was [,] most likely [,] not even made intentionally, and his working himself up out of the oyster bed to his

present position was probably a matter of surprise and regret to the Creator. (Mark Twain)

9. Fitzgerald said, "The very rich are different from you and me." "Yes," Hemingway replied, "they have more money."

10. To see how this was so, let us ask ourselves why the spheres were ever supposed to exist. They were not seen or directly observed in any way; why, then, were they believed to be there? (H. Dingle)

11. We keep one eye open, however safe we feel. Indeed, some of us keep both eyes open; others of us, moreover, wish for a third eye.

12. For him, to think meant to act.

13. To die bravely fighting, at first seemed good; later, retreat seemed better.

14. Dear Jojo,

I received your last letter. At least [,] I hope it was your last letter.

Sincerely,
Butch Butcher

15. The title role of *Elmer Gantry* (which Rebecca West, the English critic, has termed "a sequence of sermons and seductions") is played by a profligate clergyman, a ponderous monster, bleater of platitudes, ankle-snatcher [,] and arch hypocrite, whom we meet first as an "eloquently drunk" student at Terwilliger College [,] in Cato, Missouri. (H. Hartwick)

16. He had forgotten his wallet, which reposed in his green trousers; the money which he had in the purple pair that he was wearing didn't equal the amount of the bill.

Exercise No. 63

1. Courtship in animals is the outcome of four major steps in evolution: first, the development of sexuality; secondly, the separation of the sexes; thirdly, internal fertilization, or at least the approximation of males and females; and finally, the development of efficient sense-organs and brains. (J. Huxley)

2. They wanted to know "how modern man got this way": why some people are ruled by a king, some by old men, others by warriors, and none by women anymore; why some peoples pass on property in the male line, others in the female, still others equally to heirs of both sexes; why some people fall sick and die when they think they are bewitched, and others laugh at the idea.

3. He is a man; hence [,] he is fallible. She is a woman; therefore [,] she will fool him.

4. It is hard to form just ideas; wayward notions, however, come without being called.

5. A small group of people arrive: I recognize Jean Negulesco, the director; Wolfgang Reinhardt, the supervising producer; and George Amy, the cutter. (Adolph Deutsch)

Exercise No. 64

1. Dear Sir:

I have read your letter, a courtesy you apparently did not vouchsafe mine.

Yours truly,
Jojo Jones

2. There are two methods of curing the mischiefs of faction: the one, by removing its causes; the other, by controlling its effects.

3. Dr. Jucovy, a noted psychiatrist, writes: "The statement: 'People are stout because they eat more and consume more calories' no longer suffices. Now we ask: '*Why* do some individuals eat more?' "

4. All will be well: God is silent; he is not indifferent.

5. In *The Short Bible: An American Translation*, Professor Smith translated Psalms 19:1 thus: "The heavens are telling the glory of God, And the sky shows forth the work of his hands."

Exercise No. 65

1. Persuasiveness of argument, apt examples from history and experience, inner logic, and perhaps our simple need to have a part of our experience given satisfactory meaning—these have played a far greater role in the history of theories in the social sciences than strict canons of evidence and proof. (Nathan Glazer)

2. Why haven't I a butler named Fish, who makes a cocktail of three parts gin to one part lime juice, honey, vermouth, and apricot brandy in equal portions—a cocktail so delicious that people like Mrs. Harrison Williams and Mrs. Goodhue Livingston seek him out to get the formula? (E. B. White)

3. More than thirty-five million women—about 40 per cent of the nation's labor force—are in paid employment. (World Almanac, 1979)

4. My expectations were not high—no deathless prose, merely a sturdy, no-nonsense report of explorers into the wilderness of statistics and half-known fact.

5. Henry's genius—if that's the word—was sometimes indistinguishable from another man's pigheadedness.

6. To be a scientist—it is not just a different job, so that a man should choose between being a scientist and being an explorer or a bond-salesman or a physician or a king or a farmer. (S. Lewis)

7. In the country there are a few chances of sudden rejuvenation—a shift in the weather, perhaps, or something arriving in the mail. (E. B. White)

8. Why they are called comics, when people who read them—both young and old—almost always look like undertakers, eludes me.

9. Restraint, Repression, Respectability—those are the three R's that make him [Sinclair Lewis] see Red. (W. L. Phelps)

10. And we—well, we shut our eyes, then say, "We can't see a thing wrong."

Exercise No. 66

1. In the days that followed (happy days of renewed vigor and reawakened interest), I studied the magazines and lived, in their pages, the gracious life of the characters in the ever-moving drama of society and fashion.

2. As the Hebrews saw their history (Genesis to Judges), it fell into several discrete sections, writes H. H. Watts; and the author (authors?) of only the first section (Genesis 1–11) made no distinction between Hebrew and non-Hebrew fate.

3. Winchell, according to H. L. Mencken, invented *pash* (for passion), *lohengrined* (for married) and *Reno-vated* (for divorced).

4. If the rise over the Continent of North America should amount to a hundred feet (and there is more

than enough water now frozen in land ice to provide such a rise) most of the Atlantic seaboard, with its cities and towns, would be submerged. (M. K. Bennett)

5. Mr. W. M. Thackeray has published (under the Cockney name of "Michael Angelo Titmarsh") various graphic and entertaining works: *The Paris Sketch-Book* (London, 1840), *Comic Tales and Sketches* (London, 1841), and *The Irish Sketch-Book* (London, 1842).

Exercise No. 67

1. Correct.
2. Correct.
3. Enclose *generally speaking* in commas or parentheses.
4. Correct.
5. First pair of brackets correctly placed; replace second with parentheses.

Exercise No. 68

1. Bentley, the publisher of *Bentley's Miscellany*, said to Jerrold, "I had some doubts about the name I should give the magazine; I thought at one time of calling it *Wits' Miscellany*." "Well," was the rejoinder, "You needn't have gone to the opposite extreme."
2. "One of the old philosophers," Lord Bacon tells us, "used to say that life and death were just the same to him." "Why, then," said an objector, "do you not kill yourself?" "Because it is just the same."
3. "The American Scholar," Emerson's address to the Phi Beta Kappa Society at Cambridge in 1837, was termed "our intellectual Declaration of Independence" by Oliver Wendell Holmes.
4. "The so-called race between population and food supply has again come forward as an absorbing topic of conversation," M. K. Bennett notes.
5. William Keddie, in his *Anecdotes Literary and Scientific*, tells this anecdote: "A friend of the poet Campbell once remarked: 'It is well known that Campbell's own favorite poem was his "Gertrude." I once heard him say, "I never like to see my name before the 'Pleasures of Hope'; why, I cannot tell you, unless it was that, when young, I was always greeted among my friends as 'Mr. Campbell, author of the "Pleasures of Hope."' 'Good morning to you Mr. Campbell, author of the "Pleasures of Hope."'"'"

Exercise No. 69

1. science-fiction
   space-travel
   time-travel
2. four-mile
   thrice-wounded
   25-year-old
3. All-cargo
4. trans-shipment
   mop-up
   pro-United States
   middle-road
5. anti-vivisectionism
   one-focused
6. Land-rich
   money-poor
   knee-high

Exercise No. 70

1. Smith Brothers Cough Drops
2. Newton's Law
3. earth's surface
4. geese's cackling
5. hero's welcome
6. Prince of Wales' horse [Wales's would cause too many *s*-sounds.]
7. James's novels
8. Queen Elizabeth II's coronation
9. Achilles' heel [Achilles's would cause an awkward combination of *s*-sounds.]
10. anybody else's word
11. princess' gown
12. princesses' gowns
13. Xerxes' triumph
14. here's how
15. at 6's and 7's
16. *Mississippi* has four *s*'s
17. six o'clock
18. you'll
19. they'd
20. who's

Exercise No. 71

1. A.D. preceding the date: e.g., A.D. 1776)
2. A.B.
3. A.M.
4. Dr.
5. log (no period)
6. Pfc (no periods)
7. radar (no periods)
8. t.b.
9. S.D.
10. viz (period and italics optional)
11. sq. in., in.²
12. gill (not abbreviated)
13. bbl.
14. P.R.
15. cwt.
16. ton (not abbreviated)
17. Jan.
18. Mon.
19. NW.
20. C.

Exercise No. 72

1. Charles W. Morton, associate editor of the *Atlantic*, had collected examples of periphrasis, the use of three words where one would do. In the *Atlantic Bulletin*, a monthly promotion letter, he cited these horrible examples: The New York *Herald Tribune* called the beaver a "fury, paddle-tailed mammal"; the Lincoln Sunday *Journal-Star* termed milk "the vitamin-laden liquid" issuing from "a bovine milk factory"; *Travel* magazine said skiers slid down the slopes on "the beautified barrel staves." (Adapted from *Time*)
2. He sailed to Europe on the *America;* he flew back on the *Antipodes.*
3. "Sally Bowles," perhaps the best story in Christopher Isherwood's *Goodbye to Berlin*, was adapted into a mediocre play, *I Am a Camera*, by John van Druten.
4. The pull of -*or* is so strong that the pedagogues, who began calling themselves *educationists* a decade or so ago, have now gone back to *educator*, which appeared as a rival for the homely *teacher* in Shakespeare's time. (H. L. Mencken)
5. I saw the motion picture *Come Back, Little Sheba* in France, with French voices dubbed in. It seemed odd to hear Shirley Booth refer to *"la petite Sheba."*

Exercise No. 73

1. The Anglo-Saxon language was the language of our Saxon forefathers in England, though they never gave it that name. They called it English. Thus King Alfred speaks of translating "from book-Latin into English"; Abbot Aelfric was requested by Aethelward "to translate the book of Genesis from Latin into English"; and Bishop Leofric, speaking of the manuscript (the "Exeter Manuscript") he gave to Exeter Cathedral, calls it a "great English book."
2. The city of Nome, Alaska, acquired its name through error. There was a small prospectors' settlement known as Anvil City on the Seward Peninsula in Alaska. A Washington clerk, in drawing a map, did not know its name, and wrote "Name?" at that place

on the map. One of his superiors took the word for "Nome" and that name still stands.

3. *Stories in the Modern Manner*, edited by Philip Rahv and William Phillips, was published by Avon Books. Perhaps the best story in it is Gide's "Theseus."

4. The lion is a kingly beast.
He likes a Hindu for a feast.

5. It is the grace of God that urges missionaries to suffer the most disheartening privations for their faith. This grace moved Saint Isaac Jogues to say (when he came to Canada), "I felt as if it were a Christmas day for me, and that I was to be born again to a new life, to a life in Him." (Adapted from *Time*)

Exercise No. 74

1. weird	6. financier	11. cashier
2. glacier	7. feint	12. pierce
3. friend	8. ancient	13. wield
4. siege	9. conceive	14. deity
5. lieutenant	10. foreign	15. hygiene

Exercise No. 75

1. judgment	5. courageous	8. changeable
2. eyeing	6. managing	9. sensible
3. peaceable	7. lovely	10. hoeing
4. dining		

Exercise No. 76

1. occupying	5. turkeys	8. business
2. loneliness	6. tries	9. reliance
3. trolleys	7. keys	10. occupied
4. dryness		

Exercise No. 77

1. ceiling	10. referring	18. siege
2. worries	11. unbelievable	19. alleys
3. field, daisies	12. seized	20. studious
4. monkeys	13. preference	21. studying
5. hoping	14. occurred	22. benefited
6. argument	15. thieves	23. relief
7. shining	16. noticeable	24. perceive
8. ninety	17. merciless	25. truly
9. received		

Exercise No. 78

1. frolicked	6. supersede	11. secede
2. addenda	7. succeed	12. Negroes
3. pimientos	8. mosquitoes	13. exceed
4. synopsis	9. intercede	14. enemies
5. innuendo	10. mimicked	15. dynamos

Exercise No. 79

1. advice	6. dessert, dining	11. led
2. effect	7. consul	12. past
3. all together	8. cited, site	13. than
4. beside	9. devise	14. persecute
5. coarse	10. its	15. quite

Exercise No. 80

1. clothes	8. supersedes	15. judgment
2. sophomore	9. procedure	16. loneliness
3. sergeant	10. dictionary	17. pronunciation
4. effects	11. affected	18. conscience
5. recommend	12. principal	19. Arctic
6. superintendent	13. prophecy	20. weird,
7. omitted	14. interesting	cemetery

Exercise No. 81

embarrassed	cemetery	tranquillity
innuendo	hypocrisy	aggrandize
mimicking	questionnaire	repellent
mnemonic	maneuver	scurrilous
morganatic		

Exercise No. 82

a. opaque, inchoate
b. satiated, abrasive
c. cacophonic, calumnious, condign
d. acerbating, anomalous, assiduous
e. contiguous, contumacious, garrulous
f. misogynous, poignant
g. recalcitrant, viscous
h. viscid, salubrious, peccant
i. onerous, parabolic, plethoric

Exercise No. 83

invulnerable	concomitant	enforcible
aberrant	coherence	adaptable
irrefragable	feasible	adjustable
collapsible	forcible	admissible
confectionery	portentous	duties
invidious	dominance	instantaneously
hymeneal	malfeasance	

Exercise No. 84—Part 2

a. peccadillo	e. vendetta	h. sloop
b. chauvinist	f. nadir	i. zenith
c. bas-relief	g. filibuster	j. incognito
d. cajole		

Exercise No. 85—Part 2

a. bicentennial
b. incite
c. pusillanimous, cognizant, belligerently
d. incredibly, amorous, magnanimous, incognito, animated
e. cursory, animadversion, succeed, recede

Exercise No. 86—Part 2

a. fallacy, obdurate, ambidextrous
b. ductile, conduits
c. factotum, duress, perjured, factitious
d. fervid, aggrandize
e. adjure, transgresses

Exercise No. 87—Part 2

a. colloquial, loquacious, mortify, admonition, omniscience, explicate, imponderable
b. rapacious, renascence, ignominious, medieval

Exercise No. 88—Part 2

a. introspection, perspicacity
b. malevolent, virago
c. tenets, stringent, tenaciously, adversary
d. tangible, vociferously, aversion

Exercise No. 89—Part 2

a. esthete, sedentary
b. homogeneity, amalgam, demagogue
c. protagonist, misanthrope, archetype

Exercise No. 90—Part 2

a. neophyte, etymology, cosmic
b. idiosyncrasies, monomanias, neurotic
c. philologists, neologisms, cosmopolitan
d. apathetic, euphony, cacophonic

Exercise No. 91—Part 2

a. psychoanalyst, zodiac
b. archetype, prototype, stereopticon

Exercise No. 92—Part 2

incongruous	abnormal	improper
ignoble	counterplot	disinter
apathetic	disquiet	disengage
disingenuous		

Exercise No. 93

constitution	avarice	tillage
frequency	masculinity	spoilage
delicacy	denunciation	lucidity
eloquence	convocation	inversion
terrorism	supplication	superficiality
freedom	laggard	clothing
unity	devotion	

Exercise No. 94—Part 1

satiric	admonitory	derisive
maniacal	workable	accessible
virulent	continuous	fallacious
planetary	inventive	exhortatory
avaricious	British	wondrous

Part 2

liquefy	classify	regularize
integrate	hearten	itemize
exemplify	symbolize	personalize

Exercise No. 95

flurry = flutter and hurry
riffle = ripple and ruffle
smog = smoke and fog
squelch = quell and crush

Exercise No. 96

Typist's Exam

1. postpone
2. changeable
3. calumniate
4. unforgivable
5. reward
6. salable
7. disuse
8. unremitting
9. caviling

Exercise No. 97

Patrolman's Exam

1. mirthful
2. few. Although *myriad* means "an indefinitely large number" and is not closely related to *few*, it is not so distant as any of the others. Many items in the vocabulary examinations are difficult because of this quirk in the examiner's technique.
3. lucid
4. closed. *Clandestine* means "secret" and is therefore nearer in meaning to *closed* than to any of the other words.
5. irregularity
6. ilk. By a far-fetched logic, the examiner seems to indicate that *ilk*, meaning "class, family, or breed,"

has within it a variety that more closely suggests *heterogeneity* than any of the other words here.
7. many-languaged
8. *lis pendens*. This term applies in legal use to pending suit. Since *jeopardy* has a legal significance pertinent to the danger facing one involved in criminal action, it bears a closer relationship to *lis pendens* than to any other word.
9. poetic. *Terse* means "forceful but concise, elegant but succinct." The language of poetry comes nearer this adjective than *routine* or *normal*, the only other words possibly involved in the choice.
10. conspiracy

Exercise No. 98

Stenographer's Examination

1. corpulent. *Plethoric* is used generally to imply stuffy or bombastic writing. Since, however, the implication is "overstuffed," *corpulent*, meaning "fat," is the most likely choice.
2. omnipresent
3. inflexible
4. resentment
5. communal
6. slander
7. self-governing
8. insensibility
9. deserved
10. catastrophe
11. friendly
12. outcome
13. ready to believe
14. disparaging
15. transparent

Exercise No. 99

INFORMAL	FORMAL
selfish person	gluttonous person
tramp	mendicant
prominent person	executive
wife	spouse
died	deceased
greedy woman	woman who uses her wiles for financial gain
conservative	conservative
tough	criminal
car of accelerated speed	automobile equipped with a specially-constructed, high-powered engine

Exercise No. 100

1. Informal
2. Formal
3. Formal
4. Informal
5. Informal

Exercise No. 101

1. Archaic
2. Colloquial
3. Dialectal
4. Slang
5. Illiterate
6. Colloquial
7. British
8. Colloquial
9. Colloquial
10. Colloquial

Exercise No. 102

1. today
2. I believe
3. about
4. about
5. money
6. about

7. about
8. I am a lawyer
9. decide
10. I approve
11. when
12. (we, he, they) believe
13. touch (or, if the context demands it, *met*)
14. about
15. (we, he, they) direct
16. because

Exercise No. 103

1. His workmanship in jewelry is unique. (*Unique* means "without compare." He works as "a jeweler" or "at jewelry," not "in the field of.")
2. The consensus favors his retirement from office. (*Consensus* means "general agreement among many.")
3. Her complexion is pink. (*Pink* is a color: it is redundant to reidentify it as such.)
4. The modern woman makes up her mind without assistance. (*Modern* means "of today.")
5. Every genius needs a millionaire to further his career.
6. Few attended Simon's lecture. (*Few* suggests number.)
7. The vase I bought was elliptical. (*Elliptical* is a "shape.")
8. Combined, these fundamentals will teach any student to write well. (*Basic* and *fundamental* are synonymous as are *combined* and *together*.)
9. William's clothes are invariably too large.
10. Brett and Maria . . . are diametrical types of women.

Exercise No. 104

Bill Wilson, *intelligent* and *ambitious*, not only wants to improve his *economic* and *cultural* status, but consciously works towards his goal. As a *lawyer*, he reads *lawbooks*, but he widens his knowledge of men and affairs by conversing with *artists, engineers*, and *doctors*. He knows that a *broad range of information* will enhance *his effectiveness* as a lawyer. For these *reasons*, I believe that Bill will make *significant contributions* to his community and become an important member of it.

Exercise No. 105

Constitution of the United States, Ten Commandments, teachings of Jesus. The writer has combined patriotism with religious orthodoxy to ensnare his reader. *all truly good men.* The implication is that only "bad" men dare disagree.

He has not proved the connection between the Eighth Commandment and the Fifth Amendment, nor has he demonstrated logically that the New Deal violates either. After this point, almost every word and phrase is loaded: *robberies, brazen left-wingers, loyal Americans,* etc.

Exercise No. 106

1. notorious
2. embezzled; absconded
3. concisely
4. vivid
5. wit; intelligence
6. liable
7. modest
8. colossal
9. wholesome
10. cynic; misogynist

Exercise No. 107

Following are some among many possibilities:

1. slithered
2. calculated, estimated
3. roaring; plowed
4. perched; sweeping
5. leaned; wafted

Exercise No. 108

1. The governor spoke about eliminating the housing shortage. (Note that *eliminating* the linking verb helps to reduce the number of nouns.)
2. Words taken out of context do not always mean what they do in context.
3. He evaded the question put to him.
4. Shortages of raw materials cause increases in price.
5. His philosophy sought universal truths applicable only to him.

Exercise No. 109

Following are some among many possibilities:

1. warm; inept; witty
2. bitter; rancid
3. intense
4. dull, drab; fresh, gay
5. immense, huge, vast
6. consummate; insipid
7. superb; inane
8. precocious; charming; small, tiny; intolerable
9. wail; huge
10. enormous; broad; melon

Exercise No. 110

1. I intend to crusade for peace and freedom. (Mixed metaphors: *borrow a leaf* and *don shining armor*; clichés: *struggle onwards, enduring peace*.)
2. Terrified, the shivering . . . (Cliché: *sadder but wiser*.)
3. Luke entertained his friends by singing their favorite old songs. (The original is overwrought and pompous.)
4. Hayfever, epidemic during the summer, poses a constant challenge to the scientist. (Mixed metaphors: *spreads like wildfire* and *methods to iron out*.)
5. Jones alone is sufficiently forthright to battle political corruption. (Mixed metaphor: *lead us out of morass* and *beating about the bush*; cliché: *one man in a hundred*.)
6. Fish possess an instinctive wariness that protects them against fishermen. (Mixed metaphor: *fish are not uprooted*; clichés: *Mother Nature, watery home*; overwrought: *denizens of the deep, devotees of the hook and rod*.)
7. Excitedly, we watched the bride during the wedding ceremony. (The original is overwrought and trite. Note too its clumsy alliteration: *blushing bride, bated breath*.)
8. Hector's lively wit makes other comedians envious. (Clichés: *too funny for words, green with envy*.)
9. His career is finished now that his acceptance of graft has been exposed. (Clichés: *dead duck, put on the record*.)
10. A fool and his money are soon parted. (The original is overwrought and pompous.)

Exercise No. 111

1. I am fond of ice-cream, a high-caloric food. (Ice-cream is one of the few high-caloric foods of which I am fond.)
2. Emma Lazarus was born in 1848, a year of revolutions. (Emma Lazarus was born in a year of revolutions—1848.)
3. Though I like all shellfish, I rarely eat oysters.

4. A habit is a fixed response to a stimulus, acquired by repeatedly performing an action.
5. Bunt has two meanings: "a smut that destroys wheat kernels" and "a lightly batted ball."

Exercise No. 112

1. Writers often get into difficulty by not defining technical terms precisely; in order to avert the difficulty I [*or* the present writer] shall [will] begin by defining as precisely as I [he] can all the technical terms employed in the ensuing pages.
2. Readers seldom care about the history contained in a historical novel. Nevertheless, I have been careful to include no incidents which do not have a sound basis in fact. If any of them appear dubious, I suggest that the reader refer to the notes at the end of each chapter.
3. The reader will think me conceited, perhaps; but I ask him to consider my great and enduring achievements.
4. The mountaineer climbs mountains because they are there.
5. Men who live in our industrial society are different in some ways from men who live in other industrial societies [*or* from men who live in agricultural societies].

Exercise No. 113

1. Referring to authorities: Smith might be a great thinker: he has no special competence as a political analyst.
2. Misuse of statistics: A small and possibly prejudicially selected group may have been queried.
3. Non sequitur.
4. Equivocation.
5. Circular reasoning.
6. Facile assumption.
7. False cause.
8. Jack Spratt could eat no fat, whereas his wife could eat no lean.
9. Although he came of a long line of bachelors, he married.
10. Look before you leap.

Exercise No. 114

1. One cannot always guard against cheats (impostors), however irritating such people may be.
2. An extremely attractive young lady, she unfortunately possessed several grave intellectual deficiencies.
3. When the auditor asked for the telephone number of the district attorney, Mr. Cagliostro seemed to be in a serious plight.
4. I think that the man who drew five aces has been playing dishonestly.
5. I shall, as you suggest, tell you the plain truth.

Exercise No. 115

If we endeavor to form our conceptions upon history and life, we remark three classes of men. The first consists of those for whom the chief thing is the qualities of feelings. These men create art. The second consists of the practical men, who carry on the business of the world. They respect nothing but power, and respect power only so far as it is exercised. The third class consists of men to whom nothing seems great but reason. If force interests them, it is not in its exertion, but in that it has a reason and a law. For men of the first class, nature is a picture; for men of the second class, it is an opportunity; for men of the third class, it is a cosmos, so admirable that to penetrate to its ways seems to them the only thing that makes life worth living. These are the men whom we see possessed by a passion to learn, just as other men have a passion to teach and to disseminate their influence. If they do not give themselves over completely to their passion to learn, it is because they exercise self-control. Those are the natural scientific men; and they are the only men that have any real success in scientific research. (C. S. Pierce)

Exercise No. 116

In 1823 the Whitmans moved from West Hills to Brooklyn, then a country town of seven thousand people. There Walt attended public school for a few years, the only formal education he ever had. By 1831–32 he was working in printing offices and learning the trade. After four or five years of employment in printing offices in Brooklyn and New York, he taught school for a few years in several small schools on Long Island, "boarding round" at the homes of his students. Meanwhile he began to contribute to several New York journals and magazines, writing sentimental stories and poems in the tradition of the time. (G. W. Allen)

Exercise No. 117

1. After ten rounds, during which he lost precisely four teeth and about two quarts of blood, the boxer acknowledged defeat.
2. We struck hard, having penetrated the enemy's flank and reassembled our forces.
3. Men are enslaved not by force only but by fraud also.
4. Although he liked dogs and tolerated cats, he despised children.
5. When he saw, a bit foggily, the vague luminous form approach with slow deliberate steps, he faltered.

Exercise No. 118

1. Out of his surname [people] have coined an epithet for a knave, and out of his Christian name a synonym for the Devil.
2. Boswell was regarded in his own age as a classic, and in ours is regarded as a companion.
3. I come to bury Caesar, not to praise him.
4. The evil that men do lives after them, the good is oft interred with their bones.
5. The Puritan hated bear-baiting not because it gave pain to the bear, but because it gave pleasure to the spectators.

Exercise No. 119

1. Science answers many questions, but never the ultimate question: "Why?"
2. "Why?" the ultimate question, science never pretends to answer.
3. Dictatorship, as every intelligent observer knows, means not the triumph of the superior man but rather the triumph of the inferior one.
4. The Psalms, to be sure, are a passionate criticism of life.
5. Though I speak with the tongues of men and of angels, and have not charity, I am become as sounding brass, or a tinkling cymbal. And though I have the gift of prophecy, and understand all mysteries, and

all knowledge; and though I have all faith, so that I could remove mountains, and have not charity, I am nothing. And though I bestow all my goods to feed the poor, and though I give my body to be burned, and have not charity, it profiteth me nothing. (I Corinthians)

Exercise No. 120

1. A strange question to direct to traffic: "Can you deliver rain?" But the vice president of the Chesapeake and Ohio Railway had urgent reason for asking it. The reservoir of one of the manufacturing plants belonging to the company was dry . . . the plant about to shut down.
2. California, fabulous state, embraces nature's extremes. Mountains and forests bound it on the north, the Mexican desert and the Colorado River on the south. West the Sierra Nevada looms, and east stretches the Pacific. One of its many peaks, Mount Whitney, is the highest point in the nation; only forty miles away lies Death Valley, the lowest.
3. We live in a most dangerous age—an age of supersonic airspeeds, of biological warfare, of atomic and hydrogen bombs, and who knows what next. In no exaggerated sense, we all today exist on borrowed time. If we of this generation deserve no better fate, surely our children do. (Ralph Bunche)

Exercise No. 121

1. The three conspirators drew lots to determine who would undertake the assassination.
2. The crucified shirt hung from the drying line.
(adapted from J. Joyce)
3. With bent, humped back, Pope looked like a question mark.
4. Julia's dainty leg is white and hairless as an egg.
(adapted from R. Herrick)
5. No man knows what awaits him when he opens a door; Even the most familiar room may harbor surprises.

Exercise No. 122

1. What was your purpose in bringing me these two books to read from?
2. Often the man who attempts to live and die in peace is grieved.
3. The boys make a racket with their playthings.

4. Being trustful by nature, she seldom goes through her husband's trousers.
5. His mother thought his adolescent ambition to fly was capricious.

Exercise No. 123

HEADING: (see Figure 3 in text)

122 East 44th Street
Chicago, IL 60653   (note that the comma fol-
September 5, 1981   lows the city, not the state.)

INSIDE ADDRESS:

Catnip Corporation of America
Attention: Mr. John Smith
23 Hill Street
Chicago, IL 60610

SALUTATION:

Dear Mr. Smith: (the semicolon is never used
in the salutation of either
business or personal correspondence.)

BODY OF THE LETTER:

The margins of paragraph one and two are not consistent either at the left of the page or at the right.

COMPLIMENTARY CLOSE:

The complimentary close should be placed on a separate line and to the right of the middle of the page.

Exercise No. 124

RETURN ADDRESS:

William Denton (omit Mr.)
120 West Fourth Street
New York, NY 10012

ADDRESS:

Center the address on the envelope.
Follow post office directions: double space and indent each line of the address:

Mr. John Edwards, Manager
Compton Tea Company
Paterson, NJ 07509   (U.S.A. is unnecessary in national
correspondence)